Becoming ATHENA

Becoming ATHENA

Eight Principles of Enlightened Leadership

MARTHA MAYHOOD MERTZ

COPYWRITERS INCORPORATED | CHICAGO

According to Greek mythology, Zeus, ruler of the gods, feared that his wife Metis would bear a child stronger than he, and so he swallowed Metis whole. The resulting headache was so vicious that Zeus begged a divine sidekick to cleave his skull with an axe—and out sprang Athena, goddess of wisdom, fully grown and fully armed.

Athena became Zeus's favorite, entrusted with his magic shield and the knowledge of where lightning bolts were stored. She was valiant in battle but known equally as a diplomat, and for bringing the olive tree, whose branch symbolizes peace, to the Greeks.

—BASED ON *Encyclopedia Mythica*

ISBN 978-0-9749952-2-9

Library of Congress Control Number 2009920283

WRITING COLLABORATOR AND MANUSCRIPT ADVISOR

Patricia Edmonds

PUBLISHED BY

Copywriters Incorporated

A division of Greystone Global, Chicago, Illinois

116 West Hubbard, 2nd Floor

Chicago, Illinois 60654

DISTRIBUTED BY

ATHENA International

70 East Lake Street, Suite 1102

Chicago, Illinois 60601

Tel. 312.580.0111

www.marthamertz.com

DESIGN AND MANUFACTURING Carol Haralson

Printed in Canada

To Edward, with love

and with boundless gratitude for the thousand gifts
you brought to this remarkable journey

WHAT IS HONORED IN A COUNTRY WILL BE CULTIVATED THERE.

—PLATO

FOREWORD

IF YOU WOULD HONOR ME WITH A VISIT, you'd walk into my Leader to Leader Institute office on Park Avenue in New York City and the first thing you'd notice—on the table in front of the window—is a commanding and beautiful sculpture. Over a lifetime of work I've accumulated a few dozen honorary doctoral degrees and leadership awards; each was humbling and generous. So why does the International ATHENA Award occupy that first-to-be-noticed space? What qualifies this sculpture's soaring beauty to look out over Park Avenue, even as she welcomes a guest?

I was founding president and CEO of the Peter F. Drucker Foundation for Nonprofit Management (now the Leader to Leader Institute) when I learned I would be receiving the International ATHENA Award in 2001. I knew little about the award or the organization presenting it—its mission, its values, its people. So I did a fast study and was amazed at how we were, indeed, fellow travelers on ATHENA's journey. First ATHENA was on a parallel track with the vision and values of Girl Scouting; I'd been the national executive director and CEO of the Girl Scouts of the USA from 1976 to 1990. Moving from the Girl Scouts to the Drucker Foundation in 1990, I led that organization until 2000 (and still chair the Board of Governors). What this comes to is twenty-five years of common values, common ground.

Our definitions of leadership were congruent. I've said for years that "leadership is a matter of how to be, not how to do. You and I spend most of our time learning how to do and teaching others how to do, yet in the end we know it is the quality and character of the leader that determines the results." I've spent a lifetime testing my definition and it is still "the how to be leader" who will change lives, change the world.

ATHENA, and the ATHENA Awards, have had an enormous impact in the past twenty-five years. It has led from the front in a positive and powerful approach, helping women see themselves true life size, articulating Athenian leadership principles that were a battle cry for their times as they are for our times today.

Peter Drucker gave us a remarkable insight when first he said, "Focus on task, not gender." I've translated that into my own messages: "We are not women leaders. We are leaders who are women; we are not a category. And when we are successful in a position, it is because of what we bring to the job. We have a right to be there, although you and I know our gender adds a special dimension to the job. And we manage for the mission, we manage for innovation, we manage for diversity, or we are part of the past."

Meanwhile, ATHENA has taken on Martha Mertz's focus on leadership, on the eight core principles fundamental to the ATHENA Leadership Model that inspires us all: Authenticity and lifelong learning, courage and fierce advocacy, collaboration and relationship-building, giving back to and celebrating with those around us. Anywhere in the world, with women and men, these principles build the quality, the character, the success of the leader—yet it was ATHENA's vision a quarter-century ago that helped women to see their rightful place within the leadership world. What's more, Martha said women not only had a place in that world; she said women have a vital contribution to make. Women mobilized around ATHENA's vision of the future, around that vision shimmering in the distance, inspiring the sponsors of ATHENA, the contributors, the partners, the community—not only the women, but also the men. The ATHENA Award was a brilliantly conceived communications device, raising the profile of individual female leaders and simultane-ously garnering respect for the ATHENA organization itself. From the beginning, Martha understood our maxim that "communication is not saying something, communication is being heard." The power of com-munication is one of the powers of this leadership handbook, a resource for today's leaders determined to be leaders of the future.

This is an intensely personal book. Stories are open and authentic, examples are vivid, memorable—strong enough that we can appreciate them and make them our own.

"Why one more leadership book?" you may ask. The Drucker Foundation/Leader to Leader Institute has published twenty-six books on leadership with two more on the way. After serving as CEO of four great leadership organizations on my own journey, and needing to address the topic in the media and elsewhere every week of the year, I have developed a practiced eye and an inner sense when it comes to determining whether a book on leadership is relevant. Does it meet the needs of emerging lead-ers, current leaders determined to learn and grow? Does it speak con-vincingly to leaders who will head the organization of the future?

It's all here, in *Becoming ATHENA*—the history, the intensely personal stories, the documented support to those on a journey to leadership.

I urge you, whether you are male or female, a corporate veteran or an emerging leader, to take this exciting companion on your own leadership journey. Its principles will help shape your future even as they give you an appreciation of the changes from "the place for women" twenty-five years ago to where we are today. Whether it's an "evolution" or "a quiet revolution," it's all here, in this book, professional indistinguishable from personal, significance growing from page one to the closing.

This truly is a book for our times—for leaders today who will be our leaders tomorrow.

— FRANCES HESSELBEIN, 2009

WOMEN LEAD. We may not always get credit for it, or paid for it, or thanked for it—but in more ways and places than at any other time in human history, women lead. As this book goes to print, women are presidents and premiers, rulers and heads of state in nations around the world. In the United States, a woman holds the top post in the House of Representatives; in the history-making 2008 presidential elections, a woman was the Republicans' candidate for vice-president and a woman finished second for the Democrats' presidential nomination. Women today are CEOs and college presidents, generals and bishops, media moguls and opinion leaders.

It's time to recognize and savor this new truth: We are seeing the emergence of a distinctive, transforming style of leadership, one that was conceived and created by women. The point is no longer just *that* women lead. What's important is *how* women lead—and how everyone, gender aside, can use what women know about leadership to thrive in the twenty-first century.

Historically, the social order cast men as leaders and women as followers. But with every passing day it becomes clearer that leadership is not conditioned on gender. The qualities of a great leader are in fact traits that for centuries have been most common among—and most prized by—women. This "women's way" of leading transcends gender to speak to all who would be leaders.

I've spent much of my life studying this phenomenon, observing the situations in which women leaders emerge and succeed (or don't). More than a quarter-century ago I helped launch a small local program to nurture women leaders. We called it the ATHENA Award after the strong, enlightened goddess. The program sparked a movement. Today, ATHENA International has participated in award programs in more than 500 American cities and six foreign countries, and has expanded to include business mentorship and training programs as well. But the real achievement through the years has been this: We've not just honored individuals—we've honored the traits that make those individuals effective, admirable, successful leaders. And we've gathered the traits into an operational model, part bible and part blueprint.

How did we do that? By brainstorming with ATHENA honorees, surveying and interviewing hundreds of them who received the awards during the program's first two decades. We were looking for similarities in how they operated, values they espoused, precepts they followed. We were searching for the common threads that women weave into a leadership mantle that fits them just right.

We fashioned what we learned into the ATHENA Leadership Model (ALM), a set of best practices and sound principles that enable enlightened, successful leadership. At its heart we identified eight core principles that distinguish this way of leading:

Live authentically
Learn constantly
Advocate fiercely
Act courageously
Foster collaboration
Build relationships
Give back
Celebrate

Anyone of either gender can embrace these principles and adopt this way of leading, but women brought it forth. It isn't reactionary or defensive, the girls' competing version of a game the boys devised. It's as new and full of promise as the twenty-first century, for which it's infinitely well suited. And yet it's as ancient and organic as the social patterns women have woven down the generations.

Women have always lived in small circles. For centuries women were home- and community-based, rarely called upon to venture farther than the village water source or the garden plot. Rather than being stunted by this, in many cases women constructed rich and complex lives from the stuff of their immediate environments. They were the life-givers and life-nurturers, often the homebuilders as well as the home keepers. Women fed the families, tended the sick, and generally oversaw the order and care of those within their reach.

Living within a constricted environment had its benefits. Women learned to work together on projects too burdensome for one. Their work patterns also tended to be circles, everyone contributing according to their capability, adding value to the social, artistic and productive experience of shared efforts. It was less important to establish a hierarchy than to engage fully with others in the task at hand. Working together got the job done, but its value went beyond that. It was an opportunity to share ideas, experiences, and stories; to express joy and sorrow together, to build relationships, to teach others the crafts and the lore.

These practices have been carried forward primarily by women through hundreds of generations and a vast array of different cultures. From Africa to Iceland and places in between, women's ways of interacting—of living and working collaboratively, of achieving more through the hands of many together—are strikingly similar.

For centuries these shared practices were a given, anthropological wallpaper visible in the background of scenes dominated by men. But increasingly they are recognized as gold-standard behaviors—the building blocks of success in a global economy, the essence of forward-thinking leadership. The result is almost comically inconsistent. In a world still led mostly by men, the most promising "new" leadership principles derive from the age-old workings of women, who still can't get recognized as leaders in many quarters.

To be clear, not one of these admirable leadership characteristics is unique to women. But learned as they were at countless grandmothers' knees, they are time-tested and natural to women. So as women entered the professional realm, they brought these qualities and practices with them. Charged with new responsibilities in unfamiliar settings, women drew upon familiar ways that always had worked for them.

FOR YEARS I'VE RESISTED WRITING THIS BOOK because telling the ATHENA story also means telling my own story and I'd prefer to avoid that spotlight. Finally, though, I realized that was a little hypocritical. Given my conviction about women's leadership—that its unique power comes from women's shared life lessons—how could I justify not sharing my own? Throughout history, when we didn't have access to the boardrooms, barracks and academies where male leaders were trained, we've taught and learned from each other wherever we could. It only works because we all throw in our stories as wisdom and as warning. What we know about leadership can't be told through just one person's life, not even Athena's.

According to Greek mythology, Zeus, ruler of the gods, feared his wife Metis would bear a child stronger than he, so he swallowed Metis whole. The resulting headache was so vicious that Zeus begged a divine sidekick to cleave his skull with an axe—and out sprang Athena, full-grown and fully armed. When Athena emerged, she didn't ask Dad for the Mount Olympus guidebook. By temperament as by birth, she was not about "business as usual." In dealing with both allies and rivals, most of them male, she held to her own precepts and did things her own way. In 1982, we made her our program's namesake because she embodied what we considered key traits of women's leadership: strength, courage, enlightenment; resourcefulness and love of learning.

It could be said that over the years we've padded our namesake's résumé a little. Though Greek historians didn't ascribe them to Athena, there are certain traits we see again and again in those we consider her spiritual heirs. "ATHENA leaders" are fierce advocates for what they believe and committed to enriching their communities. They foster collaboration, respect diversity, and celebrate the achievements of others at least as much as their own. They build on the legacy of centuries of women who worked quietly but effectively in constrained circumstances, with little authority or socially conferred power, to lay the world's foundations.

When we launched the ATHENA Award program I explained the need to honor women leaders by quoting a man. "What is honored in a country will be cultivated there," Plato tells us. By recognizing these leaders' actions—how they perform with excellence, give back to their communities, reach out to mentor others—we say publicly and unequivocally that these actions are valuable. Not nice, not optional, but take-this-to-the-bank valuable. Singling out these leaders isn't about glorifying them personally. It's about propagating what they stand for, encouraging those who would emulate them, and giving the next generation some traction in the uphill battles still ahead.

Ultimately, it's about changing the face and nature of leadership, and at this moment in history that strikes me as critically important. Our world is experiencing crises in leadership just when it most needs to be led wisely. The challenges are so great: war, genocide and terrorism; threats to the economy and the environment; public health pandemics and widening gulfs between the haves and have-nots. Those who led us to this place cannot be counted upon, alone, to lead us out.

Make no mistake: There are leaders all around us capable of shaping solutions. But many of them are women who've never been acknowledged in that role. Stand them next to a John (Wayne or Rockefeller) or a George (Patton or Bush), and they look nothing like those command-and-control, corporate-hierarchy, cowboy-diplomacy types. And that's been the casting call for leaders for so long that many women who exhibit all the skills and achievements still aren't accorded the title. I've lost count of how often I've been on a stage before a standing-ovation crowd handing an ATHENA Award to an accomplished woman and heard her say in wonderment, "I just don't see myself as a leader."

It's time to check her vision—and our collective vision, of and for our leaders. Through shared life lessons backed by scientific research, we've outlined eight principles of the ATHENA Leadership Model. We know they're the right tools for these times because they're already proving successful for the leaders (women and men) who employ them. On the next pages, you'll see how the seeds of these precepts were sprinkled through my life and, maybe, through your own. These are old truths newly framed. These are our intuitions, finally said out loud.

Now all that's left to do is step up. We must become the leaders we've been waiting for.

I AM SO GRATEFUL to Patricia Edmonds, my writing partner. Her distinguished background in journalism (USA TODAY, NPR.org) and capability for weaving mountains of notes, interviews, and philosophical concepts cohesively has earned my highest esteem. Without Patty this book wouldn't have been possible. The project would not have been started were it not for the instruction, encouragement, and spark of ignition from Cynthia Richmond. To round out this team of magicians my accolades to Carol Haralson who designed the book to be as beautiful as the leadership model it contains.

For more than twenty-five years the ATHENA family has been drawn together by the recognition that our world is in need of balance in leadership and that we, all of us, could do something positive to help bring that about.

Enormously talented people from many places each brought their skills and left their imprint. Collectively, their contributions have built this project into an international quest. It would be impossible to finish this book without mentioning a few who have literally given years of their expertise.

In the formative times: Marge Shelden, founding partner; Linda Ackley for designing and sculpting the original graceful bronze art form and the nearly 6,000 numbered sculptures that followed; Hortense Canady, wise and experienced guide; Pat Hanes and Lamont Lator, both enhancing potential in the world for their daughters; Jim Anderton, expanding our horizons; Karen Jury, exemplifying complete dedication. These stand out among many.

Later came Mary Lou Bessette, focusing on strategy; Cathy Bolte, leading from inspiration; Ellen Ruddock, a wise and steady leadership soulmate; Yvonne Wood and Pat Pierce, master collaborators; Lynn Myers, for the remarkable journey; Linda Stevenson, who changed a corporate culture; Norma Rist, quietly, thoroughly effective; Gayle and Dutch Landen and Carole Leland, exceptional role models; Arlene Rosenthal, she of great heart; Jim Erikson and Ray Maghroori, who brought knowledge we needed; Mary Schnack, the global visionary; Dianne Dinkel and Robin Kottke, carrying our world on their shoulders. While these have been some of the major contributors to the organization, they have also become a family of priceless friends.

There are countless others, and some of their stories are told within. Many more, although they aren't mentioned here, will always be profoundly appreciated.

FINALLY, I OFFER A LOVING TRIBUTE TO MY FAMILY, which has generously listened to all things ATHENA for a long time.

To Romelle and Mary, for the profound depth of support that sisters share.

To David, my treasured and inspiring brother.

To Michelle, Michael, and Christopher, who arrived in this world as my children and have all this while been my teachers. Your presence in my life is priceless.

To my grandchildren Cameron, Ryan, Angelo, and Calvin, and to all the children of the future, for whom the people in this book and thousands more have labored to create a more balanced world. I am honored to join them in offering that gift to you.

— MARTHA MERTZ, 2009

Becoming ATHENA

ONE

Sister to King David

MY FIRST LESSON ABOUT A WOMAN'S PLACE in the universe arrived with my brother, "King David." I was three the year he was born and from then on was unwillingly enrolled in a long and steady education in the cultural significance of gender. At last my mother had her son. Though he was preceded by two daughters and would be followed by one more, his arrival signaled the ultimate accomplishment for her.

That was saying something, because my mother Irene was an accomplished person. She was unquestionably smart enough to follow her father into medical studies but did not, heeding his warning to her that "if you become a doctor, nobody will ever marry you." And so Mother followed a template in her own life that she later urged on her daughters: Girls could be nurses, or girls could be nuns. Mother chose nurse, working after my sister Romelle's birth and my birth two years later (but shelving her nursing career to care for her growing family upon the arrival of David). Years later Romelle also chose nurse, as did our younger sister Mary, born when I was eight. Nun had no takers.

And David, of course, was king—not a title he demanded or even knew I had pinned to him, but a status subtly accorded to him as the family's only male child. In our youth David didn't have to stir pudding at the stove, do the dishes, set the table, scrub the floors, or watch baby Mary while other kids played outside. When he did do chores, like rake leaves or run errands, it was always something I thought I would have liked better than my own cook-and-nursemaid assignments. Though I cherished him (always will) and considered him my favorite playmate, I resented the seeming inequities. As David matured, the list of privileges grew ominously. He could drive the family car, stay out later on Friday nights, and wear whatever he found in his closet while everything my sisters and I did was controlled much more closely. In that place and time, David and his male friends were governed by one social contract

Martha at age one,
in Rochester, Minnesota.
Photo courtesy of
Martha Mayhood Mertz.

while my sisters, my girlfriends and I were governed by another. From then until now, that disparity, and how it made me feel, influenced my view of the world.

In our small midwestern town of Rochester, Minnesota, I'm sure we looked like a typical family: father running his business, mother running the household, kids running all over the place, generally keeping their noses clean in the neighborhood and in parochial school. But from the inside, I experienced a different family dynamic. My older sister Romelle was indispensable to Mother, almost her personal assistant. Baby sister Mary was the little princess. David held his unique place in Mother's heart. I alone had no particular standing with her. I simply wasn't on her first-string team.

Luckily for me, my father Ross treated me as if I were his absolutely favorite person in the world. Family photos show us paired off doing errands or projects: a big-eyed, curly-haired munchkin and a handsome, wavy-haired man with an engaging smile. I was his sidekick, his go-fer, and he made that role seem so privileged. Weekends when he did handyman work around our house I enthusiastically trailed behind him to the basement for a building project or to the roof to pass him shingles. The soundtrack of our camaraderie was his banter, his whistling, and the occasional Spanish words sailing over my head—his way of surreptitiously swearing in my presence, I subsequently figured out.

Because Dad was a devoted boxing fan, Friday nights found us before the television with heaping bowls of popcorn, waiting for the Gillette "to look sharp every time you shave" theme song, the prelude to whatever momentous match we would watch together. Much later in life, I shuddered at how much I knew about boxing, a sport that came to seem brutal and inhumane to me. But it wasn't the boxing that drew me; it was the pleasure of sitting at Dad's knee and being his buddy.

Ross and Irene Mayhood with Romelle and Martha (at front of the sled).

Photo courtesy of Martha Mayhood Mertz.

BEING DAD'S SPECIAL PAL didn't just make me feel loved, it made me feel important, even powerful. Dad was in charge; Dad made things happen. That was the order of life not just at our house but on our street, in our town, and pretty much across 1950s America. My mother and father each brought strong opinions to the raising of their children, but when they differed, so far as I knew, his overrode hers. As partners and as parents they assumed the roles that their upbringings had prepared them for: the leading man and the woman who follows.

Irene's mother died when she was only six years old so her father Dr. Hubert Zins, a veterinarian, essentially raised her and his other five children himself. Relatives pitched in and he hired help but it was a long time before he remarried, so those years must have been pretty difficult for all of them. Irene, his middle daughter, was his favorite child—and no wonder. She was a bright, positive-natured girl and an outstanding, scholarship-level student. She was reliable and industrious, and while her siblings sometimes questioned their father's authoritarian, German, homespun wisdom, she soaked it up like a sponge. Irene adored her father and her deep respect for his values and opinions lasted a lifetime. (Even the nickname we grandkids called him signaled respect as well as affection: He wasn't just Grandpa, he was "Grandpa Doc.")

While my mother would speak freely about her early years, my father was exceedingly reticent about his. He told us he was born on a farm in Minnesota, the fourth of six siblings, but little more. Piecing together what relatives said over the years, I came to understand that there had been hardship and tragedy. His youngest brother died in a fire and his oldest brother suffered severe lung injuries in the rescue effort.

The first and last time I saw my father's father, Walter Mayhood, was at his funeral. All of ten years old, I stood by his open casket and searched his face for family resemblances. Later, I learned that my grandfather had been an alcoholic and that my grandmother Alma did most of the heavy lifting for her brood. I will always believe that my grandmother's strength and steadfast resolve to make the best of the circumstances framed her son Ross's model of an ideal woman, strong in capability while soft in manner, focused yet fun-loving, persevering but not severe, and unquestionably devoted to her family.

Ross Mayhood could have been the boy in the World War I–era novelty song "How 'Ya Gonna Keep 'Em Down On the Farm (After They've Seen Paree)?" For him, "Paree" was Chicago, then Scotland, then Mexico. He was adventurous and ambitious, with a powerful work ethic. From their modest beginnings, he and his siblings did well. One brother became a multi-term Minnesota state senator and one sister a prominent business owner, as was my father.

I found so much to value in each of my parents. I admired my dad's absolute love and respect for my mother, his ease with people from all social tiers, his ability to fix or figure out or build anything he set his mind to, projects he approached with a stubborn streak of perfectionism. I admired my mother for her love of learning and her wicked ability to win at bridge, her wide range of volunteer activities in our community, her constantly-expanding social circle, and her devotion to her church. In our household Mother performed the tasks of a CEO but Dad held the title *Pater Familias*, and they worked in utter harmony.

Our household was like so many others in middle-class, mid-twentieth-century America. But when the world outside took stock of my parents, somehow Dad's talents and accomplishments gave him a social standing, a market value, well above Mother's. To me, from early on, that seemed neither right nor fair.

DEVELOPMENTAL PSYCHOLOGISTS TELL US—no surprise here—that children draw their first sense of their competencies from those who raise them. Parents give us wings and boundaries. I loved how my dad let me attempt so many different things, never hobbling me with warnings

The growing Mayhood family: Above, Irene and Ross with Martha, David, and Romelle. At left, Romelle, Martha, David, Mary.

Photos courtesy of Martha Mayhood Mertz.

that I might not be up to a challenge. And I chafed when my mom drew tight circles around what I could or couldn't achieve, must or mustn't do, because I was female. She absolutely believed what she said about those confines, even when her own brimming talents belied it.

One Easter, when I was five, our family was driving from Minnesota to eastern Wisconsin to visit relatives, a lengthy trip and a big deal in the days before freeways. My father had purchased a new four-door car, the kind with back doors that opened toward the front. We were heading onto the last leg of the journey, little David in the front seat with my parents, Romelle and me in the back snacking on fruit and ranging about (seatbelt-free, in those days). Looking out the rear window, watching things recede from view as we sped on, I was spellbound by the lesson in perspective. It occurred to me that if I threw my banana peel out the window I could watch it, too, shrink and disappear. Finding the car's window frozen shut, I decided to open the door just a little to throw out the peel, then scamper up on the seat to catch a view of it. As we drove across some railroad tracks, I pulled the door handle. Because the door opened toward the front, the wind caught it, flinging it wide open and taking me with it. I landed head first on those tracks and the door was wrenched off its hinges.

We raced to the nearest hospital emergency room, my scalp bleeding from an ear-to-ear gash. I have a fleeting memory of trying to peer through grit at people across the room whose voices bounced like sounds in an echo chamber. The doctor, without taking any vital signs, told my mother that I was gone. "Take her home and bury her," he counseled.

By nature, my mother always deferred to doctors. By training and instinct, she knew better this time. My parents packed me up and drove well over 200 miles back to Rochester's St. Mary's Hospital, which offered some of the best medical care in the world at that time. I had suffered a fractured skull; I was unconscious for three days and spent a month in the hospital.

The Menominee, Wisconsin, newspaper printed my obituary, a copy of which was sent to us. Mom later heard that the doctor had been barred from practicing medicine because of an addiction to narcotics. Had she not been there—"just a nurse," she'd have said, but willing to override a slipshod doctor—I would not be here. (Remarkably, I suffered no long-term effects from the accident though when the story was retold in family circles David liked to suggest that I'd lost half my marbles that day. After considering that possibility, I told him to just imagine, then, how much smarter I would have been with a full set.)

FOR YEARS, BEMUSED NUNS CHIDED ME with the New Testament verse "Martha, Martha, you are busy about many things." It's what Jesus is supposed to have said to his friend Martha because she rushed around waiting on him while her sister Mary sat learning from him. The Bible relates it as an admonition; somehow, for me it's been more like a mantra.

I liked to do things the neighborhood boys did: play softball, draw treasure maps, lead playmates on parades. I wrote a newspaper and sold subscriptions up and down the street. Because each one was handwritten and illustrated, the whole enterprise only lasted through one edition. (I never did return the five cents to my subscribers for any subsequent "publications." Now more than fifty years later, I'm sending my apologies.) In the third grade, in the only pugilistic outing of my life, I beat up the class bully (a girl!) during recess while her victims cheered me on.

And the summer I was eight or nine I gathered the motley crew of neighborhood children together to teach them how to fly. A stone wall separated our driveway from the yard next door, two feet high for most of its length but rising to four feet at one end. I would line up our group along the lower wall, then solemnly climb to the high point and demonstrate the very precise maneuvers required. Stand straight with arms rigidly at one's sides. Raise arms straight out at shoulder height, then into a wing position. Begin to bend at knees and waist. Jump from wall onto neighbors' grass. For some reason this was both wonderful and dramatic for my audience who then proceeded, one after another in orderly fashion, to emulate my actions. On those hot afternoons, we'd stage jump after jump, and, since flying was the story, we thought we were.

If leadership is convincing others to imagine what they can accomplish and then take a leap of faith, I suppose that was one of my first efforts to lead. No one broke a leg, either.

SOMEWHERE ON THE ROAD FROM CHILD TO TEEN, I lost my leader, my mentor—my father. Maybe he anticipated losing me to adulthood and so pulled away first. Maybe it seemed to him improper to stay close as the tomboy girl became a young woman. For whatever reason, he put me at arm's length and the distance was unbearable. He seemed chronically angry at me and irked at my interests; he bridled at the music that floated or pounded from my room, at the clothing I wore, and especially at any young male who dared to express interest.

I took to having conversations with myself that I longed to have with him. "If only you would hug me," I imagined saying. "I'm looking for where you are. Why can't I find you any more?" I never had felt that special bond with Mother, I'd somehow lost my exquisite closeness to Dad, and so, in adolescence, I felt I didn't have either parent. Because none of my siblings had the same experience, they didn't understand.

As I look back on it now, I suppose there's a part of me that is grateful; not being able to lean on Dad forced me to be stronger in standing up for myself. But it was a sad and painful time, trying to find my footing, trying to find out what life was going to be about for me.

As Dad withdrew, Mother came into sharper focus and what I saw in her became harder and harder to reconcile. Irene Rose Zins Mayhood was talented, tireless, and smart across a wide range of interests. While cheerfully carrying most of the load of raising four children, she led or participated in numerous civic organizations. She seriously collected stamps and coins (and had us kids sift through endless rolls of pennies to find the rare 1909-S VDB). She didn't just sew on her Singer machine, she tailored; she'd try on suits at expensive shops and then come home and make elegant copies for herself. She played contract bridge with uncanny skill, seeming to know every card in her opponents' hands as soon as they bid. She loved to entertain and brought people from all over the world home to dine with us. Because our hometown, Rochester, also was home to the internationally-known Mayo Clinic, we'd receive guests who had come from Hungary, El Salvador, Japan, Egypt, the Philippines.

I was struck by the enormity of her gifts—and by her absolute belief that they could take her only so far because she was a woman. With all those outsized talents, how could her sense of herself be so small? She didn't just tolerate the social structure that assigned her this cramped, second-class spot. She embraced it and thought that I should, too. She took all that energy, smarts, and skill (enough to run a small city) and poured them into a well-trimmed collar, a church rummage sale, or some other approved pursuit.

I remember heated conversations with my mother about "a woman's place." I remember her adamant defense of the hierarchy—in society, her church, and our home—that set men above women. I questioned her, I wanted to debate. Why aren't there women priests, women in this role or that? We frequently squared off, a pesky kid battering the foundations on which her mother's whole life rested.

Mother wasn't the only authority I questioned. As the three Mayhood girls trooped through Catholic schools, I was the one most often elbowing the boundaries. My least favorite teachers were the ones who expected us to do everything in lockstep. My favorites were the few who didn't. There was Mr. Biewen in English Literature, who urged us to

think for ourselves and then, when we did, showed respect for and interest in our ideas.

And there was Sister Jane Francis in Latin I, who cared about our
mastery of the language but ultimately cared more about our integrity.
I still struggle with the conjugations as, years later, I strive to learn a
bit of Spanish. But I never have forgotten how she wove her convictions
into every class. A tiny, seemingly ancient woman garbed in dark brown
Franciscan robes, Sister Jane Francis was a soft voice but a large presence.
Daily she'd walk up and down the aisles reciting the lessons and then
punctuating them with one admonition: "To thine own self be true."
Subject as I felt to so many layers of authority—the pope, the principal,
and my parents, just for starters—the idea of listening to myself had an
almost subversive appeal. Plus, Sister Jane Francis was such a trusted figure, and she said it so often, that I resolved to take it to heart. It took
decades of trial and error for me to learn what being true to myself really
meant but, all those years ago, Sister Jane Francis laid the foundation for
my understanding of authenticity.

In every class and subject, my favorite projects were the creative ones:
posters for our bulletin boards, lettering and designs for the classroom,
drawings and articles for in-house publications. I played clarinet in the
band, built floats for school parades. I wanted to try it all. "Variety is the
spice of her life," said the yearbook blurb by my photo.

THE MID-1950S brought a new book to our school library: *Profiles in
Courage,* written by a charismatic young senator from Massachusetts.
In my very Catholic family and parochial school community, John F.
Kennedy was a source of tremendous pride. So when he singled out eight
leaders and presented their stories as the essence of courage under pres-
sure, we embraced them as exemplars. From John Quincy Adams to
Daniel Webster, all eight profile subjects were senators so, of course, all

eight were men. The presence of women in the book was confined to the occasional wife or daughter posed primly in official photos and Kennedy's dedication, "to my wife," Jacqueline. The book was Kennedy's ode to courage, which he called "the most admirable of human virtues." But it was an admonition, too. A nation that has "forgotten the quality of courage" displayed by its past leaders "is not as likely to insist upon or reward that quality in its chosen leaders today," he warned. "And in fact, we have forgotten."

While my Minnesota schoolmates read Kennedy, the news headlines from Arkansas offered a different study in courage. The 1954 Supreme Court ruling outlawing racially segregated public schools didn't have much impact in Rochester, where we could count the number of black families on one hand and still have fingers to spare. But the pictures we saw from Little Rock showed nine black students, kids about our age, trying to enter Central High School while the governor, the state national guard, and angry protesters tried to keep them out. It took an order from President Eisenhower and a shield of a thousand United States Army paratroopers, but on September 25, 1957, the nine black students, six of them girls, entered the school.

In news photos of the girls, I saw shades of my friends and me on the first day of school, with hair carefully coiffed, pretty new clothing, books hugged tightly to chests. But there the similarity ended. I remember thinking about how scared they must have been and admiring the bravery it took to face that kind of fire. But mostly I remember being horrified by the raw hatred of the crowds, the people who looked like me. Men, women, and even children expressed a sickening, shocking depth of rage at these students who simply wanted a decent education. I remember wondering what it would take to bring all these people into some kind of harmony. I remember hoping fervently that such a significant change could happen during my lifetime.

MY PARENTS MET in St. Mary's Hospital in Rochester, Minnesota. Ross Mayhood had been pheasant hunting in the fields outside of town with a group of friends, mostly doctors. He dropped his shotgun while climbing a fence and reached for the muzzle just as the gun went off. His right hand was shattered. Luckily, he was with people who knew what to do and who got him to St. Mary's, where Irene Rose Zins was one of the nurses on duty.

Although raised on a farm, Ross had been to the big city—in his case, Chicago—where he'd picked up a little sophistication. So there he was in the hospital, a good-looking young bachelor dressed in silk pajamas, flirting with the nurses. Irene, four years out of nursing school, fell for him hook, line, and sinker.

With months of skin grafts, surgeries, and physical therapy, doctors eventually were able to stabilize Ross's hand into an open clench, giving him just enough flexibility to hold onto some objects. The accident dashed his hopes of a career in golf, at which he was talented enough even in his youth to have competed at St. Andrews in Scotland. But until his death in 2002 he delighted in playing the sport and in being married to his fetching former nurse.

My parents' marriage was one of the most harmonious relationships I've ever known. I do not remember a time when we kids were able to wheedle our way by setting one against the other, although there was great sport in trying. They were an impenetrable force, always in agreement. My father deeply respected my mother and loved her with a devotion that amazes me all the more now that I've had my own marital journeys.

Through adolescence and teen years my parents kept us girls on very short leashes. It was less an issue for Mary as she was much younger, though she too would later rebel. Romelle found subtle ways to get around the restrictiveness, but I faced it head on. "Why are you doing this?" I'd ask my parents, which of course only made them clamp down harder.

I longed to prove that I was competent, reliable, independent, all those things that I and others admired in my dad, who was successful in his business and esteemed in the community. So as soon as I turned sixteen, I got a job working part-time for Donaldson's Flower Shop. To support his wife and five children, Mr. Conrad "Con" Odegarden ran the shop frugally, leasing a small space within a big Rochester department store. He was kind and patient in teaching me shop tasks; I worked all the hours I could get, after school, Saturdays, and on summer break.

I'd been working there about a year when Con, overworked and exhausted, was diagnosed with pneumonia and ordered to bed. He asked me to mind the shop for him. I felt honored, trusted, and prepared.

I didn't count on a visit from the wholesaler who provided the shop's merchandise. But when he came in, rather than bother my boss in his sickbed, I put together the order myself. Who knows what I based it on, but at the time I felt confident in ordering 1,000 roses, 300 chrysanthemum plants, and various other florae. I thought I was doing really well. Only when I told him what I'd ordered and heard a stricken silence on the phone line did I realize my order was way beyond what the shop could hope to sell.

The next day in came the flowers, out of bed came Con, and we had an enormous sale. Even at a dollar a dozen, we worked like dogs to move those flowers, for which there certainly wasn't room in the cooler. I remember the ads in the paper, the signs on the windows, the long hours asking people to tell their friends, and seeing people leave the shop with their arms full. But what I remember most is Mr. Odegarden, wrapping and ringing up sales while trying not to cough on customers, never saying one word of reprimand to me. Nothing since has taught me more about what it means to treat co-workers, no matter their station, with compassion.

OUTSIDE OUR FAMILY, I saw what freedom was like, and I sought that. Inside our family, I saw my mother comfortable with constraints imposed by gender, and I fought that. Much as I admired her gifts, she could not be my role model. Neither, at his distance, could Dad. While I could learn from role models like Sister Jane Francis and Mr. Biewen, I wanted something more.

And then, when I most could have used her presence, my Aunt Erva left. Erva Mayhood, my dad's youngest and favorite sister, was the first fulltime female professional I knew. She was the buyer of linens and other goods for The Emporium, a big St. Paul department store. Her job meant frequent trips to New York City, and she always looked the part of the urban sophisticate. A beautiful woman with prematurely silver hair (a family trait), she dressed in chic gray from her tailored dresses to her designer shoes and handbags. The only place I was allowed to spend the night outside my own home was at Aunt Erva's in St. Paul. Every visit was a special occasion, whether it involved an outing to the circus, dinner at a restaurant, or just staying in and playing with her fragile collection of Hummel figurines. From my limited glimpses, Erva's life looked unbounded, her career fulfilling. Whatever put her beyond the structures that hemmed in my mother, I wanted a piece of it.

I was in my teens when, around 1959, Erva disappeared from the family. No one knew where she was, no one heard from her. She just vanished. Even a search by Dad's friend in the Social Security Administration turned up no traces. A few years later, when Dad and Erva's older brother (a former Minnesota state senator) was killed while trying to break up a fight, Dad so wished for Erva to be there to share the grief. Then their mother died and again he grieved without his sister.

Erva was gone from our lives—almost. Sometime in the 1980s, a postcard arrived at my parents' Arizona home, postmarked Hawaii but with no return address. It said, "Dear Ross and Irene: This is a beautiful place. Wish you were here. Love, Erva." And then, nothing.

TWO

Forever and Ever

LOURDES HIGH SCHOOL, ROCHESTER, MINNESOTA. Whether thanks to alphabetical order or his own plotting (as he later claimed), a lanky star athlete was seated behind me in geometry class. My school uniform included the standard-issue, navy-blue cardigan sweater and, as I tried to listen to Sister Finbar, the sophomore began picking at a stray strand of yarn. Feeling something brush my back, I leaned forward, turned around, and saw my sweater unraveling at the hand of M. Michael Mertz. He was quarterback of the football team, lead guard of the basketball team, a talented high-jumper, and a good student, as much into hitting the books as having fun. He also was, as my mother observed, a nice young man from a good family.

Within months, he announced matter-of-factly that he was going to marry me and that he had this slogan for us: F-A-E, *Forever and Ever.* I was as puzzled as I was pleased. Mike clearly was smitten and I didn't think myself the smiting type. I was almost a year younger than most of my female classmates, still girlish and scrawny while they were willowy, womanly. But I found what he said compelling, so ardent, so certain. Here was a young man saying "You will never leave my life."

In uniform, Lourdes High School, Rochester. Photo courtesy of Martha Mayhood Mertz.

Throughout my senior year of high school (his junior year), we were a couple. When I moved to St. Paul as a freshman at the College of St. Catherine—casually, St. Kate's—I saw Mike on trips home but also dated guys from the nearby University of St. Thomas.

People like my parents sent their daughters to St. Kate's for two reasons: to get a very good education, and to be held in a protected, controlled environment. But as tight a ship as the Sisters of St. Joseph ran, after how I'd been raised St. Kate's seemed like an oasis of freedom and self-rule. That first year, it felt like everything was changing for me, everything was possible. And when I looked around this new landscape for people to admire, I found Sister Vera.

A spirited and gorgeous woman, Protestant-raised Vera Chester had converted to Catholicism and then entered a convent. At St. Kate's she taught theology. But to students just beginning to look at the world in a more sophisticated way than we had in high school, she offered so much more.

Hands down, Sister Vera was the best professor I had. She had a stunning command of the material and an ability to present even ancient, often-heard texts in fresh and provocative ways. Her obvious passion was contagious and inspiring. Though she wore the habit of one of the most hierarchical organizations on the planet, she made it clear that she did not need to be "above" in order to be effective. She listened to her students and challenged us to test our intellectual freedom. She seemed as eager to learn from us as we were to learn from her.

To a young woman like me, restlessly searching for exemplars, Sister Vera was a revelation. She conveyed a sense of very deep self-awareness, of generosity of spirit. She embraced her own growth along with the growth she fostered in her students. Even within the confines of the convent, she seemed to have found an internal freedom that made her confident, centered, and serene. How my mother must have rejoiced. While I hadn't picked Mom's option of *being* a nun, at least I was eager to be *like* one. It wasn't Sister Vera's vowed life that impressed me so much as other qualities, traits I would only later recognize as the hallmarks of a born leader.

THE SECOND YEAR I WAS AT ST. KATE'S Mike enrolled at St. Thomas, and we became an exclusive couple. I was drawn to him in part because of his witty way of expressing his feelings, including anger. I was angrier about many things than I'd ever said out loud: Dad's estrangement from me, Mother's modest distance. Maybe Mike's wit could manage my anger, too. Forever and ever.

Mostly, I was so affirmed by the attention Mike lavished on me, as I deeply wanted to be esteemed for exactly who I was. If I had had a stronger vision of my academic and career potential or had felt more affirmed in some other parts of my world, had his not been by far the strongest gravitational pull, we might have made other decisions. But we didn't. At

Christmas that year, young and in love with a lifetime of hope in front of us, we embarked on an entirely new adventure and were married in a small family ceremony.

I have an indelible memory of one scene from that time: the provost of St. Kate's, looking at me across her beautifully carved desk in her intimidatingly spacious office. My academic records were spread out before us, and she kept pointing to notations and shaking her head in frustration. These are your grades (all good). You've done this and this and this (leading and excelling at a range of activities). This is what we think of you (universal praise from my teachers). "I can't conceive of you leaving school at this point to get married," the provost said. Then she closed my file.

Maybe I had buried any reservations about this path we were choosing. Who knows if that's where my subconscious was going when, shortly before I left school, I had the most bizarre dream. It starred Sister Ann Denise, St. Kate's strict and efficient assistant provost and the overseer of my dorm floor. In the dream I was running through the tunnels that connected the buildings at St. Kate's with Sister Ann Denise chasing me, black veil flying wildly behind her. I remember two things most clearly about the dream: that it was terrifying, and that Sister Ann Denise never caught me.

MARRIAGE BROUGHT A TOTALLY DIFFERENT LANDSCAPE with a pioneering quality, a we-have-each-other-and-the-future-is-ours-to-design approach. We did just that despite a predictably tiny budget. I enjoyed setting up a household, learning how to cook, managing the meager finances. Our daughter Michelle was born in 1962. She was a healthy nine-pound baby with typically anxious first-time parents. Michelle took all her cues from me, an overly-solicitous new mom, and for our first several months together we struggled with adjustments. She developed colic; I couldn't bear to hear her cry. So we walked and rocked and hummed and soothed each other until the rhythms of our lives became synchronized.

We lived in half of the second floor of a circa-1920s Victorian home that had been sectioned into apartments. Ours consisted of what seemed like two closets and a hallway. When we first moved in, two truck drivers occupied the other side and we shared the bathroom, which meant I cleaned it every time we used it. I did not miss them or their grimy bathtub rings when they moved out.

The new tenant was a tiny middle-aged woman who resembled Dolly Parton and went by the nickname Blondie. She fell madly in love with baby Michelle and after her daily waitress shifts would sit and play with her for hours. She'd also bring us food from the restaurant where she worked; it probably showed that we didn't have much, but neither did she, beyond her very good heart. She didn't own a car, so she walked back and forth to work in spiky heels, her bleached-blonde hair piled high atop her head.

I HAD MANAGED TO GET MY BEARINGS as wife, mother, laundress, cook, when the world outside was placid. But then I found myself walking a colicky baby by the light of the television screen as a national crisis unfolded. A sober-faced President Kennedy told the nation that the Soviet Union was building nuclear missile sites in Cuba and that the United States was imposing a naval blockade to keep the Russians from moving more weapons to the island.

At the time it was breathtaking in a most terrifying sense of the word. Never had the history of distrust and enmity, the cultural differences and communications barriers, the huge capacity of sinister weapons and firepower collided in such a massive exercise of power. It was a game of chicken gone global. Everyone on earth was invested. The tension-drenched voices of newscasters reporting this standoff held me riveted while I rocked and soothed my infant daughter wondering what, if any, future she would know.

In our community, as across America, the fear was palpable. Neighbors rushed to the grocery stores to stock up on canned goods and to weapons stores for guns and ammunition. Some who had built fallout shelters in the 1950s re-stocked them; those of us who hadn't wondered where we'd go.

In a second-floor apartment in the middle of the country with my little family, I watched and waited, utterly attentive and utterly helpless. Many of the tense conversations among U.S. and Soviet leaders—President Kennedy, Soviet Premier Nikita Khrushchev, U.S. Defense Secretary Robert McNamara, Soviet Foreign Minister Andrei Gromyko—were revealed only much later. But what Americans did hear was terrifying: the most powerful men in the world in the full cry of confrontation. Military men, lawmakers, and ambassadors stood on the brink of nuclear war, hurling insults and threats.

Here's how historian Alice George remembers the time: "As a ten-year-old, I saw my world come perilously close to dying. I remember the look on my fifth-grade teacher's face when she told us that nuclear war might begin at any minute. The first Soviet ship was approaching the American naval blockade around Cuba, she explained, and, soon, we might be dismissed from school, presumably to die at home with our housewife mothers." While numerous historians have studied the diplomatic and military events of that time, little was written about its impact on U.S. civilians until George wrote *Awaiting Armageddon: How Americans Faced the Cuban Missile Crisis.* Her book is full of the kinds of poignant moments recalled from that frightening time (as from the Pearl Harbor attack before it and the 9/11 attacks since). Clois Williams, a forty-year-old African-American single mother, cleaned white families' homes in Hickory, North Carolina, to make a living for herself and her thirteen-year-old daughter Katherleen. The day after Kennedy's speech announcing the blockade, she recalled, an employer "had me take her vacuum cleaner downstairs and look in all the cracks and get rid of the spider webs so the basement could be their fallout shelter. And to tell you the truth, that dark basement scared me more than Khrushchev." Returning from work, Clois found Katherleen so alarmed by the attack drill at her school that she had run home in a panic, triggering an asthma attack. Between bellicose leaders and basement bomb shelters, Williams said, "folks were just scared."

From her reading of history in general, Alice George would argue that women "often tend to take a less confrontational approach to problem solving." But, she would add, "we have no way of knowing whether a woman would have handled the Cuban missile crisis more effectively because there were no female heads of state in 1962." In this game of brinkmanship, the key players all were men.

Cradling my baby girl, I looked to these leaders for reassurance and for weeks found very little. We saw photos from the oval office of JFK bent over his desk, overwhelmed with the sheer burden of decision. We watched TV footage of a belligerent Mr. Khrushchev (who once memorably pounded his shoe on a United Nations podium to make a point).

As far as the watching world could see, George notes, "the only official who pushed for negotiation and compromise was United Nations Ambassador Adlai Stevenson—and he acquired a bad reputation in the administration for suggesting talk rather than action." This was a face-down moment, a battle of wills and egos with the armaments of both countries as the ultimate threat.

Then after nearly two weeks, the Soviets agreed to stop building the sites and remove the missiles. "What we know now and didn't know then," George says, "is that Kennedy did use secret diplomacy to avoid nuclear war. Robert Kennedy's clandestine meetings with Anatoli Dobrynin played a big role in ending the crisis without a military conflict.

Behind closed doors JFK did what an enlightened leader of today might have done publicly: He offered to remove U.S. missiles from Turkey in exchange for the removal of missiles from Cuba."

After the Soviets backed off, one top U.S. Air Force general advocated bombing Cuba anyway. But when the possibility of atomic Armageddon had drawn terrifyingly near, Kennedy and Khrushchev, two men with the world's future in their hands, had moved past saber-rattling to negotiation.

Announcing in late November that the blockade was over, Kennedy told the nation, "There is much for which we can be grateful as we look back to where we stood only four weeks ago." In averting the crisis, he credited not only U.S. military might but "the calm determination of the American people."

AS WE HAD PLANNED, Mike continued his education, pursuing a dual track of coaching and history. He also continued to play basketball; it wasn't high-level college ball, just junior college and sometimes pickup games, but something he loved. He also worked at a local drug store, bringing in the salary that kept us afloat. Our rent was $50 a month, utilities included. He needed our one car nearly all the time so inevitably I became isolated and lonely—and pregnant again.

Our second child, Michael, arrived in a smooth glide. Easy birth, easy baby. He was barely six months old when Mike was recruited to play football at Yankton College. So off we went, with Mike's beloved dad, Baldy, leading the caravan, to South Dakota, where we settled into spacious new student housing. Our fellow tenants were families in similar circumstances, pursuing educations while raising young children with limited budgets and moms at home. We had a social circle!

Mike's football career was tragically short. During one of the first days of practice, he was tackled by a beefier teammate, suffered a concussion, and hung up his cleats. But the scholarship continued so we stayed. He went to school and I worked part-time as a psychiatric assistant in a state hospital, earning $1 an hour. In this utterly foreign and sometimes dangerous setting I was the rookie. So I drew the day room assignment, spending my shifts among patients lost in catatonic trance or pacing and conversing frenetically with voices only they heard.

The one patient on the ward who seemed entirely normal was in there for murder. She had killed a rival for her lover's affections and, because South Dakota had no women's prison, was serving her sentence at the state hospital. A relentless observer of both patients and staff, she delighted in giving me hints about managing this one, avoiding that one. I learned to keep my back to something solid to minimize sneak attacks and to brace for violence out of nowhere. Once a skinny teen flew at me, her clenched fist drawn back to strike. Though I was just too stunned to react, she read me as too tough. She stopped in mid-motion, announcing, "If you had flinched I would have punched you." Her arms were lined with self-inflicted stripes of gouged skin.

More troubling than the patients were a few staff members, the Nurse Ratcheds, as my murderess informant called them, after the vicious character in *One Flew Over the Cuckoo's Nest*. They represented a sorry truth of human nature: Faced with weakness and vulnerability, some authority figures will respond with meanness, even brutality. Happily, most of my co-workers were not Nurse Ratcheds but kind, straightforward midwestern farm women. Little as I felt or looked the part, I had to act like an authority figure too; my credibility and safety depended on it. But I was able to choose which kind, the Nurse Ratched type or the other.

One day in the medium security ward, which was filled mostly with chronically ill people with little chance of improvement, a patient smacked a tall, heavy window pane with the backs of her hands, shattering it. She then wrenched out two long, dagger-like shards and took a stance facing the staff office. Only two employees were on duty: the psychiatric nurse in charge, Lucille, who was my favorite mentor—and me. "Stay calm," Lucille said evenly, "and come with me." We crossed the very large room, past other patients in various states of alarm, toward the menacing-looking woman whose hands dripped blood as she brandished the glass daggers. We came with soft words, nothing else. Lucille spoke gently. In almost a caress, she took hold of the patient's arm and asked her to release the glass. To my amazement, the patient dropped the shards, one and then the other. Her hands were cut deeply, palm and back. Lucille called to alert the medical unit and then headed there with the patient.

That left me to manage the glass, the blood, and the eighty other patients, many clearly upset by the scene. I knew such a disturbance could trigger any number of reactions. And I knew I was on my own. No backup, no mentor, no one to lead me out of the moment. Lucille could not tell me what to do now, but for months she had been showing me. Commanding but kind. Calm. Empathetic. Meeting as many eyes as I could (steady gaze, reassuring smile) I fetched the cleaning supplies.

As I swept and mopped the patients' anxiety subsided. The atmosphere in the room closed back down to the customary: the hushed murmurs, the pacing and rocking, the droning of the TV, the heavy weight of time passing slowly.

IN 1966, fresh out of college, Mike joined a national seed company as a regional representative. He traveled a lot, leaving most weeks on Monday and not returning home until Thursday night or Friday. When he did get home, he'd be exhausted and ready to have some "time off," so I was soloing with the kids a lot. Mostly I loved our time together playing, reading, going to the park; young as I was, I was growing up with them. Everything that could be was made into a game. As adults, my kids joke about how I conned them into cleaning up by scooting a "train" of bowls across the floor to collect scattered toys and bits of litter as "passengers." But there also were times when the constancy required for parenting, the never-ending responsibility, seemed pretty overwhelming.

By the time our third child, Christopher, was born in 1967, our little family had moved to Des Moines, Iowa. Before Christopher turned two we had lived in a total of nine towns throughout Minnesota, South Dakota, Indiana, and Michigan. Moving as frequently as we did was not the lot of only Mike and me; it was standard procedure for corporate sales managers in those days. Though it never was openly stated, the intent clearly was for the company to serve as community, even family, for its employees. If you didn't have time to set your roots in one community and become part of it, if you kept being moved around, then your only close ties were to the company. And that really was the way it worked, by corporate philosophy and practice.

I used to try to laugh off all the relocations, saying that was the way I did my spring cleaning. I just moved. But I thought then, and I absolutely believe now, that it was very destructive. The company leaders devised the system to maximize their employees' dependence on the company with no apparent regard for the impact it had on families. I couldn't have found these words for it then but now I'd call that my first real brush with a toxic model of leadership, one that treated employees like movable assets instead of valuable partners.

One particular relocation, to Hammond, Indiana, seemed to represent what my life was becoming: a neighborhood of little houses all in a row downwind from the Gary factories, with air quality so wretched that for nearly a year I didn't see stars in the sky. I nearly forgot about them. Every day husbands would leave those little houses for their company jobs and wives would gather, first on one small porch, then another.

I never really felt that I fit in with the women there, the neighbors and the spouses from Mike's company. I didn't know any professional women whose chief focus was career. I knew plenty of homemakers, women who might once have honed work skills or aimed for careers but whose energies were now centered on home. I didn't want that single focus; I didn't think I needed it to be a decent wife and mother. I itched to reach beyond that, but toward what I didn't know.

In every day's news, it seemed, horizons were expanding. Golda Meir became Israel's first woman prime minister, only the third woman in the world to hold the office. New York Democrat Shirley Chisholm became the first African-American woman elected to the U.S. Congress. Some of America's most prestigious all-male colleges—Princeton, Georgetown, Yale—began admitting female students. The U.S. Supreme Court ruled that women who met the physical requirements could work in previously male-only jobs. And on courts around the world, Billie Jean King was winning virtually every tennis competition open to female players.

I remember feeling that I had made my decisions to marry, to have a family, and that I was truly making the best of them. But I often felt very alone and like the Little Red Hen of the children's tale, with so many things to be done and no one else to help that just I'd do them myself.

THE FIRST HOME WE BOUGHT was a 1,050-square-foot ranch on about an acre of land, close to a nice shallow swimming area on Lake Lansing in Haslett, Michigan. We'd been in the house less than a year and the children were ages three, six, and eight, when the company relocation office called us again.

> Mike: "Guess what? I'm going to be transferred to Little Rock."
> Me: "No! Our kids need a place to be from."

Of course, the decision wasn't that simple, two sentences and done. But ultimately Mike got off the bandwagon. He left that company, toyed briefly with opening a restaurant, and then hired on with a regional supermarket chain, in a position that paid a bit less but was infinitely better for the family. Finally we were able to settle into the community, get to know the neighbors, plant trees, and experiment with minor improvements to the house.

As first-time homebuyers, we had been a little panicky, a lot ignorant, and thus terribly vulnerable to choosing badly in one of the most important financial decisions of our lives. That realization and the whole home-buying experience fascinated me.

With house payments to make, Mike around more, and two of the three kids in school, I saw my opening to seek work outside the home. At the time, I had no sense of stepping onto a career track. I joked that I wanted to "make enough money to buy throw pillows" and other household extras.

But this wasn't about the income. It was about dipping into the outside world, exercising my mind and interests, playing with grown-ups for a change. The money mattered chiefly because it would buy freedom, paying for babysitters as needed. Both my mother and Mike's mother expressed some dismay at the idea but Mike was quite supportive.

I studied for my realtor's license with one clientele in mind: the first-time buyers that Mike and I so recently had been. Such novices typically needed the most education and hand-holding, had a paltry sum for a down payment, and could afford only the least expensive properties. Seasoned agents considered these buyers a lot of work for only half of a seven-percent commission but for me, having earned nothing in years, the pay looked just fine. I didn't care if it was a niche nobody else wanted; I still was carving myself a niche in a competitive profession. Plus I liked the fact that I was doing something good for these people, as Pollyanna-ish as that sounds.

One of my first sales netted me the impressive commission of $260. Meanwhile, my brother David had earned an advanced degree in nuclear physics and was traveling around the world under the ocean on a nuclear submarine. Playing faintly but constantly in the background, I could hear my mother's doctrine: A woman's reach is finite, a man's is infinite...

WHEN WE WERE CHILDREN, my father loved to play Monopoly with us. From him I learned the thrill of taking risks with money, buying properties and building little empires, savoring the convergence of luck with strategy. (It was no mistake that my first big venture into real estate development was a commercial property we named Central Park Place. I'm still waiting to build Boardwalk.)

By 1974, it was clear that real estate was a good fit for me. I thoroughly enjoyed the new dimension working brought to my life. Thanks to some good sitters, some schedule accommodations, and my husband's expanding forays into cooking, our home life continued to run smoothly. I went well beyond earning enough for throw pillows, gradually becoming a significant contributor to the household income. And I still could be there to enjoy and participate in my children's school endeavors.

More and more women began streaming into the workforce, seeking opportunities to develop professional skills as well as make money. "Entrepreneur" wasn't the commonly-used term it is now and certainly not often applied to women. So when a friend and I decided to try our hand at a new venture, I calmed my nerves by harking back to my Monopoly days, thinking of the stake I was risking as "play money."

Rising through the ranks at a small but respected real estate company, I had gotten to know Roger Drobney, our in-house custom residential builder. I liked the designs he conceived and built for clients, and I had become a very good source of sales for his homes. One day, he asked me what I thought I'd be doing in five years. Was this a part-time job or a career?

It was the first time I had to seriously consider the question of professional stature. I told Roger that my professional endeavors were providing a sense of balance in my life. I think that answer and the consistent sales record I was building led him to believe I'd be a good small-scale investment partner. He and I each scraped up $500 to invest, put the $1,000 down on a tract of land with a lot of road frontage, and signed a contract with the balance to be due in one year. We then split the land into three nice-sized segments and sold them to his clients for new home sites. His buyers were pleased and we were too. Well before the year was up, Roger and I paid out the contract and realized a gain of $9,000. I had taken the first step in what became a long-term investment partnership, one through which I was to build a significant portfolio.

As I learned my profession I looked closely at the really successful men in it. Most, it seemed, were involved in commercial rather than residential sales. The advantages were clear. They typically worked regular business hours rather than the evenings and weekends that residential buyers often spend searching for their dream homes. Commercial clients based their choices on location, space, and cost, so there were far fewer possibilities to sift through. They didn't fret about the blue carpeting in this property or the ugly chandelier in that one. And the payoff, on commission, was much greater. I decided to give it a try.

My first big prospect was a businessman from a neighboring community seeking a location for a new fast-food franchise he'd just purchased. Little as I knew about the restaurant business, I remember thinking his then-unknown hamburger chain would never prosper; after all, who could compete with McDonald's? But I was confident that I knew enough about my business to help him find the right location.

After some research I found the perfect spot. It was on a main road, across from a new mall, and I'd learned that the county's freeway plans envisioned an off ramp running right alongside the property. Jackpot! Excitedly, I made an appointment to show it to him.

On the appointed day I waited at the site for forty-five minutes but he never arrived. I called his office, set a second meeting time, and again waited a long time at the site for him to arrive. No sign of him. This time

People

Courage, wisdom pay off for developer

Mertz cleared a path for other women in real estate industry

By Teri Banas
Lansing State Journal

By any standard or gender, Martha Mayhood Mertz has become a professional success story, a builder of Lansing-area landmarks and trailblazer.

She developed award-winning office buildings and shepherded a pivotal renovation in downtown's Pere Marquette building. She made her mark raising the upscale Central Park Place across from the Meridian Mall in Okemos.

And she did it by starting her Okemos real estate business 18 years ago under a ruse of sorts.

Mindful of gender bias, she called her company Mayhood & Mertz to infer a male partner. She became the first woman to broker commercial real estate in mid-Michigan.

She's become a champion for women's business development. Now one of Mertz' top achievements will help showcase the town where it all began.

The international Athena award Mertz launched in the '80s is coming home. The success was borne of the struggles women have had cracking the glass ceiling in business groups like the Chamber of Commerce.

"A lot has changed over the years, and Martha has certainly been at the helm, helping women in our industry and others participate

GREG DeRUITER/Lansing State Journal

Building partners: Deborah Lentz Arnold, left, said she was encouraged by Martha Mayhood Mertz to switch careers from legal secretary to real estate developer. They now are partners. They are standing in one of their projects, the American Board of Emergency Medicine building, which won awards for construction and design.

and drama, landed in Okemos in th '70s after a job transfers for her hu band. With three small school-ag children, she was encouraged to se real estate, exclusively residence at first.

She discovered she had a knac for it, and liked helping young fam ilies make what was often their fir big financial purchase.

"Maybe that's one reason I valu this community and its growth an development over the years," sh said recently while sitting in he Okemos office.

Located in the shadow of the bus Meridian Mall, it sits in one of th few turn-of-the-century histori brick buildings in modern Okemos "We selected this community to liv here. I don't take it for granted.

"Once you invest in land, you'r sort of planted," she added.

The Pere Marquette project cam in 1991. She and other partners con verted the 100-year-old, run-dow warehouse into a trendy new offic home for tenants such as the Great er Lansing Convention/Visitor Center. The renovation showed oth ers the possibilities of saving histor in downtown Lansing.

Today, the Mertz-Arnold partner ship has diversified, branching be yond the Lansing area.

They built the award-winnin American Board of Emergenc Medicine building in East Lansing They also help companies with sit selections and building purchase here and beyond the Lansing area

Arnold, who joined Mertz 1

At right, Martha in front of the national headquarters of the American Board of Emergency Physicians, a Mayhood/Mertz project recognized for its architectural design.

Photo courtesy of Martha Mayhood Mertz.

I got him on the phone and asked why he'd missed our meetings. I recall his words exactly: "Lady, I would never buy a piece of commercial property from a woman."

His statement stunned me to my socks. But instead of feeling defeated, I felt challenged. I showed my investment partner Roger the property and my research on it. We found a way to buy the entire piece ourselves, all fifty-five acres, though frankly the deal was way over our heads in terms of cost and complexity.

With the property under contract, I called the businessman back. I told him that if the property interested him, he would have to "buy from a woman" because I was now the owner. For the prime 1.87 acres he needed he paid handsomely, about half of what Roger and I had spent on the entire parcel.

Though the man's sexism was appalling, his business judgment was not. His franchise, a Wendy's, is still going strong decades later.

I was right on the location.

THREE

Marge,
Mr. Mayhood—and Athena

AFTER WORKING FOR OTHERS in real estate for seven years—the term of an apprenticeship in the old European tradition—I felt ready to take the helm. Having bought the fifty-five acres of land, I felt that it needed its own company to market it; plus, relocating from downtown Lansing to suburban Okemos would put me closer to both the property and my kids' school. In late 1977, I resolved to start my own company.

I mentioned it to a few business associates, who all strongly advised against such a move. They predicted I would fail and backed up their predictions with grim stories about others (men) who had. Feeling alone, scared, and overwhelmed by the prospect of the huge investment and risk involved, I desperately needed someone to confide in.

In my community there was one company headed by a woman (with her husband), but I was too intimidated to approach her. Finally I went to the woman sales manager of another real estate firm in town, took her into my confidence, and asked for her advice. Within hours after I left her office, she called the firm where I worked and reported my intentions to my boss. So much for mentoring! Still, I stuck to my plan.

After my experience with Mister Wendy's, it seemed wise for my company to have at least the appearance of a man involved in running it. People in our community knew me as Martha Mertz. Since I was a transplant from Minnesota, no one in Michigan knew my family name. On January 2, 1978, I signed papers establishing the firm of Mayhood/Mertz Realtors, serving both residential and commercial customers.

For years I would receive calls from prospective clients asking for Mr. Mayhood. I would genially inform them that Mr. Mayhood was out of town (which was true; neither my father nor my brother lived there) but that I was Martha Mertz and would be happy to assist. The little ruse proved effective and it's been a good story to tell on myself—but how sad to look back at a time when such pretense seemed necessary.

The elusive Mr. Mayhood got no calls from certain of my clientele. When those well-served, first-time home buyers started trading up to larger homes, they returned to me in droves. Some families moved four or five times within our community, and retained me every time. One couple told of overhearing their daughter, in a game of make-believe, proudly identifying herself as "Martha Mertz, Realtor." I was on a rising tide.

I'D NEVER SEEN A CHAMBER OF COMMERCE BOARDROOM and it was daunting to walk into one. It was late November 1980 and I was attending a reception for new board members. Around me clusters of men, apparently well-acquainted, chatted in that easy male banter that seems to establish or reinforce dominance. I knew only one man there and sought him out so that I wouldn't be stranded. Some glanced at me, taking in my gender and small stature. I think they presumed I was part of the staff.

I had not sought to join this board. The invitation had come after I'd (politely) refused to shut down our local branch of an initiative the

Chamber had started and for which it had sent us a staff member. The initiative was intended to facilitate dialogue between business and government officials. I was the chair of our little group and we found the discussions valuable; the Chamber, in retrospect, thought they consumed too much staff time and was calling it quits. I simply advised the staff representative that our group intended to continue, thanks, and frankly I had never seen any reason to have the staff there, or the Chamber for that matter. So all the other groups obediently closed down and we remained active. That put me on someone's radar screen and soon thereafter I was joining the Chamber board.

The men around the table were high-profile, high-powered city leaders. Although it was utterly intimidating to be among them, I was fascinated. Never before had I heard conversations in this all-male "business dialect." It was direct, certain, articulate, and effective. When it wasn't effective enough, the speaker turned up the volume to try to win the day. There was no hesitation, qualification, or rumination. This was a complete departure from the way most women at that time couched their statements, with "Would you consider . . . " or "How about . . . " or "I've been thinking . . . ."

I moused along for a year at those meetings while learning that language, which was an absolute prerequisite for joining the conversation. It also took me that long to figure out what value I could contribute to that board. What I could bring, I decided, was others like me. I felt neither comfortable nor effective being the only woman there. I'd been given the title of vice president of membership services, in charge of overseeing events the Chamber sponsored for members. Though there was kind of a Dolley Madison feel to the job, it served my needs at the time perfectly; I learned the purpose and background of Chamber functions and got to know the women on the staff who did all the work for those functions.

Quietly and cautiously, I was taken under the wing of the Chamber's office manager, Marge Shelden. Everyone in town knew her as "Marge-at-the-Chamber." Over the more than twenty years she'd been there, some bosses and members had grossly underestimated Marge, treating her as a functionary, a coffee girl. But she truly was the heart of the organization. During her long tenure Marge had watched as one executive after another ran the Chamber in the style of the old boys' network it was. On occasion Marge would suggest bringing women in as volunteer leaders and one woman had actually held the presidency for a year. But she left without having brought any other women in and Marge's idea was met with neglect if not derision.

My arrival must have been quite a surprise to a lot of people but perhaps especially to her. We quickly established a camaraderie and began to explore what the Chamber did for its women members. This wasn't a part of the strategic plan, it was our initiative. As a volunteer I had a fair amount of latitude but Marge, as a Chamber employee, was risking ire, even her job, by joining me. Marge began showing me the ropes, sharing insights about what was important and how to do things effectively within the organization. For example, the Chamber's weekly executive committee meetings were at 7:30 A.M. in downtown Lansing, a particularly dark, cold, early, and inconvenient time for me, a mom driving in from the suburbs. But even if other VPs sometimes skipped the meetings, Marge knew I should not. That was where the real work got done. So, for more than seven years, I made those meetings.

At Marge's urging, I sought an appointment to the Chamber board's nominating committee. When I got it, I was thrilled and determined to bring more women onto the board. Though I'd become pretty fluent in that male "business dialect," I still felt drowned out in the all-male conversations because my ways of prioritizing issues or dealing with circumstances and people were not the same as theirs. To get my approaches and ideas a fair hearing, I needed other women—or at least people whose perspectives and priorities might be more aligned with mine—at the table.

I came to the nominating committee session with a folder containing names and biographical information of at least five women I considered great candidates for one board role or another. The four men on the committee listened to my suggestions. Then one by one, they rejected every woman I'd proposed with some version of the statement, "She's just not a leader." This person was rejected because she didn't hold the top position in her company; that one because she was "not prominent enough in the community." I didn't get one woman on that slate. I did, however, get my fellow nominators' message loud and clear: Women are not leaders!

I thought differently and set out to change their minds.

OF THE CHAMBER'S 1,200 registered members, only forty-five were women. I wanted to meet with them, so I composed an invitation letter on Chamber letterhead. To this day I am aghast at (and a bit proud of) the moxie it showed. The opening of that letter read:

> *Dear Chamber member:*
> *Why are you a part of this old boys' network?*

After it was mailed and too late for revisions, I found myself second-guessing the cheekiness of that wording. For a while I lived in fear of an angry phone call from some member who'd gotten wind of it but none ever came. It might be the one time I benefited from higher-ups not paying much attention to what I was doing.

To my amazement, thirty-nine women came to that gathering. Soon we had a structure, a mission, and a dedicated group of professionals meeting regularly as the Business Women's Council (a new committee under the Membership Services area I headed). We had two primary goals. We wanted to appoint as many qualified women as possible, as quickly as possible, to leading positions on Chamber committees. And we wanted to influence the Chamber to promote women's leadership.

To advance that second goal, we decided to create an award to be presented to a woman leader within our community, underscoring her professional excellence, her commitment to the community, and her pattern of helping other women achieve their full potential. We figured such public recognition would accomplish several things. First, business and professional women would see that the Chamber was an organization recognizing (and welcoming) women. Second, as women achieved leadership positions, they would be inspired to help others do the same (a concept that would become known as mentoring). And finally, because the award emanated from the Chamber, our male leaders would come to recognize women as leaders, creating a much-needed shift in perception. Our Chamber president-elect, local banker Mike Hoffman, agreed to the idea and approved us presenting the award at the Chamber's most visible gathering, its annual dinner.

With a core planning committee (women and men) offering input on every aspect of the award, the discussion was lively. After someone earnestly suggested that the award take the form of a painting on black velvet, I volunteered myself as a one-person search committee to find something a bit more artistically refined. Since we had no budget, I approached the Michigan State University art school, seeking a student who might be able to create our award economically.

Her name was Linda Ackley. She was a graduate student in the art department, in the latter stages of achieving a master of fine arts in bronze sculpting. She had carved out a space on the second floor of a cavernous building and was the only one around the day I climbed the steps and met her. She seemed pleased to take up the challenge and agreed to accept the $350 that we had scraped together.

A week later Linda showed me two draft renditions: a stylized open-door shape and a rectangular frame lined with jagged bits of wood. I saw where she was trying to go. The jagged rectangle could symbolize the difficulties women leaders had to overcome; the open door could suggest

Linda Ackley as a Michigan State University graduate student in gear for a bronze pour. Linda designed and created the first ATHENA Award, and would in time make nearly 6,000 more, using the lost wax process. Each sculpture is a numbered work of art. Photo courtesy of Linda Ackley/ Third Millennium Fine Arts.

opportunity. Somehow, seeing what she did not express in these forms made me realize what we had to express—and that was the exhilaration of achievement. Neither one of us had fully experienced such leadership achievement yet in our professional lives but we could imagine how it would feel: the satisfaction, the validation, the pride and flat-out joy. The award needs to look like success feels, we agreed. You're getting where you want to go. You're celebrating. As we talked, I threw in some body language, triumphantly thrusting my arms over my head.

The next time Linda showed me a rendition, I was blown away. She had drawn an abstract shape subtly suggesting a woman's form with arms uplifted in a graceful and celebratory pose. Where the head would be, a crystal prism rested. She proposed casting the design in bronze and setting it on a wooden base.

All that was left was to decide what the award would be called. We listed inspiring women from history, namesakes who exemplified the kind of excellence we had in mind. But as remarkable as many were, no single name—not Rosa or Indira, Amelia or Eleanor, Sacagawea or Susan B.—embodied everything we wanted to associate with women's way of leading in the late twentieth century.

Ultimately we decided that if one mortal female couldn't convey it all, maybe an idealized, mythic female could. Linda volunteered to spend some library time researching goddess figures. Within a week or two, she came back with a file full of mythology clippings and a one-word recommendation: Athena.

OF ALL THE CHARACTERS IN GREEK MYTHOLOGY, nobody makes a better entrance than Athena, daughter of Zeus, king of the gods, and his first wife Metis (whose name means "wisdom"). Here's how the *Encyclopedia Mythica* tells the story: "In fear that Metis would bear a son mightier than himself, Zeus swallowed her and she began to make a robe and helmet for her daughter. The hammering of the helmet caused Zeus great pain in the form of headaches and he cried out in agony. Skilled Hephaestus (Zeus's son, and a blacksmith) ran to his father and split his skull open—and from it emerged Athena, fully grown and wearing her mother's robe and helmet."

Small wonder that she was worshipped as the pre-eminent goddess of Greece: Athena had it all. As Zeus's favorite child, she alone shared his protective shield and his arsenal of thunderbolts. She was the goddess of wisdom, of war, and of the domestic arts (spinning, weaving, pottery). She was an inventor (the chariot, the plow, the flute), a wise judge and counselor, and a protector of some of mythology's best-known leading men (Herakles, Odysseus).

In the early 1980s as we sought a namesake for our award, we looked hard at Athena's checkered history. She had, after all, sprung from the mind of a man, and with no real birth mother and no girlfriends throughout mythology she is seen aligning herself mostly with men. Still Athena embodied so many of the traits we believed women would need to achieve their full potential in that uncharted time: courage, wisdom, strength. And as recounted in Greek myth, her actions seemed so consistent with enlightened, twenty-first-century leadership.

Take her approach to conflict resolution, when she and her uncle Poseidon both laid claim to a certain city in Greece. Again, from the *Encyclopedia Mythica:* "It was decided that the one that could give the finest gift (to the city) should have it. Leading a procession of citizens, the two gods mounted the Acropolis. Poseidon struck the side of the cliff with his trident and a spring welled up. The people marveled, but the water was as salty as Poseidon's sea and it was not very useful. Athena's gift was an olive tree, which was better because it gave the people food, oil and wood." Athena won and named her city Athens.

From the outset, I didn't care for the martial aspect of Athena. "Goddess of war" seemed at odds with valuing women's more collaborative, less confrontational way of leading. But over time I've thought it through in ways that work for me and so have others who have studied and analyzed Athena. Scholar Elinor Stebbins contends that "In spite of (her) birthright of armor, Athena was not known to have a bellicose nature, nor did she bear arms except when her country was threatened or attacked, or when she came to the aid of heroes such as Herakles, Perseus, and Odysseus." I thought that squared nicely with what we saw in contemporary women leaders: tough when they had to be, to defend what they valued or to come to the rescue of others.

The ancients built shrines to honor their important figures. Today, we build Web sites. Google Athena and you'll find online tributes characterizing her as "the first career woman" and the mother of all multi-taskers. Name a pursuit important in ancient Greece and she was a patron of it, from animal-taming and agriculture to shipbuilding and shoe-making. She was a creator of beauty and an artisan, a trusted advisor and a strategic thinker. With such diverse strengths, she was well-prepared to meet whatever challenges arose, obviously an important capacity for modern leaders as well.

In his book *The Homeric Gods,* William F. Otto calls Athena "the goddess of nearness." It's a particularly intimate way to describe a deity so expansive. Athena was as likely to draw close to heroes in battle as to maidens preparing for their weddings. In short, she was a mentor to those who needed her support, a role model that seemed particularly apt for emerging women leaders.

The more we learned of Athena, the more we admired her. There was this sense of totality, of an integration of mind, body, and spirit. Again and again, stories demonstrated that indispensable dimension of integrity, woven into the legend right down to her name. According to Greek scholar Walter Burkert, Homer's description of the goddess "calls her by a higher name, 'divine intelligence,' as though to say: This is she who has the mind better than others." But more, Burkert says, Homer "wished to identify the goddess with moral intelligence (*en ethei noesin*) and therefore gave her the name Ethnooe, which . . . either he or his successors have altered into what they thought a nicer form, and called her Athene."

This went to the heart of what we wanted our award to exalt: that moral compass, that ethical framework, that consistency of values and behaviors without which a leader cannot be trusted. In dealing with both allies and rivals, Athena held to her own precepts and stayed true to herself. And as for her unorthodox birth, I decided to consider it a parable for how a strong woman is a man's headache—until he comes to terms with sharing responsibility and opportunity with her.

We had our paragon. Athena would be recast as a modern ideal, a twenty-first-century avatar of strong, womanly leadership. Our Chamber working group pressed ahead with organizing the honors program and unofficially we gave ourselves a new name: The ATHENA Society.

WITHIN ONE FOURTEEN-MONTH SPAN, the following occurred: I filed for divorce and moved out of the family home. I watched my young company come to a standstill as Michigan's economy tanked. And I led the planning and execution of the first ATHENA Awards program.

Talk about putting an axe to your head.

Yet I think a lot of people have experienced what I did during that period. In horrible times that try our souls, we somehow convert anguish and upheaval into extra energy. I applied that energy to a half-formed idea about honoring women leaders, and out came ATHENA. The pain brought the inspiration!

But the pain was intense and it permeated the family. My daughter Michelle, by then a college student who had chosen to take a sabbatical with a couple of her girl friends, was enjoying Florida sunshine and waiting on tables. My son Michael was heading to college on a full scholarship. Only Christopher, a sixteen-year-old high school junior, was at home. One of the best things that Mike and I had done together was raising the kids. It was as if the gears of our lives had meshed there. But beyond that, as I became more involved in business and women's issues, the rest of our lives had diverged, leaving almost no shared interests or endeavors.

After working with and without counselors for years to find a way to bridge our differences, we parted. Taking only my clothes and a stereo, I moved into a townhouse nearby. Intellectually, the kids understood the split; emotionally, it was brutal for them and horrible for me to see them hurting.

As the marriage ended, Michigan's economy hit its worst slump in years. With interest rates sky-high, everyone wanted to sell their real estate and no one wanted to buy. My company was moribund; my earnings for the whole year hovered around $4,000. Throughout my industry, there literally was nothing to do. So, I figured, better to go out and do something else. With the help of a therapist, I began to delve deep into my psyche and history, the family issues, the anger and hurt. Mostly, I spent long hours at the Chamber working on every aspect of the fledging ATHENA Awards program.

Through my work both in counseling and at the Chamber, I arrived at the same realization: Unequal treatment of women had been and remained a defining issue for me. The burgeoning women's movement resonated so strongly with me because it described what I had lived, the limits on girls' aspirations, the belittling of women's achievements. If the era's emerging feminist leaders could be heard, then so could we all. The question for me was how to use my voice. The country had this problem, all this anger about women not being dealt with equally. But instead of anger (of which I'd had enough) I wanted to create something positive, something that let everybody win. A leadership award program would honor and encourage deserving women. It would reflect well on the sponsoring individuals and organizations. And it might even begin to identify what leadership could look like with a female face.

In fashioning criteria for selecting our honoree for the ATHENA Award, we purposefully ran counter to what other award programs often emphasized. Our recipient would be honored for more than being just The Top or The Only. This wasn't going to be adulation for those we had come to call The Queen Bees, women who had become the first to rise in their profession and then so enjoyed that position that they turned their backs on others seeking opportunity. Our award would be for the less ego-driven leader, the often quieter voice, the striver who focused on others' advancement as much as self-advancement.

On one level, ours was a nuts-and-bolts task: to list the judging criteria for this new award program. But in reality we were doing much more. Around a coffee cup–littered conference table in a Lansing, Michigan, boardroom, we were redefining the core principles of leadership.

We agreed that the award would identify and celebrate an outstanding individual, usually a woman, who had excelled in these ways:

(1) She had achieved the highest level of professional excellence in her field.

(2) She had given of her time and talent back to her community.

(3) Most importantly, she had opened leadership opportunities for others, especially for women.

As we talked about recipients, we could see them in our mind's eye. They were achievers in the classic sense, visibly involved in the community and passionate about making a difference. Unlike Queen Bees, they were eager to provide encouragement and advice to other women— women who were beginning to dream of their own possibilities, women who were inspired by the examples recipients were setting, women who

Nation's Business   August 1990

Women In Business

*Ideas, insights, and information to help women
compete and succeed in the marketplace.*

RECOGNITION

Courting Women By Honoring Them

By Anne Merick

In a 1982 telephone survey of companies in the Lansing, Mich., area, business leaders were surprised to discover that more firms than they had expected were run by women.

But it's no surprise that today, just eight years later, the percentage of women members in the Lansing Regional Chamber of Commerce has more than doubled—from 9 percent to more than 20 percent—and the number of businesswomen on its 28-member board of directors has risen to eight from one. The credit for this increase in female involvement goes in no small part to Lansing's "Athena" program, an awards project designed to recognize outstanding businesswomen in the community.

The Athena award, now part of a national program, was conceived by Martha Mertz, an Okemos, Mich., real-estate developer who in 1982 was the sole businesswoman on the chamber's board. She discovered that in the 70-year history of the Lansing chamber, only one woman had ever been honored for her business leadership. "I felt most women didn't have time to wait that long again," says Mertz.

She also felt that her organization was not a network only for business*men*. The world was changing, she reasoned, and if women who owned businesses were not involved both as members and leaders in the chamber of commerce, they were missing out.

In 1985 Mertz was elected president of the Lansing Regional Chamber, and the following year she herself won the award she had created.

Mertz looked to Mount Olympus for her inspiration and chose the Greek goddess Athena as her model. The daughter of Zeus, Athena embodies the

Anne Merick is a free-lance writer and media consultant in Bethesda, Md.

virtues of courage, wisdom, and strength—"qualities today's women must have to succeed in the business world," says Mertz. A statue was commissioned by the chamber and was designed by Michigan State University fine-arts student Linda Ackley, now herself a successful entrepreneur with her own studio in Lansing.

The bronze award is an abstract figure of a woman with uplifted arms holding a crystal prism. Ackley says

Inspired by *developer Martha Mertz, right, the Athena Award Program is directed by Marge Shelden.*

she chose a surface with a lot of texture, likening it to the life of a successful woman. The prism symbolizes the multifaceted nature of women and their ability to shed light on the community.

The award has been given annually

since 1982 to individuals in recognition of their business accomplishments, service to the community, and support of the goals and efforts of professional women.

The Oldsmobile division of General Motors, which is headquartered in Lansing, agreed five years ago to sponsor the Athena program nationwide through its network of automobile dealerships. Today 250 chambers in 45 states are participating in the project in partnership with their local Oldsmobile dealers. Marge Shelden, national director of the project, expects to have more than 350 local chambers involved by the end of the year.

"The program increases public awareness of the outstanding contributions of women," says Shelden. Noting projections that half of all businesses will be owned by women by the year 2000, she adds that more chamber marketing efforts should be directed toward women.

A packet of materials promoting the program tells Oldsmobile dealers that as sponsors, they "receive increased recognition and direct attention from one of the most influential and sought-after markets ... the women's market."

Some of the proceeds from the sale of statues and jewelry modeled after the sculpture go to the Athena Foundation for use in the Lansing area. Last year, funds were made available to the Lansing Community College Women's Resource Center for scholarships for women in need of education to re-enter the work force.

An exhibit of the Athena sculpture is on display this year at the Michigan Women's Hall of Fame and Historical Museum in Lansing, and an exhibit is scheduled to begin at the National Women's Hall of Fame in Seneca Falls, N.Y., in September.

More information on the program is available from Marge Shelden, director, Athena Award Program, Lansing Regional Chamber of Commerce, 510 W. Washtenaw St., P.O. Box 14030, Lansing, Mich., 48901; (800) 548-8247. In Michigan, call (517) 487-6340.

PHOTO: ©WILLIAM DEKAY

An article in *Nation's Business,* a publication of the U. S. Chamber of Commerce, featured Marge Shelden, left, and Martha.

were themselves reaching for that next level of credibility and success. We thought of recipients not just in terms of who they were today but in terms of how their actions would shape the future. When asked by colleagues to recommend a worthy candidate for some job or opportunity, these recipients would confidently make the case for a person who hadn't yet had the chance to prove herself. They would be willing to take the time to listen, to relate aspects of their own journey, to invite along, to introduce, to coach, or to compliment—in short, to respond in large and small ways, each gesture giving heart and hope to the aspiring woman. That's what we believed women needed to gain a better footing in the professional world and that's what ATHENA recipients, women and men, would provide.

The award, we hoped, would serve a second purpose. It wouldn't just recognize a few recipients, it would raise up many more like them. Along the way a new friend of mine, Edward Ingraham, had given me a little slip of paper with a quote he thought described our vision. It was from Plato and it became the defining motto for the meaning of the award: "What is honored in a country will be cultivated there." By praising leaders who were excelling, giving back, and reaching out, we would reinforce the value of those behaviors. And when others in the community saw those values being rewarded, they'd make an effort to emulate them. By changing the concept of what was esteemed, we aimed to change the face and nature of leadership.

On January 27, 1983, the first ATHENA Award was presented at the annual dinner of the Lansing Regional Chamber of Commerce. I was present that evening, watching from a table off to the side, as Chamber President Mike Hoffman described this new award and announced, with proper fanfare, the identity of our first recipient—Dr. Marylee Davis.

Marylee worked for Michigan State University in a community outreach capacity, serving as an important link between academia and business. She had previously lived in Washington, D. C., working for the Carter administration. She was polished, articulate, generous with her time, a positive model of an effective woman. She was well known to both the "town" and "gown" populations, serving essentially as an ambassador between the two, representing her beloved MSU well and quietly opening opportunities for women in both realms.

The selection of Marylee also set an important precedent, though at the time only a few insiders knew of it. Not surprisingly since the award program sprang from Chamber and business circles, some of our committee members initially wanted to require that award nominees be business owners and Chamber members. I argued against those restrictions, convinced that ATHENA had to stand, above all, for inclusiveness. Ultimately, that approach prevailed—an ATHENA Award could go to anyone who embodied our core leadership principles, no matter the nominee's field of endeavor, age, station, gender, or Chamber membership.

Obviously Marylee was to have been our guest of honor at the award ceremony. But a few days before the dinner her car had been struck head-on by the pick-up truck of a drunk driver. On award night, Marylee was in a hospital intensive care unit, fighting for her life. When her name was read as the first ATHENA Award recipient, her boss strode onstage and, with tears on his cheeks, said he would take the sculpture to her directly.

Then I heard a rolling thunder that at first I couldn't identify. It was the sound of 1,000 chairs moving against the floor as the entire audience rose to give a standing ovation. The gesture recognized a woman, a leader—a woman leader. Athena was born again.

FOUR

Leadership's Female Face

T HE FIRST ATHENA AWARD was so well heralded in the local press that three things happened. The Award officially became an annual program, as Lansing Chamber leaders gave us permission to plan for a second year's event, and then a third. We began getting calls from beyond Lansing, from Chamber and community leaders interested in starting their own ATHENA Award programs. And our Chamber's president, Mike Hoffman, suggested looking for a corporate sponsor to support the program and help take it nationwide.

As president of Lansing's largest bank, Mike knew most of the community's top employers. In no time, he and I were booked for lunch with two top marketing executives for Oldsmobile, a General Motors division then headquartered in Lansing. One was a gentleman; the other was a sharp, slender woman named Lynn Myers.

The Oldsmobile executives were lovely lunch companions. Then came time for the presentation. I showed them the ATHENA Award sculpture I had brought along and outlined the ATHENA Award concept.

The gentleman looked at me as if I were speaking some foreign language. As far as I could tell, he simply could not see how honoring these leaders fit with selling cars.

At the end of the lunch, I felt sure the gentleman wasn't interested in any part of what I had said. As I walked with Lynn toward our cars, on an impulse, I handed her the award sculpture and asked her to hang onto it for a while so she could "think about it." I wasn't entirely sure what I was doing, I just knew I needed to make a connection with her if not with her colleague.

When I checked back with Lynn a few months later, she told me that she went back to Oldsmobile, where she was the only female at her level in the organization, and put the sculpture on her desk. Over the weeks, various male executives would come into her office to kick around ideas. They'd perch on the corner of her desk, idly play with a paperweight or pencil—or the sculpture—and then end up asking, "What is this?" She found herself repeatedly describing the award and the ideas behind it. Pretty soon, she found she had started to believe in it.

At a news conference in August 1985 Oldsmobile announced a generous in-kind sponsorship of the ATHENA Award program. Oldsmobile would encourage its 3,200 dealers nationwide to purchase award sculptures and organize award banquets and news conferences for their communities' honorees, often in collaboration with a local Chamber, university, or women's group, and to promote the program in their advertising. While Oldsmobile touted the program to its dealership network, we would seek support from the National Chamber of Commerce to promote the program to its 1,500 member chapters.

I came to know and admire Lynn Myers. Across our differences, me the entrepreneur and she the corporate executive, we have become great collaborators. We met at a time when, professionally and personally, we were both trekking in uncharted territory, designing the course of our lives without benefit of role models. At that critical time, our admiration

Lynn Myers, retired Marketing General Manager for Pontiac-GMC, an ATHENA International past president and an ATHENA International Award recipient. Photo courtesy of Lynn Myers.

and support for each other was mutually uplifting. She remained an energetic proponent of the ATHENA program as she rose through the ranks at GM to head the Pontiac-GMC division. We've established a tradition of having dinner together once a year and have thoroughly enjoyed comparing the tracks of our careers and the ongoing adventures of our families. I'm proud to say that in 2007-08, Lynn served during a very important year as president of ATHENA International, the organization's most important volunteer position.

ATHENA, NATIONWIDE! All of a sudden, with the Oldsmobile sponsorship, our award program was much bigger than the Lansing Chamber. While that was great for the promotion of women's leadership, it had its down side for one woman in particular: Marge Shelden. Her paycheck came from the Lansing Chamber and its focus was on the local community, not on this now-national project. Marge and I were straying outside the boundaries of the Lansing Chamber's mission and that didn't please some of the senior leaders of the Chamber who hadn't much liked the program to begin with.

Unveiling the ATHENA Wall of Fame at Lansing Community College: Martha (holding scissors) with, from left, ATHENA Award recipients Dr. Marylee Davis, Michigan State University; Lucille Belen, Lansing City Council; Sister Janice Belen, chief executive officer of Sparrow Hospital; Allison Steele; and Debbie Stabenow, Michigan House of Representatives.
Photo courtesy of ATHENA International.

The ATHENA Award had gained enough support in town that it just couldn't be dumped outright, so the top Chamber staff offered a compromise. Marge was allowed to remain in charge of the program but it was made clear that it shouldn't interfere with her ever-increasing office-manager duties. I didn't know for years that she was taking work home at night in order to get it done. She didn't complain once. She was the best gift those leaders could have given us, because Marge was invaluable. But it also meant playing a cat and mouse game much of the time to keep ATHENA growing but not so visibly that her superiors would notice and change their minds.

Marge became the voice of ATHENA as people around the country called a newly-installed toll-free number for guidance in launching local programs. Because the office manager sat in an open reception area within earshot of Chamber co-workers, Marge often used her break to walk to a pay phone and make ATHENA-related calls. When she and I had ATHENA business to do, we "had lunch" away from the office and worked more than ate. Finally on some pretense about better use of Chamber office space, she and I lugged a big desk into an unused office with a door that closed so she could work with more privacy.

ATHENA hummed along through 1985 and 1986 when, probably to the chagrin of its critics, I served a year as Chamber president. At the outset, we had structured the Award program so it covered its own costs and even made a little money through sculpture sales. I thought that would motivate the Chamber to keep the program going. It never occurred to me that someone might find a way to keep the proceeds but not the program.

The Chamber leaders did. In 1987 it was announced that the local chamber needed to spin off the national program—sort of. The ATHENA Award still would be presented at the annual dinner. The ATHENA program would have use of office space, the toll-free phone number, and Marge, but a board-of-directors agreement gave the Chamber leaders equal control of the organization. As for funding, in consideration of the money the Award program was bringing in (somewhere between $10,000 and $20,000 a year at that point), the Chamber would give the program an annual operating stipend—$1,000.

We lacked the resources and the maturity as an organization to separate completely from the Chamber. We took the deal. But some at the Chamber weren't stopping there. Among their choices for ATHENA board directors was Jim Anderton, a prominent local businessman. We figured Jim was assigned to the board to help or at worst to keep an eye on things. We learned only later that he had basically been given the task of closing ATHENA down.

We learned that because Jim told us. He joined the board generally sharing the sense that the Chamber would be well rid of the program. But once he spent some time with ATHENA supporters—working on building the foundation and the award program, seeing its positive effects in a rapidly growing number of U.S. communities—his perspective changed completely. He began pulling with ATHENA, not against it, giving it the benefit of his considerable business skills.

Jim's knowledge of organizational management helped lay a sound foundation. He encouraged actions such as broadening the geographical representation on our board that would make us more truly a national enterprise. Perhaps most importantly, he envisioned and helped lead efforts toward a national gathering of ATHENA recipients and supporters, a conference where people could form connections and create a network. With full support from this man who'd once been sent to discourage us, the ATHENA Foundation sought and received tax-exempt status as a 501(c)3 organization, thanks to hard work by two board members who were accounting professionals, Lamont Lator and Carol Fitzgerald.

In 1992 the news for women was mixed. America got its first female poet laureate, Pulitzer Prize winner Mona Van Duyn. The Church of England allowed women to be ordained priests. America's vice president decried the bad morals of a woman who didn't even exist, the single-mother lead character of the TV series *Murphy Brown*. And America's Navy secretary resigned over a scandal involving women sexually assaulted by Navy personnel at a gathering known as Tailhook. At their summer 1992 presidential nominating conventions, the Republicans and Democrats both featured powerful women speakers in primetime. Two of them were HIV-positive mothers, Democrat Elizabeth Glaser and Republican Mary Fisher, who implored their parties for action and compassion for those with AIDS.

And in 1992, after nearly twenty-five years at the Lansing Chamber, Marge Shelden was preparing to depart. The time was right. The ATHENA Foundation (named to reflect the modest grants we gave from our $1,000 Chamber agreement) announced it was ready to become an independent organization, and the Chamber leaders went along. For the transition, they even gave us Marge's services fulltime for her last three months on Chamber payroll. I assumed the foundation's presidency as a volunteer position (which it still is). We renovated an inexpensive space in a downtown warehouse, moved our files, and set up an office for ATHENA's first executive director, Marge Shelden.

Roseanne Stead, Executive Director, with Martha introducing ATHENA at a 1993 regional gathering of Chamber of Commerce executives. Photo courtesy of ATHENA International.

BY 1993 the ATHENA Award had been presented to nearly 1,500 individuals through programs in 300 cities. To bind these leaders into a national organization, we needed a national meeting. So invitations went out for "Forging the Future," the inaugural national conference of the ATHENA Foundation, to be held May 19-21, 1994, just outside Washington, D. C.

The invitation rang with the enthusiasm and optimism we all felt. "It is time to unite the excellence, power and vision of our ATHENA recipients and those who sponsor us. This conference will chart the course of the ATHENA Foundation. We will plan strategies for heightening the relevance and effectiveness of ATHENA in our nation and in our communities . . . . We will learn about remarkable local programs and leadership ideas worth taking home . . . . We will do far more than sit and listen: We will frame the ideas that will guide us in the years ahead."

The conference drew nearly 100 people: ATHENA Award recipients, Chamber and other community leaders and sponsors involved with local Award programs, and national ATHENA underwriters, including Oldsmobile and First of America Bank Corporation. It was an impressive crowd, 90 percent women and 100 percent fired up about our mission. One recipient, Dr. Joyce Murphy, came from Anchorage, Alaska. She was a veterinarian ophthalmologist who worked with seals and other Alaskan wildlife. Another, Mary Lou Bessette, managed the *Arizona Business Gazette.* Terri and Dave Hedges came from their printing business in Nashville. Ellen Ruddock, a recipient from Indiana, Pennsylvania, took time off from Career Dynamics, her management consulting firm. Dr. Marylee Davis, our first recipient in Lansing, was there. Even Edward and my daughter Michelle came, though at the time they both were still forming their opinions about the whole idea.

We worked hard over three days: organizational planning, educational workshops, brainstorming sessions and interactive, team-building exercises. We played a little, too, taking in a National Symphony performance at the Kennedy Center. At our conference dinner, I remember looking out from the dais at all the glowing faces and thinking, "These people are so impressive, so accomplished, and they've come from so far to be here. We are all envisioning the same possibilities, we are all willing to commit our time and talent because this is truly important for our times." That night it seemed I was able to step outside of myself and view the experience through a different lens. It all seemed a bit removed from reality, like in my dreams. That same "out-of-myself" experience would happen many times over in the years to come, in moments when the power and resonance of the ATHENA ideas generated an almost unbelievable outpouring of enthusiasm and commitment.

At the conference we also named our first nationwide ATHENA Award recipient. When ATHENA Foundation board members had surveyed the national scene, looking for leaders to consider for this inaugural award, we identified three in one spot.

National Public Radio journalists Cokie Roberts, Linda Wertheimer and Nina Totenberg seemed to embody ATHENA's core criteria: displaying professional excellence in their field, giving time and talent back to the community, and opening the way for other women to flourish. A recently published *New York Times Magazine* profile described how the three were "revolutionizing political reporting" while remaining "the closest of friends." The wisdom of the day was that women could neither work together—too competitive, too insecure—nor be counted upon to reach out and help female colleagues. Yet here were three top-flight professionals who appeared to be doing just that.

Of the three, Nina Totenberg stood out. In 1991 she was one of two reporters to break an incendiary story. Anita Hill, a University of Oklahoma law professor, claimed she had been sexually harassed in the 1980s by Clarence Thomas, then President George H.W. Bush's nominee for a Supreme Court seat. Both Totenberg's gender and her hard-charging reporting made her a target in the political firestorm that the revelation sparked. But she stayed on the story, and her coverage forced the question

Nina Totenberg, first National ATHENA Recipient, with Bill Bleau of GM, Martha, and Linda Ackley in Washington, D. C., 1994. At right, Marilyn Carlson Nelson, CEO of Carlson Companies, Inc., with Ellen Ruddock, past president of ATHENA. Photos courtesy of ATHENA International.

of whether the Senate Judiciary Committee members (all men) had seriously investigated Hill's allegations.

In early 1994 Totenberg's husband Floyd Haskell, a former U.S. senator from Colorado, suffered severe head injuries in a fall on the ice near their Washington home. When the ATHENA board approached her about being our award recipient, she was keeping a schedule all too familiar to working women. One moment she was at a desk fulfilling her work responsibilities, the next moment at a bedside nursing a loved one.

And so it was that Nina Totenberg became the ATHENA Award's first national recipient.

FAST FORWARD TO WINTER 1997. For three snowy days we met on the Wellesley College campus, seven women and men who believed in the ATHENA program and were committed to its future. I led the retreat with the help of Dr. Peggy McIntosh, a brilliant Ph.D. and associate director of Wellesley's Center for Research on Women. Others in the room included Carole Leland, Ph.D., of the Center for Creative Leadership, a prestigious leadership development institution; Dr. Peter Mitchell, a college president and ATHENA award recipient; and business owner Ellen Ruddock, also a recipient who would become a beloved leader of the organization in years to come. Together, we analyzed where ATHENA had been and strategized about where it should go next. The organization would continue doing what it did best, honoring women's leadership through the ATHENA Awards. It would press for more local and national dialogue on the need for gender balance in leadership from the highest ranks on down. In addition it would develop more mechanisms to link our aspiring leaders with lifelines: coaches and mentors, partnerships and resources.

We came away convinced that what we were developing was more than just a collection of programs, a menu of services. One word kept cropping up in our discussions: *model*. Taken together, all those principles and behaviors we were exalting amounted to a distinct and revolutionary model of leadership—an ATHENA model.

As we planned how ATHENA would empower women leaders of the future, one of the most powerful women in my past resurfaced.

Just before I left for Wellesley, my sister Mary had called with an interesting proposition. She had mentioned to an acquaintance of hers, a talented Internet sleuth, that her aunt had vanished thirty-five years before. He flatly declared that with a birth date and a Social Security number, he could find Erva Mayhood, no matter where she'd gone and how long she'd been missing.

In no time at all, he introduced us (on the computer screen) to Anne Craig, the identity Erva had taken when she broke from her old life and embarked upon a new one. Scrolling through Web pages, he showed us she was in business, the owner of Anne Craig Real Estate in Scottsdale, Arizona, just across the valley from Sun City where my parents had retired. We even could see information about where she shopped (Saks—it had to be her!) and, ultimately, how to contact her. So we did, keeping our discovery a secret from Dad until we could better gauge the situation. After I finished at Wellesley, Romelle, Mary, and I met in Arizona and went to visit Erva/Anne.

She was just who she always had been to us, gracious, dignified, and warm, still lovely inside and out. We had brought her flowers, candy, and an abundance of love and joy for the blessing of this unexpected reunion. On that first day, we learned a bit about how she had rewritten her life story. For a time she had lived in Hawaii, then moved to Arizona. She started a real estate business just in advance of the area's population explosion, worked hard and prospered. She acquired a young business associate, Jim, an earnest and talented person; he and his personal partner, Mark, had become like family to her.

There was, however, the matter of the rest of her family: her one remaining brother, our father Ross, living just across the valley. We asked if we could take her over to see him and somewhat to our surprise she said yes.

When we arrived at Dad's, my sisters went inside to bring him out to where we were waiting. He said hello and waited to be introduced to this lovely silver-haired lady whom he didn't recognize and assumed was some friend of ours. When we told him who she was, he was speechless for a few seconds and then blurted, "Where the hell have you been?" It was the last time he would ask. Her reply—"None of your business, Ross"—closed the door to any further prying.

When we went inside, Dad headed for his den and within seconds came back holding the postcard Erva had sent from Hawaii years earlier. He had kept that bit of paper, that token of her, at his fingertips all that time. But now that she was back he was overwhelmed with hurt and anger. *Where the hell have you been?*

Where Erva had been was ultimately revealed to us nieces through Jim and Mark, her adopted family. She had been with her mate, Maggie, a woman with whom she had enjoyed life until Maggie's death in the late 1980s. They had not lived openly as a couple. In their cover story, they had each lost a husband and were widowed roommates. In this way they were able to live together in privacy, carve out successful lives, and spare their families what Erva believed would be an utterly unacceptable truth.

Through the lost years my mother used to wonder aloud if Erva had been kidnapped and "sold into white slavery." I mourned her disappearance as a family tragedy and a deeply personal loss. But after Erva reentered our lives, I understood her vanishing for what it really was: an act of authenticity. She believed she could not stay where she was—in the Twin Cities, in the retail world, in our family—and be who she was, with Maggie. And so she gave up a very successful position, forfeited the comforts of family, paid an incredible price. But she chose authenticity, bet on the future, and went forward.

Though my father had his sister back for five years before his death in 2002, I don't think he ever completely got over her disappearance or forgave her for it. My siblings and I had an easier time with it. For us, reconnecting with her was a gift. She assumed the position of grand matriarch for all our families, as well as Jim's and Mark's. She lived to be ninety-two, serene and content in the embrace of so many. Because she had been such a model for me in my youth, everything I thought a highly-accomplished woman should be, it was fascinating to see where her life and mine ran in parallels. She had a real estate company, as did I. She was involved with her local Chamber of Commerce, as was I. She had made me believe, decades before, that women could achieve professional success—and she had, as had I.

Because we found Erva, at least the story has an ending. I might even go so far as to say it has a moral. Over Erva's long life, she had given up one incredible career and prospered and excelled in another. She had lived many years with a beloved partner, but without any member of her blood family. I may never fully grasp what I missed of her but I think I understand what I retain from her, and it speaks to a cardinal virtue of ATHENA leaders: being true to one's authentic self.

When I learned of Erva's last wish after her death in 2007, I felt her draw close one more time. She asked that her ashes and Maggie's be scattered near my home in the Sedona hills she had loved.

FIFTEEN YEARS after we'd given the first ATHENA Award, the movement was flourishing. Scores of organizations around the country, Chambers of Commerce as well as other sponsoring groups, had presented the awards to more than 2,300 leaders in their communities. Every few weeks, another local organizer would call to ask about starting

an ATHENA event in another city or to send us a copy of the commemo-
rative program from an event. Flipping through the programs, we'd see
the honorees smiling confidently from the pages. Most were women but
beyond that, they were people of all ages, backgrounds, and professions.
Reading their biographies, we'd glimpse the accomplishments and contributions that earned them the honor.

At first I just reveled in looking at those faces and thinking *leader*.
But as the list of recipients grew, I found myself wanting to know more.
We had established that these people were leaders, but what kind of leaders? Virtually none of the women had been brought up to assume they'd
fill those roles in society. Virtually none had been routed early into professional leadership tracks or training, as men often were. So how did
they become leaders? How did they achieve such leadership excellence
that their communities said to them, "You're the role models we want to
emulate"?

The question became a quest with two goals: (1) Let's see what we can
learn about how these people lead; and (2) let's distill those distinctive
ways of leading into a model that other aspiring leaders could follow.
I knew that I personally operated differently as a leader than many of
the men around me and I had a hunch that other women did too. But it
seemed important to really pin this down in order to identify common
elements in women's ways of leading: to understand the traits, to examine the rationales, and to scrutinize the outcomes.

Now we'd gone from a question to a quest to a research project, and
for that we needed partners. We applied to the W.K. Kellogg Foundation,
asking its support for "a project to identify, articulate and share the values
and characteristics ascribed by the ATHENA philosophy of leadership."
In June 1998 Kellogg gave us a $45,000 grant. With research assistance
from the Center for Creative Leadership and one of its visionary fellows,
Dr. Carole Leland, we would survey ATHENA recipients, gathering their
insights, experiences, and opinions about leadership. Armed with that

research, we'd convene a panel of national authorities on women and leadership and we'd hammer out the definitive statement of the leadership principles ATHENA embodied.

When we chose which ATHENA recipients to invite to participate in the survey, we were intentionally inclusive. Participants were involved in every sort of professional endeavor and came from workplaces of every size. Most were drawing a paycheck but some were unpaid volunteers. All had made important contributions to their communities. To my knowledge, not one had received any formal education in or preparation for management or leadership. The vast majority had not grown up with the expectation that they would assume a leader's mantle. Most amazing of all, most of them came to us still insisting they did not see themselves as leaders, even though their communities had singled out their accomplishments by handing them ATHENA Awards.

Most survey participants had found their voices as leaders without all the acronyms, the MBA degrees and the C-level titles (CEO, COO, CFO). They emerged as leaders because they attracted and inspired followers. They generally did that by bringing three things to the table: their own talents and expertise; a passionate focus on the purpose and potential of their pursuits, and an ability to compellingly communicate their vision.

The survey was straightforward. Define leadership, it prompted. Identify the qualities that separate leaders from followers. Identify leadership challenges for the twenty-first century, including both impediments and opportunities for women to assume greater leadership responsibilities. Finally, we asked survey participants to share their thoughts on a central goal of ATHENA: achieving balanced leadership. The award program had sprung from my head (so to speak) as a way for women leaders to be acknowledged and encouraged as much as men. But fifteen years later we saw leadership out of balance by other measures: race/ethnicity and socio-economic background as well as gender. As people of integrity, ATHENA leaders would need to address that imbalance as well.

More than 400 ATHENA Award recipients answered the survey. When we reviewed the responses, what we saw was remarkable. Though the participants did not know or communicate with each other, the leadership characteristics and attitudes they described were so similar that it was startling, almost magical. Their approach to leadership also was significantly different from the prevailing leadership models of the day, the models created chiefly by men.

From the responses a common set of characteristics emerged, distinct but interrelated traits and principles that these women brought to leadership. These principles were not codified in business schools or mandated in corporate manuals; rather, they were drawn, unselfconsciously, from centuries-old practices learned at grandmothers' knees. Neither our survey participants nor our panel of experts believed that these principles were unique to women. The study findings suggested more that they were reflexive to women, so second-nature that when women moved into professional and leadership roles the principles went with them, shaping and guiding all they did.

For three days in a suburban Detroit hotel, Dr. Carole Leland led nine of us through the process of drafting our leadership model. The group included Dr. Peter Mitchell from the Wellesley meeting as well as internationally-known experts on aspects of women's leadership: Joline Godfrey, an authority on financially empowering women and girls; Dr. Yolanda Moses, an anthropologist specializing in gender, class, and racial inequality; Shaunna Sowell, an advocate for moving more women and minorities into technical fields; and Dr. Margaret Wheatley, a pioneer in organizational management and learning.

When I recently rediscovered my scrawled notes from that retreat, I was amazed. I don't even remembering jotting down some of the ideas but however they registered then as we brainstormed about our vision of leadership, they hold deep meaning for me now that ATHENA has passed the quarter-century mark. "Women's leadership ways are what we choose to note," I wrote. "Working differently together . . . deeper energy . . . non-ego involvement . . . expressing our gifts." In summary, I noted that this approach struck me as "how we behave when we realize we belong together."

Peter Mitchell and Carole Leland had turned the fruits of our discussions into a draft; it was reviewed by the ATHENA Foundation board, revised, and edited. The resulting monograph was distributed in print and on a CD-ROM at the May 1999 ATHENA International Conference in Pittsburgh with Carole Leland formally introducing it. After her presentation we pulled conference participants into small, facilitated discussion groups, a format we called ATHENA World Café, to discuss what they had heard. One participant's comments were so representative and so moving to me that they stand out to this day. She said that our new statement of ATHENA leadership "made me feel validated ... that my style, both my compassion and my strength, were honored ... that they

were okay—so much so that they formally became a model that will be taught! For once, I will be represented and included."

Our movement now had its manifesto. The ATHENA Leadership Model.

Dr. Carole Leland, who oversaw the development of the ATHENA Leadership Model, 1998. Photo courtesy of Dr. Carole Leland.

FIVE

The ATHENA Leadership Model

F
ROM THE OUTSET, we envisioned the ATHENA Leadership Model (ALM) as a "living" model, one that could evolve and be adaptable in different settings, accommodating to specific circumstances. Over the years, we've periodically reviewed and revised the principles' wording in order to speak to the times and the many new places that ATHENA programs took root. Most recently, we reworded the principle "foster collaboration" to more explicitly reflect the global reach and value of ATHENA ideals. But we never have departed from the fundamental understandings drawn from our survey of ATHENA Award recipients. When leaders strive to live by the ALM's principles and then share what they've learned, the principles are reinforced, gaining dimension, credibility, and context.

As we distilled the original study findings into the ALM, we found that its eight principles fell naturally into three categories. The first two principles concern how people understand and develop themselves as leaders. The next three principles concern how ATHENA leaders live out their convictions. And the final three concern how, in leading, they embrace and encourage others.

When our work was complete, it was summarized this way: "The ATHENA Leadership Model is a new paradigm attuned to the needs of a changing world. It consists of eight principles or qualities found inherently in the ways that women lead. Taken together, these principles capture the essence of effective twenty-first–century leadership."

The ATHENA Leadership Model

Live Authentically ~ Being true to yourself. An inner clarity centered in core beliefs, grounded in ethics, and honed through reflection. A sense of purpose, pursued with integrity. Authenticity is the single most important quality of leadership.
Leaders know their values and remain true to them.

Learn Constantly ~ Continuous development of skills and competencies, regardless of your level of achievement. Understanding built on experience, intuition and self-directed learning. The art of listening; the ability to learn from role models, bad as well as good.
Leaders seek knowledge.

Advocate Fiercely ~ Passionate, personal devotion to something that deeply matters. Acting with unswerving commitment tempered by respect and compassion. Generating a powerful force for good.
Leaders champion what they believe is right.

Act Courageously ~ The willingness to stand alone and speak the truth, to question assumptions or challenge the status quo. The determination to act honorably, consistent with your values, even in the face of fear or loss.
Leaders dare.

Foster Collaboration ~ Valuing the gifts each individual brings, with a perspective that is global and a spirit that is inclusive. Deepening understanding, awareness, and knowledge through diversity. Encouraging participation from those who are often overlooked.
Leaders welcome others to the work of leadership.

Build Relationships ~ Connecting genuinely with those around you. A willingness to bond with others, profoundly and productively, with trust and respect; to reach beyond status and self-interest in search of meaningful connections.
Leaders engage, empower, and trust.

Give Back ~ Leaving a worthy legacy for your community and the world. Recognizing that with success comes a responsibility to enrich the lives of others. Generously devoting voice, position, and resources to advance the greater good.
Leaders serve.

Celebrate ~ The age-old practice of gathering to mark important times. Strengthening bonds of unity through creative expression, rituals and traditions. Memorializing moments, triumphant or tragic; sharing joyful or solemn reflection.
Leaders remember and rejoice.

I'VE BEEN ASKED where vision appears in our model, in which of the eight principles—and my answer is, in all of them. If the ALM principles are tools we use to lead, our vision is those tools' power source, the essential ingredient that gives the principles force and life. Vision begins with the ability to dream, to lift the eyes of the soul beyond the familiar to behold the unimagined. Vision identifies possibilities; vision ignites passions. It is the depth and scope of a vision, the innovative, charismatic, transformational power of it, that opens the way for leadership.

Those who express the potential of a vision ("I have seen the mountaintop . . . " M. L. King) resonate with an energy that is compellingly, intensely hopeful. Little wonder that others are drawn to join them in a shared journey of significance and possibility.

Over the years, one of the things I've found most gratifying is this: None of these original core concepts of the ATHENA Leadership Model, these eight basic principles, has had to fall away. The care we took at the beginning to articulate principles that were true and sturdy, specific yet expansive, has paid off.

As the essence of the ALM has held true, so has the heartfelt description of it written by leadership expert D. L. "Dutch" Landen, a dear friend and collaborator who validated and reinforced the importance of this model for me: "The ATHENA Leadership Model focuses on service, interpersonal relationships, courage, and celebration—all of which are natural aspects of women in leadership. The ALM's moral tone emanates from the challenge it imposes on all who aspire to be leaders of both ideas and people. It holds forth new ways of thinking about leadership in today's world; it charts pathways to higher standards of personal morality and professional integrity. The ALM speaks loudly that the search for truth and goodness never ends; that mutual learning is at the heart of fulfillment; and that giving voice to our wisdom is a test of both our sincerity and our resolve."

SIX

Live Authentically

THE AUTHENTIC SELF IS THE SOUL MADE VISIBLE.

—SARAH BAN BREATHNACH

I N FRAMING the ATHENA Leadership Model, it has always felt particularly appropriate that the first principle should be this—"live authentically"—because it is focused upon the core and substance of a person. Knowing and staying true to one's authentic self is the solid foundation, the base for every other principle, trait and value. It's about acting with integrity. In both senses it's about being an integrated person, all parts of life and spirit meshing and in harmony. A leader could manifest every other ATHENA principle and still be waving in the wind unless that leader is grounded in the bedrock of her authentic self.

Some of the other ATHENA principles describe what we do (or at least aim to do): act courageously, learn constantly, build relationships. Authenticity is not only about what we do but about who we are.

Today it seems clear that each of us has an original way of being human, but within the long sweep of human history, that concept is relatively new. I like how philosopher Charles Taylor describes its evolution in his landmark 1992 book *The Ethics of Authenticity*. In centuries past, Taylor says, people generally were born into a fixed identity, defined by their families' station in life and expected to share in the behaviors, mores, life's work and habitat accorded to their group. Rare was the individual who strayed far from the prescribed path.

The end of the eighteenth century, Taylor says, saw the birth of an "ethic of authenticity." It drew from the notions of individualism pioneered by philosophers such as René Descartes and John Locke. It asserted each person's responsibility for formulating a moral code for himself or herself rather than adopting as unalterable the prevailing social or religious code. As education became more widely available, people were encouraged to develop and refine their personal understandings and opinions. By exploring an expanding array of religious, scientific, philosophical and political thinking, they could determine for themselves the ways they would interact with the world.

Taylor believed that by the early 1990s this idea had "entered very deep into modern consciousness," and it seems even more entrenched now. Individuals in the twenty-first century each claim and shape a distinct identity—who they are, "where they're coming from." We paint the backdrop against which our desires, opinions and aspirations make sense. We devote ourselves to realizing our full potential, we set goals for self-fulfillment. We struggle with and against the tensions of social conformity. We learn to articulate our views in a voice that is uniquely ours.

To me, Taylor's description of this quest reads almost like poetry: "There is a certain way of being human that is my way. I am called upon to live my life in this way, and not in imitation of anyone else's. This gives a new importance to being true to myself. If I am not, I miss the point of my life, I miss what being human is for me. This is the powerful moral ideal that has come down to us. . . . Not only should I not fit my life to the demands of external conformity; I can't even find the model to live by outside myself. I can find it only within."

Living authentically is a state of being whole, in touch and in tune with one's core, and thus so much more capable of being in tune with others. It's a state in which ego takes a back seat. We don't need the strok-ing, the constant reaffirmation of our value, because we carry inside a solid sense of worth. Living authentically does not confer invincibility. We still take hard knocks, get shaken to our foundation, and go away feeling horrible. But if we stay true to our beliefs, even though we suffer defeats, we are not diminished.

Think about those we call leader in political office or community life, in our businesses, churches, and schools. Rarely does one of them stand before us and announce, "Today I completely threw off my principles" (except, of course, when caught red-handed at it). Most of the time, a leader retreats from principled living by degrees—a little rationaliza-tion here, an uneasy compromise there, an intentional blindness to an ethical departure. Eventually, the leader's onetime standards are just a faint point in the distance. The leader still may still trot them out when needed, for public display, but they're conveniently remote from the day-to-day decisions where staying true to oneself can be unpopular, profes-sionally costly, or even dangerous.

Fortunately for us all, there's no three-strikes-you're-out rule for authentic living. We can fail ourselves and others in the quest to behave with integrity, then get up the next day and try to do better. ATHENA leaders make living with authenticity and integrity a lifelong pursuit. They strive to keep their consciences fine-tuned. They surround them-selves with trusted intimates who will call them on their missteps and help them get back on track.

Leaders strive to live authentically because someone or something has implanted in them, as Sister Jane Francis did in my long-ago Latin class, that personal imperative, "To thine own self be true."

BY SUMMER 1983, my friendship with Edward Ingraham had deep-ened into affection. This felt like a relationship we both could grow in, a partnership of mutual interests. I was delighted (and only a little nervous) to be invited to meet his relatives. So one sunny afternoon we spent an hour on Fayerweather Street in Cambridge, Massachusetts, at the home of one of his favorite cousins, Mary Ingraham Bunting, Polly for short.

Edward had told me to expect "an utterly unpretentious person," and Polly was just that. An energetic seventy-three-year-old with silvery bobbed hair, she received us warmly. We chatted about everything and everyone but her, as she and Edward caught up on the doings of the large family circle. I've come to identify that visit as one of the most pleasant missed opportunities of my life. There I was, a year into the ATHENA Award program, just starting my inquiry into women's leadership, and I never even broached the topic with one of the nation's true pioneers of equality and opportunity for women. Polly Bunting, fifth president of Radcliffe College and tireless advocate for women's professional advancement, didn't "talk shop" about gender issues during our social call. As Edward had told me, it was not her nature to draw attention to herself or her work. I deeply regret that I never got another chance to discuss our shared passion for women's advancement with Polly.

Writer Elaine Yaffe didn't know Polly at Radcliffe. Elaine graduated from the school shortly before Polly arrived there. But like me, as Elaine came to know Polly's history, she became more and more impressed. And then Elaine did something about it. She sought and received Polly's permission to write her biography, *Mary Ingraham Bunting: Her Two Lives*. One of the great rewards of the ten-year book project, Elaine says, was collaborating with Polly: "She taught me a great deal about how to live." One of Elaine's great regrets, she says, is that Polly did not live to see the book published in 2005. Between Elaine's research, Edward's recollections, and memories shared by Polly's sons Chuck and Bill Bunting, I feel privileged to have entered Polly's world, however late. Hers remains one of the best examples I know of a life lived authentically, true to herself and committed to what she knew mattered.

Edward tells great stories about spirited Polly in her youth. Born in 1910, she was raised in a closely knit, intellectually lively family in the "silk-stocking" area of Brooklyn. She was a daring child, hopping rides on passing garbage trucks. While her brothers went to school, Polly often was (or claimed to be) too sick to attend, and essentially schooled herself in what interested her. She once said she had studied history "without dwelling on the wars as much as what people were thinking"—and by age ten, she had read extensively in the Koran, Confucious, and the Bible. Back in formal school at fifteen, Polly fell hard for one subject: "Nobody had told me that anyone could count the molecules in air! I certainly knew that much as I loved literature and history, it was science that I would pursue."

Polly went to Vassar during the worst of the Great Depression, was both fascinated by and gifted at her science studies, and graduated with honors. Graduate school at the University of Wisconsin in Madison let her spend time with her uncle Mark Ingraham, a mathematics professor who later became dean of the College of Letters and Science, and his family (soon to include her infant cousin Edward). Polly wasn't easy to keep up with. Edward still chuckles to retell the family story of how, determined to break up with a beau, Polly took him on a long, cold hike around local Lake Monona and that was that.

On her way to earning her Ph.D. at twenty-four, Polly found a soulmate in grad-school colleague Henry Bunting, a son of two doctors who was studying medicine. They married on June 22, 1937, and were not only adoring partners but great fellow scientists, hashing out theories, tending each other's experiments. While Henry's obvious talents led to advancement—Harvard Medical School, a residency at Yale—Polly's just-as-obvious talents did not. In 1930s academia in general and in the sciences especially, even brilliant women rarely rose beyond instructor rank or got to pursue their own research; if they were awarded grants, male professors often had to sign for them. Yaffe notes that Polly betrayed "not a

Polly and Henry Bunting on their wedding day, June, 1937, at the beach house in Northport, Long Island. Photo courtesy of the Bunting family and Elaine Yaffe.

trace of bitterness or even of frustration" at these obstacles. She simply pursued her work.

Because both loved the country, Henry and Polly settled in Bethany, Connecticut, a quiet village twenty miles northwest of New Haven. In that idyllic setting they created a family, a daughter followed by three sons. As wartime made gasoline scarce, Polly opted to stay home, where she was just as industrious as she'd always been in the lab. She grew and canned vegetables, tended chickens and sold eggs, kept bees, repaired equipment, entertained friends, worked on civic efforts—and even arranged to spend some library time each week following a strain of research she'd started years earlier. Henry, now a highly-respected doctor, taught at Yale.

And then, before most who loved him even knew he was ill, Henry was gone, dead at forty-three from a malignant brain tumor. Nothing could have prepared Polly for the loss. A close friend said the grief was so profound that Polly seemed "in another state of being." But the full weight of her responsibilities was clear. She would have to provide for daughter Mary, thirteen, and sons Chuck, eleven, Bill, nine, and John, seven. Thus ended what Yaffe called the first of Polly's two lives, "the life she wanted and had assumed would always be hers—doing research that interested her, living in the kind of rural place she loved, bringing up her children in the way and in the place she and Henry had chosen together."

A onetime teaching colleague's query launched Polly into her second life: Douglass College, the women's affiliate of Rutgers University, needed a new dean. Was Polly interested? Hard as it was to trade Bethany's serenity for city life in New Brunswick, New Jersey, and to shelve her scientific research, Polly saw this as a job she could do and still tend her family. She had never considered a career in academic administration, had never envisioned any of this. But she set a new life course and seemed never to look back.

When Polly arrived, Douglass was poised to move beyond the "finishing school" model of women's education to academic excellence. Polly had both the scholarly credentials and the boundless energy to take that on. Like many women thrust into leadership roles without formal preparation, Dean Polly essentially invented her position, drawing from past experiences and her own internal wisdom. She invited the faculty to help her reconsider everything from academic programs to campus traditions. Even as the Little Rock Nine struggled to gain access to education, Polly worked on increasing black student enrollment at Douglass. She lectured students about their health, encouraging sports and physical activities. She urged them to achieve in the sciences and aim for graduate studies, advice that ran counter to the "ring by spring" creed so often preached to co-eds.

Since she fit none of the standard molds anyway, Dean Polly seemed fearless about breaking them: taking fresh approaches, engaging the whole Douglass community, unleashing cooperative and creative energies for the benefit of all. As her son Bill Bunting told me, "She never believed in being doctrinaire. She always thought that rules were made to be broken, within reason." Yaffe notes that during five years leading Douglass, "without setting out to be an example, Polly became one. For many of the students she was the first single mother they had encountered, the first working woman with a significant job. By skillfully balancing her competing responsibilities she showed them what a woman could achieve. And when Douglass students spoke of her years later, it was her courageous, independent spirit, her being a single mother who raised her children alone, had an important job, served her community—combined it all and flourished—that they remembered most and thanked her for."

In her own life and work Polly never felt she'd been hurt by gender bias, but at Douglass, surrounded by so many women who did feel disadvantaged, she began to reevaluate. Then in 1958 came what Polly would call her "awakening" to the magnitude of the inequality women faced. She had been invited to join a prestigious National Science Foundation panel focused on the development of scientists, a task made more urgent by the Russians' launch of Sputnik and America's desperation to catch up. To guide the NSF's efforts to train more scientists faster, Polly's committee asked for data on one question: Of the nation's brightest high school students, which ones did not proceed to college?

A few weeks later, the findings came in. Among American sixteen- to nineteen-year-olds with the highest IQs, nearly 99 percent of those who did not go on to college were female.

Polly found the statistic "earth-shaking . . . mind-boggling." But even more stunning was her NSF committee mates' response: essentially, nothing. They just moved on to the next agenda item. "These were nice men, not sexist people, and they just sort of set this aside," she later recalled. "Nobody on the Advisory Committee or the NSF staff proposed to do anything about this loss of talent. I was deeply puzzled. I felt that I was looking into a great dark cave that had been right beneath my feet all my life without my knowing it. Beneath their feet, too."

Too baffled to say anything right then, Polly took the experience home and thought hard about it. What "turned the light on for me," she said later, was juxtaposing the NSF reaction with a quote she had read from Carnegie Corporation president John Gardner: "A society gets the kind of excellence it values."

At last, Polly understood. The leaders at NSF, and many of their brethren throughout the country, "didn't think educating (women) would give them a group of people who were going to make a difference . . . . This country didn't expect women to do important things. That was why so few women bothered to go on in the sciences or other demanding fields." Recognizing this "climate of unexpectation," as she named it, revolutionized Polly's view of the world and what she had to do in it.

Later in life, Polly would describe the life change this way: "My divining rod had found a flood that would run with me where I was running." Immediately she set about changing the "climate" where she could, at Douglass. First she targeted women whose education had been interrupted by marriage, children, and other responsibilities, people much like her. Most colleges would not admit women who couldn't shoulder a fulltime course schedule, a policy many Douglass administrators supported. For a year Polly worked with and around the opposition until she finally prevailed. Douglass opened admission to older, part-time students, but to just ten of them at first. Those women proved to be such dedicated and exemplary students that within a few years opposition vanished. The program flourished and was the great achievement of Polly's Douglass years.

Then came an even greater challenge. In 1959, at age forty-eight, she was offered the presidency of Radcliffe College, Harvard University's college for women. There, Yaffe told me, "Polly sized up immediately what the problem was. The women were being treated as second-class citizens," though they took classes (and paid tuition) along with the male students. One example: Harvard housed students in "lovely river houses with beautiful paneled dining rooms, while Radcliffe had these Motel 6–type accommodations," Yaffe said. And yet Polly found Radcliffe's brilliant, gifted students somehow feeling powerless to address the disparities. In simple ways, Polly set about challenging that defeatism. For example, Yaffe says, "she brought in all of the student government people and asked them, 'What do you think, what should we be doing?' . . . and then she gave each dorm $1 per student and told the students to tell her what they did with it, but they could do anything they wanted. That was her approach to empowering people, to take people who had felt denigrated and give them a sense of what they could accomplish."

Again at Radcliffe, Polly looked to serve women whose careers had been interrupted (often by family obligations) but who longed to return to professional endeavors and creative projects. She envisioned a center that would foster research into the factors shaping women's status. It would give resident scholars space to live and work, financial support, and access to all Radcliffe's and Harvard's resources. Her idea was, of course, in direct contradiction to the prevailing attitude of the time that once a woman was married she should do nothing but attend to her family. "She wanted to make these women visible again," Yaffe says, "and to create a place that was collaborative, non-competitive. As she often said, 'Life doesn't have to be a racetrack, it can be a garden.'" Skeptical trustees wouldn't let Polly tap existing donors to fund the enterprise— "an interesting way to tie my hands," she later said, which she took as "a challenge from the old curmudgeons." She raised grant money herself and, in fall 1961, her garden was planted: the Radcliffe Institute for Independent Study.

The first Institute class included poet Anne Sexton. She would go on to a distinguished career, as would other Institute alumnae: writer Alice Walker, psychologist Carol Gilligan, performance artist Anna Deavere Smith, former Vermont Governor Madeleine Kunin, geophysicist Marcia McNutt. After their "Bunting years," several fellows received MacArthur "genius grants."

Though the Institute was her crowning achievement, it was hardly the only history Polly made in her dozen years as Radcliffe president. In 1964, she became the first woman on the federal Atomic Energy Commission. Through the mid- and late 1960s, she was a mediator, and target, as anti-war, Black Power, and other student demonstrations rocked the campus. And while those issues blazed, Polly worked on a quieter one— the integration of Radcliffe into Harvard.

Polly came to Radcliffe convinced its semi-separateness from Harvard benefited women. But, ever the scientist, she kept testing that hypothesis as more and more eminent universities went co-ed, admitting women on equal footing with men, and when she became convinced that merger with Harvard was the right course, she drove toward that.

Polly's son Chuck Bunting, a Harvard-trained scholar who went on to his own eminent career in higher education, says Polly talked to him during that time about "the irrationality" of students attending the same classes to earn degrees that said Harvard if the graduate was male and Radcliffe if female. "To her, it was illogical, absurd and wrong," Chuck told me. "A kind of class-system of degrees—that really stuck in her craw." Though many in the Radcliffe community opposed her bitterly, late 1970 brought a compromise that Polly blessed: a "non-merger merger" that would keep a Radcliffe identity but give Harvard and Radcliffe students equal standing and resources.

Polly stepped down as Radcliffe president in 1972, then spent a few years working on a range of educational issues as a special assistant to Princeton University's president. In 1979, after a quarter-century of widowed life, she married longtime friend Dr. Clement Smith, a retired pediatrician also widowed years earlier. From then on, a framed photo of Clem sat on her dresser near the one of Henry she had kept there always. During this happy, re-settled part of Polly's life when I met her on Fayerweather Street, the fruits of her life's efforts were all around. A *Boston Globe* article in 1983 dubbed the Institute "America's think tank for women." Gauging the Institute's impact in an article on its thirty-fifth anniversary, the *Harvard Gazette* quoted novelist and Institute alumna Gish Jen: "There is no place in America that has enabled so many women to make such a difference in the world."

Empowering others was not just something Polly did. It was the authentic expression of who Polly was, at heart.

DR. PEGGY MCINTOSH is associate director of the Wellesley Center for Research on Women, a key contributor to ATHENA's direction over the past dozen years, and a powerful public speaker. I once heard her discuss the intuitive gifts that are frequently attributed to women, using a notion she calls "the mad woman in the attic." This mad woman, as she explains it, is the occasional internal voice we hear, suggesting some action, something that might lie outside our normal behavior, or lack an obvious rationale, or require an extra dose of courage. Whatever we choose about heeding her in a given moment, surely "the mad woman in the attic" is a part of our authentic selves.

You might say Tamara Woodbury heard her "mad woman" on the frigid slopes of Mt. Rainier. She was twenty-three, a college-student leader of eight senior Girl Scouts who had been training and raising money for two years to make a mountain ascent. "We originally were supposed to climb Mt. McKinley," she recalls, but at the last minute the scouting organization's insurance company said it wouldn't insure a trek up that 20,320-foot mountain, the highest in North America. "When we asked them, 'Why didn't you tell us you wouldn't insure this two years ago?' they said, 'We didn't seriously think you'd be able to do it.' So we came up with something they would insure," a climb up 14,410-foot Mt. Rainier in Washington state.

Tamara, the eight girls and a mountain guide started their climb up Mt. Rainier on June 21, 1981. Aiming to take advantage of a window in the weather, the climbers set out at 3:30 A.M., their path lit by headlamps. They had none of the sophisticated communications and technical gear that aids climbers today. But after six hours of steady climbing, Tamara says, "we had traversed the Ingraham Glacier and were above 12,000 feet. We were crossing the area called Disappointment Cleaver when a massive serac (a large block of ice) broke off the mountain and tumbled down 100 yards from us—and I had just a terrible feeling in my gut, a sense that we had to get off the mountain." She conferred with the group's guide and made the call. They would head back down, not up to the summit. The pain of that moment still is fresh decades later, Tamara says. "It felt like a big betrayal to these young women, who had worked so hard for this moment.

"On the way back down the mountain, we ran into a group of climbers on the way up. We told them about the conditions that concerned us. They looked at us like, 'What do these girls know!' and they went on. We got off the mountain, we began the long drive home, and the girls were so upset that they weren't even talking to me.

"As we drove, the news came over the radio that there'd been an avalanche on Mt. Rainier, at the place where we had been, and that eleven climbers were buried and could not be rescued. It was the group of men we had met." The event remains the most deadly avalanche in the history of mountaineering on Mt. Rainier and the worst climbing tragedy, in terms of lives lost, in American history. The men's bodies remain buried

Girl Scout executive Tamara Woodbury, center, ATHENA Award recipient from Phoenix, Arizona, with scouts at a national convention. Photo courtesy of Tamara Woodbury.

and frozen in the ice of Mt. Rainier. Tamara's unpopular gut feeling and courageous choice very probably saved her team's life.

"And so it was confirmed to me, about listening to my intuition," Tamara says quietly. "That the internal voice is the best guide."

While training her team for the mountain trek, Tamara had met Frances Hesselbein, CEO of the Girls Scouts of the USA. Hesselbein insisted that Tamara should make the climb and then come for tea someday to tell her about it. Three years later, Tamara took Hesselbein up on the invitation and recruited her as a mentor. Since then, Tamara has built a career in leading organizations that encourage girls and women, and she has been a relentless student of what makes good leaders. She has studied leadership at institutions including Harvard Business School, Smith College, and Yale University, and has learned from pioneers in the field including Hesselbein, Peter Senge, and Peter Drucker.

Since 1993 Tamara has been CEO of the Phoenix-based Girl Scouts' Arizona Cactus-Pine Council. "Our mission is to help girls find the courage, the confidence and the character to make the world a better place," she says. "To draw from that essential self, to practice authentic leadership—and that doesn't look anything like the leadership of 'command and control.' It's leadership that cannot serve ego, that doesn't serve to the disadvantage of others; it's leadership that can't serve anything other than what's good for the whole. That's the kind of leadership that will change the world."

In 2007 the Greater Phoenix Chamber of Commerce presented its ATHENA Award to Tamara Woodbury.

EARLY IN MY WORK ON THIS BOOK, during a conversation about college days, I was asked a provocative question: If I could have given someone an ATHENA Award when I was a student at St. Kate's, whom would I have chosen? As so often happens when a question takes me unaware,

I found myself answering almost before thinking, and yet, as I said the name, the answer seemed unquestionably right: "Sister Vera."

After decades submerged in memory, her face was again before me, her voice as vivid as if I'd heard it that very day. Why did she make such an impression? Maybe she was the first person I'd ever met who seemed to be utterly in love with what she was doing and with being who she was. Maybe it was the energy with which she transformed a plain text into poetry, or the artfulness with which she drew us into learning, unraveling metaphors and stories until deeper meanings appeared. Always she radiated a kind of unalloyed joy that seemed to rise from her core.

Though the Internet sleuth who found my Aunt Erva seemed like a wizard in the mid-nineties, we've all learned a few Web-search tricks since then. And so in short order, I'd found a contact in the Sisters of St. Joseph of Carondelet religious order to relay my email query, and had gotten back Sister Vera Chester's sunny response: "Dear Martha—After all these years! How nice to get a great compliment from a student. I stayed in the theology department at St. Kate's and taught there for almost forty years . . . . I retired from full-time teaching in 1997 . . . . Good luck with your book! If you want to set up some sort of interview with me, that'd be fine."

We set a date for a phone call. As the day neared, I thought about my hopes for the conversation. I wanted to know more about her, who she'd really been back then, and who she had become since. I wanted to thank her for her impact, that strength of being that she had emanated and that had stayed with me, much more than anything in the course syllabus. Honestly, I think I also wanted to feel as much as I could, across phone lines and four decades, whether her authenticity, her clarity, her essence still would resonate.

Down the phone line, the voice was remarkable—the same! The laughing wit and the crackle of energy, with the slightest crinkle of age to it. I dug right in with questions. She had taught me theology with such energy and conviction that I'd always wondered: What were her own religious roots? Turns out she was raised in a family of non-practicing Lutherans, visited synagogue with her Jewish best friend, and at various times attended Methodist, Episcopal and Presbyterian churches—but she tells it best:

> I never saw my parents in church. Everybody in my public school went to Sunday School so I just got into carpools. I was a good second alto from about eleven or twelve so I went where I could sing, first in the Episcopal choir, then the Presbyterian Church. What really got me going to the Catholic Church was after my mother died when I was fourteen, my father remarried, a Roman Catholic woman . . . . He came to me and said, 'I don't care where you go to church, but you have got to go to church every week because I know it's driving your stepmother crazy.'

Sister Vera Chester, Ph.D., former theology professor at College of Saint Catherine, St. Paul, Minnesota. Photo courtesy of Sister Vera Chester.

Singing at the Presbyterian Church meant early Sunday morning rehearsals, but attending noon mass allowed Vera to sleep in—"so it was sloth that got me really well-acquainted with Catholicism," she concludes with a laugh. Ultimately, she says, "it was other students who converted me: these bright young women who had prayed their brothers and uncles through the war. They didn't talk Catholicism, they just went ahead and lived it."

Through high school and the start of college at St. Kate's, Vera never saw the church as a career path. But in her junior year, finishing homework with a friend at two o'clock in the morning, talk turned to the future and each asked the other: Have you ever thought of being a nun? "And I said, 'I have this awful feeling that's what I'm supposed to do. I don't really want to—but I don't know that I can not.' It was a sudden revelation to have said it out loud. My friend asked me, 'How will you know?' And I said, 'Well, if Bobby doesn't come up to the mark over the summer'—a nice Italian kid, terribly good looking—'then I guess I go into the convent.'"

Vera had no sooner mentioned the idea to a sister at St. Kate's than she was signed up to enter the novitiate and ushered in to meet the bishop. "He said, 'You must promise me you will not go out on dates between now and then' and I said, 'Oh no, I won't promise that.' He asked, 'Do you have any vices?' And I said 'I smoke and drink a little bit, and I'm not going to stop doing that until I have to.' So he kind struck out with me as far as that was concerned." She and I laughed as she told the story, two onetime Catholic co-eds scorning Mother Church's call for conformity. But while I moved away from Roman Catholicism later in life, Vera moved wholly into it; she just didn't lose her independence in the process. As she had told her dad upon choosing vowed life, "I'm not going to come home unless they send me—but I'm not going to change for them.'"

After three years' religious training, Sister Vera devoted herself to both teaching and learning. The Sisters of St. Joseph sent her to teach at co-ed high schools in the Dakotas and rural Minnesota, then brought her home to teach at St. Kate's. While on the faculty there, she earned master's and doctoral degrees from Marquette, gathering material for her dissertation while on a Fulbright Award at England's University of Birmingham.

Since I had known her for just months, in a St. Kate's career that spanned decades, I wondered if we would see her legacy differently. I told her, "I think your great strength as a teacher was encouraging your students to seek and speak truth as we perceived it." And she responded:

> You know the story of that saint that set out to go to Ireland, taking with him a harp and a sword, for poetry and militancy? I think I spent my teaching life trying to put the sword in the hands of young women. Girls (as we were called in those days) and women are not well-trained and encouraged in the kinds of things that happen in public discourse. If a young woman makes a statement and someone else says, 'That's the stupidest thing I've ever heard,' the young woman feels hurt which is so beside the point! I tried to teach students to have the kind of give and take where, if you don't want somebody to tear it apart, you don't say it, but you own what you say.

Sister Vera says she knew she had succeeded in emboldening one class "when, after a month, the students announced, 'Sister, you talk too much!' They gave me a timer, and from then on I had the last twenty minutes of class to speak, and they ran the rest. It was wonderful—they had the sword in their hands."

By the time she retired, Sister Vera says, something had changed. "The teachers I knew in the '60s, '70s, and early '80s were empowering women. Then somewhere along the line there crept in a notion of nurturing women. It all turned too touchy-feely for me . . . . If I had been 'nurtured' like that, I wouldn't have gotten where I am." In her first decade of retirement, she stayed active doing lectures at the University of St. Thomas senior center; her topics were provocative, her delivery feisty, and, she says, "I had a nice following of mostly Christians and Jews, plus one or two rabid atheists who still thought I was swell." Lately, she lamented, a creaky hip was cramping her style.

Shortly after our reunion conversation, Sister Vera had hip replacement surgery, not an easy undertaking at any age. When I checked in a few weeks later, again came an email sounding so like her voice, sunny with a touch of sass: "My surgery went very well, and I am now walking more easily and standing straighter than I have in four or five years. I still have plenty of complaints, but being more mobile and having a non-hurting left hip sure help a lot. And I seem to be functioning okay from the neck up!"

Hard to quarrel with that. And so it is with living an authentic life. We own our own truths, good and bad. We know, accept and respect ourselves. We trust in our core beliefs, we live and lead from them, and thus we earn the trust of those we would empower.

SEVEN

Learn Constantly

A LEADER WHO IS THROUGH LEARNING IS THROUGH.

—JOHN WOODEN

MEDICAL SCIENTISTS once thought all they needed to know about the human heart could be learned by studying one kind of human: the male kind. Through many years and countless millions of dollars, cardiovascular research was conducted overwhelmingly on men. The best medical minds in the world apparently did not seriously question whether the phenomenon of heart disease might differ depending on the patient's gender.

That one-size-fits-all approach seems utterly bizarre, given what we know today. Women, it's now clear, are physiologically different from men when it comes to heart health, different in critical ways, from how accurately some tests diagnose our conditions to the ways we feel symptoms of heart attack.

Single-sex cardiology research didn't get at the whole story. Neither does a single-sex approach to most other fields of endeavor. The ATHENA Award was conceived as a way to tell the whole story about leadership— not just male chapters with female footnotes, and not just women's stories to the exclusion of men's. The goal was a balanced, all-embracing perspective, a 360-degree understanding.

Just as that kind of understanding isn't fixed by gender, it can't be frozen in time. Neither leadership nor learning is a static proposition, a body of knowledge that gets settled and stays that way. Leaders wake every day to some new challenge in leading—and thus, a new need to learn. It's folly to imagine otherwise. As long ago as the eighteenth century, English satirist Alexander Pope was warning that "Some people will never learn anything for this reason: because they understand everything too soon." Pope's admonition rings even more true in the digital age. How could any of us believe we're ever done learning, when what we learned two minutes ago may be obsolete three minutes from now?

And so when ATHENA leaders commit to constant, lifelong learning, it's because we think futurist Alvin Toffler got it right with this prediction: "The illiterate of the twenty-first century will not be those who cannot read and write, but those who cannot learn, unlearn, and relearn."

John Wooden might look like a guy who'd have nothing left to learn about basketball. The UCLA men's basketball teams he coached in the '60s and '70s set record after record—ten NCAA championships, including seven in consecutive years. Born in 1910 and still going strong in his late nineties, Wooden co-authored more than a dozen books, for kids, for sports fans, and for would-be leaders. In his 2005 book *Wooden on Leadership,* the man who's been called "the greatest coach who ever lived" had this to say about such superlatives: "You must never become satisfied with your ability or level of knowledge . . . . It is easy to get comfortable in a position of leadership, to believe that you've got all the answers, especially when you begin to enjoy some success. People start telling you that you're the smartest one around. But if you believe them, you're just the dumbest one around. That's one of the reasons it's extremely difficult to stay at the top—because once you get there, it is so easy to stop listening and learning."

Wooden's wisdom took me back to a scene in an elegant bank board-room. It was the early 1990s, when corporate takeovers weren't the common occurrence they later became. I was there as a board member, working in concert with my board colleagues and the bank's CEO, a seasoned executive. In impressive detail, he laid out possible strategies for the bank's future, including the acquisition of other institutions.

Eager to contribute to the discussion, I asked a "what if" question: What if another institution sought to acquire this bank, against his wishes? It was as if I had dropped a bomb. That would never happen in this gentleman's arena, he said icily; and his response made it clear he considered it both ignorant and inappropriate for me even to have asked. The CEO never mentioned that episode to me again. (I can't say I was unhappy when he retired. His replacement, recognizing the change sweeping across America's corporate landscape, worked with staff and board to prepare the institution for whatever might occur, so when the takeover bid did happen, he was ready.)

In my memorably intimidating encounter, the CEO might have seemed like an all-knowing expert lecturing a know-nothing neophyte. But the lesson he left with me wasn't about banking; it was about the peril of assuming you've learned all there is to know. Since then I've met others like him, people who seem to feel they must possess (or at least profess) all knowledge to justify their title, status, or paycheck. The trouble is, by assuming the job description "font of all wisdom" they've backed themselves into a corner. Their every act or statement must reinforce how learned and clever they are; anything less could crack the façade.

At one time or another, we've probably all been tempted to play the all-knowing sage. It isn't easy, as a professional in your field, to admit not knowing something. It's painful, as a leader, to deny someone an answer when they so ardently wish for one. We may chide ourselves: What's wrong with me! I should have expected that question, I should know that, I should. But admitting what we don't know is vastly better than fudging an answer in hopes of getting lucky, or dancing around an issue trying to look like we're answering, or spouting bromides aimed at making others feel good without delivering real information.

ATHENA leaders understand that the goal of learning isn't just accumulation of knowledge. It's wisdom. The Greeks sought wisdom as the ultimate prize; my old friend Plato was all about it in his concept of the Philosopher King. The ancient Hebrews had a special word for it, *chogma*, and it was what distinguished the prophets and "wise men" (including the three bringing gifts to a manger in the New Testament). Wisdom is not just knowing a bunch of facts. It's understanding how the facts fit together in a cohesive view of the world. It's holding a worldview that is realistic and reliable. It's knowing the truth when lies are bombarding you and having the moral and civil courage to act in ways consistent with that truth. Wisdom isn't always popular, especially when it contradicts what "everybody knows." But it is a rare and remarkable commodity.

ATHENA leaders don't risk looking foolish by trying to look all-wise. They are generous with what they know and honest about what they don't know. They embrace social critic Eric Hoffer's notion that "in times of change, learners inherit the Earth, while the learned find themselves beautifully equipped to deal with a world that no longer exists." ATHENA leaders are curiously, happily, hungrily trying to learn all the time, from everything and everyone.

AROUND THE WORLD IN 1989, all sorts of barriers were being broken. Germans poured exultantly through the breached Berlin Wall. David Dinkins's election gave New York City its first African-American mayor, and Douglas Wilder of Virginia became America's first elected African-American governor. Still, some barriers held fast. Though thousands of pro-democracy demonstrators marched and several hundred died, the military prevailed in Beijing's Tiananmen Square.

In the Business School at the University of California, Irvine, Professor Judith B. Rosener was documenting another kind of revolution. In a research study using the members of the International Women's Forum, a global leadership organization, as her primary sample, she surveyed female and male leaders of similar age and station, asking about their leadership philosophies and practices. When the *Harvard Business Review* published her findings the next year, the landmark report's title was "Ways Women Lead," and its subtitle was, at that time, a revelation: "The command-and-control leadership style associated with men is not the only way to succeed."

The report documented a dramatic shift. While the first women entering the executive ranks tended to play by the rules as they found them, the next wave of women executives were not "adopting the style and habits that have proved successful for men." Instead, the report said, they were "drawing on the skills and attitudes they developed from their shared experience as women, on what is unique to their socialization as women—and creating a different path to the top." These women leaders achieved the required bottom-line results, the report said, but "in a different way. *They are succeeding because of—not in spite of—certain characteristics generally considered to be 'feminine' and inappropriate in leaders*" (emphasis mine).

Nearly two decades later, Judy Rosener is still doing research, still publishing breakthrough information about gender and leadership issues. When we spoke recently, she was at work on a book about the need to erase policies and practices that disadvantage women. And, as I discovered in our conversation, she has a charmingly roundabout way of discussing herself and her contributions.

She talks about her Depression-era family and the standouts who rose from it through education: her aunt, a psychiatrist who worked with Nobel winner Dr. Linus Pauling and discovered schizophrenia's roots in an imbalance in the brain; her cousin, a neurosurgeon who pioneered the concept of male/female brain differences. Of herself, she'll say she was "always a leader, president of everything" in school, then modestly suggest that stemmed less from her gifts than from self-confidence instilled by "my wonderful family. I had the security that whatever I did, it was okay, I could be who I was." That essential self, in Judy's case, is an inquisitive, insatiable learner.

The weekend Judy received her B.A. degree in sociology from UCLA, she married Joe, her World War II–pilot sweetheart. In Orange County, California, she stayed home to raise their three children. The kids were in high school in 1964 when the University of California opened its Irvine campus nearby and Judy and Joe went to a dinner party with the founding faculty. Judy remembers exactly her conversation with one of them: "He looked at me and said, 'I wonder if we can teach middle-aged women anything.' I looked at him and said, 'You've got to be kidding.' And the next day I said to my husband and kids, 'I'm going to go back to school.'"

For her master's degree in political science, Judy wrote her thesis on the exercise of power, chiefly in a political context. But a larger question about power nagged at her. Why did women and people of color have so little of it? Completing her master's at age forty-seven, she was approached about teaching college classes but learned that to be a professor, she'd need a Ph.D. So she got one, at age fifty—a rarity at that time.

At the university, Judy was plunged into that withering "climate of unexpectation" that Polly Bunting described: no women deans, no women chancellors, not many women full professors. But she'd been inoculated against it, in a sense, by her own family's history of achieving, intellectual women. So instead of taking this disempowerment of women as a setback, she made it fuel for, and a focus of, her research.

After "Ways Women Lead" was published, Judy recalls, "I was criticized by women academics. They said, 'We're not different!' And I said, 'You say that because you see different as deficient. I see different as adding value.'" With that simple but profound distinction, Judy laid the foundation for a global conversation that continues today. And she stated a proposition that would run through not only her life's work, but my work with ATHENA. If we can agree that the genders' approaches may be different without branding one inferior to the other, then the stage is set to find complementarity and balance.

That was the ideal. The reality, though, was much more what she calls the "one best model" message that to be a leader was to be male. When the models many of us saw in our homes—woman as nurturer, man as authority—migrated to the professional world, the male model was installed as the exemplification of what leadership looked like. That substantially closed the door on other, different ways of leading, even those that might have worked better in a given time, place or population.

Judith Rosener, Ph.D., author of the landmark 1990 report "Ways Women Lead." Photo courtesy of Dr. Judith Rosener.

Since the mid-1990s, Judy has been nudging that door open using a proven instrument of leverage: the profit motive. In a 1995 book entitled *America's Competitive Secret: Women Managers,* she expanded on her earlier research. Women's ways of leading were not only different from men's, as useful as men's and complementary to men's, she contended. They were a vast, "underutilized economic resource." Fully exploiting the talents of professional women "will lead to more innovative, productive and profitable organizations," she wrote. And "any country whose businesses fully utilize their professional women—which means including them in top management—will ultimately be more competitive at home and abroad."

Although Judy modestly claims she is "not a rigorous researcher," she packed *America's Competitive Secret* with data and case studies showing the distinct value women add. One of Judy's favorite examples involves Jill Ker Conway, the first woman president of Smith College, the nation's largest liberal arts college for women. When Conway joined the all-male board of sports equipment and apparel giant Nike, Judy says, its president was still describing Nike's approach to the women's market as "take a male product, color it pink, and sell it." Judy says it took Conway a year to convince Nike seriously to consider women athletes' needs and preferences, but once it did its women's division was quickly a success: "At the point that I wrote the book, women's products constituted 40 percent of their profits," she says.

As she approaches her eightieth birthday, Judy is pushing her inquiries about gender into a new frontier: brain science. While socialization shapes male and female behavior, she says, so do biological differences between male and female brains. For example, she says, when solving problems, if men tend to think in a linear way while women take a more holistic view, "it's because women generally use both hemispheres of the brain while men tend to use one at a time. We now have scientific findings to substantiate what this means for ways of thinking and acting. "

Judy Rosener's research also has given her a new perspective on the stereotypes of "scatterbrained" women versus "logical, rational" men. She says brain studies confirm that women "have information scattered all over the place" and manage to bring it together with both reason and intuition in play. If that way of thinking hasn't been called logical or rational, she says, it's only because "those are words men have reserved for their own way of thinking." From a brain-science perspective, she says, women's way of bringing information together is no less rational, just different.

"If you're not on the edge, you're taking up too much space." That's the mantra Judy says she lives by. "I've always been 'out there'; I've never been afraid to say what I think." She says flatly that women leaders who try to act like their male counterparts are making a mistake. But she spares a little sympathy for men who still resist women's emergence into leadership. "The glass ceiling for those below it—mostly women—is the floor for those above it, mostly men. So if you take away our ceiling, you take away their floor. Of course they'd have a fear of falling."

Always, she draws the distinction she first made two decades ago in her landmark research report. "It's important not to think of male and female ways of leading as better or worse; rather, they are different. I don't believe that women should rule the world, any more than men should rule the world; we need both men and women as leaders."

WHEN LINDA ACKLEY AND I first pored over mythology texts seeking a goddess namesake for our new leadership award, we were doing something most nineteenth-century American women could not do, at least not in the original Greek and Latin texts. Those, the basic sources for the myths, were privileged knowledge. They were taught only to white males in schools closed to females and people of color. Further, a chief source of myth stories, Ovid's *Metamorphoses,* was "off-limits to girls because of the sexual content," says author Marie Sally Cleary. But all that began changing with the 1855 publication of Thomas Bulfinch's masterwork *The Age of Fable*—a bestselling book so rooted in American culture that many of us know it simply as *Bulfinch's Mythology* (and some later editions took that title).

Like many of us, Marie Sally Cleary loved *Bulfinch's Mythology* as a child. She went on to become a teacher and was the first woman appointed to the Department of Ancient Languages at the highly-regarded Boston Latin School. And she studied Bulfinch, focusing on his passion for opening the classics to all. Bulfinch, Cleary learned, had no patience for a caste system in which Latin School boys could fully "get" the many mythological references in everyday life, but those untrained in ancient languages, women and minorities, could not.

Bulfinch didn't set out just to popularize mythology, Cleary writes in her book *Myths for the Millions*. He aimed to "democratize it … to make it work for social equality and against usurpation by power and wealth. *The Age of Fable* opened up, more widely than ever before, the mysteries of mythology to people of both sexes" and of all colors and stations.

When we aim to learn constantly, we open ourselves to delightfully random encounters with knowledge. I had seen Thomas Bulfinch's name countless times as I read up on Athena (or Minerva, the Roman name he calls her). But until I stumbled upon Cleary's scholarship while researching this book and got in touch with her, I had no idea that Bulfinch and ATHENA shared a passion: expanding opportunity for women.

I am grateful to Cleary for her teaching—and for a sort of blessing. In a kind note, she expressed her conviction that if Thomas Bulfinch "were alive today, he would fully approve of your (ATHENA) project." I so hope she's right.

Kim Thompson, sixth from left, with SWAT teammates in Los Angeles, California.
Photo courtesy of Kim Thompson.

FIRST, KIM THOMPSON learned enough to be the first woman to pass the physical agility test for the SWAT team of the Los Angeles County Sheriff's Department. Then she learned some more, on the job, and used what she learned to invent a better way for law officers to do their jobs.

Here's how Kim told her story to Cynthia Richmond, a talented writer and dear friend who has helped me collect oral histories of ATHENA leaders:

> One night I was called to a scene where six people had been shot. A fellow deputy and I saw the gunman at the same time and took off in full pursuit. We cornered the guy in an old garage, contained the situation, and then I was left to rummage through my briefcase trying to find everything I needed. I realized in that moment that there needed to be a portable command post with all materials at hand, ready to go, so that I could focus on more important issues—do all the guys have bulletproof vests, where's

my long rifle, which hospital is closest, and so on. I was used to setting things up on the hood of the car, taping things down, but that night I had to move the car six times, it just wasn't practical. I was discussing this with my superior in his office when I saw a large, corrugated cardboard box that was going to be thrown away.

That night I cut the box to fit the hood of a squad car, taped six panels together, and laid things out—a pocket for the forms I use at an arrest, blank paper to draw a diagram, all the procedures laid out, a place for the maps, a sign-in sheet for personnel, a listing of hospitals, a list of who was on duty, and so on. It was Mickey Mouse, cardboard and tape, but now we had an organized command post at the ready.

One night when my supervisor called and asked me to bring it to a chaotic crime scene, I knew that I had something there. I had twenty guys under me at the training bureau and I started making command boards up for them as a gift for their promotion. I got a little fancy, adding a dry erase board and leather straps. It became a security blanket for them.

One day I got a call from a guy who had been recently promoted. He said he loved my command board and he'd thought every field supervisor should have one. I had already thought of the different types that could be utilized: missing child, hazardous materials, bomb threat. So this guy says he thinks they should be manufactured and available for sale and he's going to show his board to some other guy that he knows. I don't know where this came from, but all of a sudden I heard myself saying, 'I have a patent pending.' Then I called my dad—he's a retired FBI agent and attorney—and I said 'Dad, how do I get a patent?'

A friend gave me a little space at his booth at the local Law Enforcement Conference and Exhibit. I had two samples made to show the officers and ended up taking 500 orders that day! Soon fire departments were asking me to customize them for their needs, schools wanted them, and then the military called. Today Marines are using my command board in the front line to counter terrorism. Homeland security trains on my board. The Pentagon ordered some. As of today we've sold somewhere between 11,000 and 13,000 command boards, over $5 million dollars in sales.

Law enforcement is traditionally a macho, male-oriented world, it's a tough nut to crack, and they aren't quick to make changes, especially not ones suggested by a woman. I've learned that you have to believe in yourself, don't be afraid to fail, just put your ego out of the way and do it. My business has impacted the world and saved lives. If I'd realized how overwhelming it would be when I first started, I'd never have done it. I had to learn so many new things. But I did one at a time, and I still am learning. Teachers seem to show up when you need them.

TODAY, women are or have been top officials at many of the nation's most prestigious institutions of learning. At this writing, women are presidents at Princeton, MIT, and Harvard, and at four of the eleven Big Ten universities.

"The numbers are improving," says one of those Big Ten leaders. "But you'll know it's successful when nobody remarks upon it, and we're not to that stage yet." Meet Lou Anna Kimsey Simon, twentieth president of Michigan State University. She came to the school's campus more than thirty-five years ago as a graduate student; she kept taking on challenges, as teacher and learner, and simply never left.

My husband Edward Ingraham, who spent four decades at MSU as a faculty member and administrator, remembers first meeting Lou Anna in the late 1970s when she was an intern in the university president's office. "We were in a meeting when some fairly complex statistics were being presented by the administration and I approached her after the meeting with a couple of questions," he recalls. "Her answers were almost intimidating for the complete control of the numbers they demonstrated. I left thinking that this was a person to watch and a mind to reckon with."

Over the years, as Edward watched Lou Anna rise through the ranks, his admiration grew. He thinks of her as having "one of the quickest, most penetrating minds I have known." But what he found even more exceptional, he has told me, were other traits: "an unusual depth of character, based on firmly held values, exceptional loyalty, and consideration of others." When I began listing leaders to interview for this chapter—people who epitomize the ATHENA ideal of lifelong learning—Lou Anna topped the list.

The baseball card in Lou Anna's office makes delightful sense once she explains it. The card shows a smiling Yogi Berra with the inscription, "I always wanted to be a college president!" The gag gift refers to Lou Anna's fondest dream in childhood. "I always wanted to play for the New York Yankees," she says with a chuckle. As improbable as that seemed

Lou Anna Simon, president of Michigan State University and an ATHENA recipient.
Photo courtesy of Michigan State University.

for a girl growing up in tiny Atlanta, Indiana, her family never discouraged her dreams. She says, "Most people in small-town America had very strong gender constraints and also were limited in some ways by what their parents and grandparents knew. I really was fortunate that my parents and grandparents did not limit me and encouraged me to learn what they did not know." Instead of a Yankee, she decided to become a coach and math teacher; she was the first in her family to go to college.

Michigan State, once a small agricultural college, was on its way to becoming one of the world's largest research universities when Lou Anna arrived. At MSU, she earned her doctorate in administration and higher education, rose through the teaching and research faculty, served as assistant provost, associate provost, and then, for a decade, provost. In that role, Edward remembers, Lou Anna regularly convened breakfasts where staff and faculty discussed the university and were encouraged to tell or ask her anything. He also remembers how in 1993 the university's presidential search process seemed to look right past her—and yet she stayed, ably supporting the administration as she had for years, until 2005 when she was appointed president.

Compared to the climate when she entered academic leadership, Lou Anna says there's now "more space for individual variations of style— and as more women are involved in leading, there are more ways the forms are different, and I think that's good." She notes that historically, "the more collaborative approach, the value of being a good listener, the value of the *we* as opposed to the *I*, those were more typically a part of the way in which you'd describe women leaders. But now if you look at the literature, that's the way it tends to describe leaders."

Asked to share stories of experiences that shaped her leadership, Lou Anna sounds like the coach she trained to be. "I tend not to replay the past—those innings are over." Instead, to grow as a leader, she focuses on "learning from a lot of people, the best-practices approach"—then balancing what she learns with "that internal gyroscope. It's important to be grounded, who you are and what you believe in, in your own personal way of addressing the world. When you couple that with being a lifelong learner, it provides a very dynamic environment—very similar to the ATHENA leadership principles. You have to be value-based, vision-based but also blend it with good execution. The way we've described it here is, developing a style of leadership that has trifocals. We aim to have good long-term vision for the institution; a good sense of the intermediate, things beyond my reach now that will be the near-term legacy for somebody else; and then a good sense of the short-term, actions you take now to move an initiative forward. So part of leadership is balancing those three vision sets."

Lou Anna's leadership vision has taken her to, of all places, the United Arab Emirates. She notes with pride how MSU is expanding its global vision and reach. In 2008, it ranked second among U.S. universities in sending students to study abroad. In 2009, the university opened a campus in Dubai, a move that meets Lou Anna's trifocal-vision test for serving the school in many ways. The campus will put MSU "in the Mideast marketplace" with other big U.S. research universities, and near the many Fortune 500 companies who have headquarters in Dubai and might do business with Michigan. It will allow MSU's American-born students to learn in the Middle East, MSU's administration to explore development and research exchanges, and it even will allow MSU "to offer an American educational experience to Emirati women who aren't permitted to go to America."

Once she had researched, consulted and taken that "internal gyroscope" reading, Lou Anna moved confidently on the Dubai venture. But realistically, she says, it may be an "all or nothing" proposition, a venture that will be either a real success or a real bust. That raises another point about leadership, she says: "A lot of leadership is about how you deal with your mistakes, because if you're bold and aggressive and want to move and grow, you're going to make them. . . . You have to figure out how to deal with all that in order to keep the momentum, and how to judge for yourself what constitutes a serious error, because it may not be what people tell you. If I have any credibility here, it's built on the fact that people believe if I make mistakes, I make them for the right reasons, not to advance me as an individual but to advance the institution. That gives you an enormous amount of capital to work through the difficult times, as opposed to if they think you're doing if for your own aggrandizement."

Yankee or not, that's a team player talking. A team leader, and a learning leader.

IT'S ONE THING TO LEARN FROM A SYMPOSIUM, a database, a TV documentary, a museum exhibit, but there's something more compelling about learning from and with another person. In the best situations, learning is a transaction that rewards both the one who gives and the one who gets; it makes the same kind of soul-satisfying connection as feeding and being fed.

When I learn something valuable with and from another person, I retain some essence of them along with the knowledge I've derived. And when I teach what I've learned, that essence gets passed, on and on, almost like a sacrament. Such a skein of learning, over many years, connected me to Max De Pree.

When West Palm Beach, Florida, gave its first ATHENA Award in 1998, the recipient was Gayle Landen. A talented organization development consultant with a high-wattage smile, Gayle soon became involved in national ATHENA efforts, and joined the board steering the organization. She teamed with me to lead facilitated discussions about leadership (the events we would come to call ATHENA World Cafés), and to turn the fruits of those discussions into research data.

Only some months into our collaboration did I discover the bonus that came with knowing Gayle. The more her husband had learned about the ATHENA movement, the more he was drawn to it, and Gayle's husband was Dr. Delmar L. "Dutch" Landen, an industrial psychologist and nationally recognized expert on leadership.

During a quarter century at General Motors, Dutch directed the automaker's organizational research and development group. One of the largest and most influential groups of its kind, this GM team, under Dutch, literally was revolutionizing the way business operations were led. From this group sprang the concept of QWL—Quality of Work Life, as gauged by employee attitudes and motivators in the work environment. Dutch's group also led GM's development of so-called socio-technical plant systems, where elements that foster good human relations are consciously built into plants' technical workflow. To every division within GM, Dutch brought a fascination with the ways of leadership, and the research, insight and training to make them work better.

Among life's greatest gifts are the occasional muses who bring larger, clearer visions of our dreams. Dutch was that for me. He was learning about leadership at the highest levels, he was testing what he learned in the corporate world, and he was then sharing both his knowledge and his enthusiasm with me to benefit ATHENA. Dutch's work brought him into contact with some of the great leaders and leadership theorists of the times. One was Jim O'Toole, then president of the Aspen Institute, known worldwide for its seminars and initiatives to foster enlightened leadership and open-minded dialogue.

Dutch introduced me to O'Toole's groundbreaking work on "values-based leadership," in which he used the presidents on Mount Rushmore as examples of remarkable leaders. Of George Washington, Abraham Lincoln, Thomas Jefferson and Theodore Roosevelt, O'Toole wrote, "Their many biographers use the same vocabulary in describing their leadership characteristics: courage, authenticity, integrity, vision, passion, conviction, and persistence." And, O'Toole stressed, "They were

Max De Pree, noted author of *Leadership is an Art,* former CEO of Herman Miller.
Photo courtesy of The De Pree Center.

all recognized as masterful teachers." O'Toole's traits of values-based leaders spoke to our notions of ATHENA leaders, and so I kept reading, reflecting, learning.

When O'Toole wrote about chiseling a Rushmore of corporate chiefs—"exemplars of outstanding leadership"—he said the first person he'd portray there was Max De Pree. For more than four decades, Max was a groundbreaking leader, ultimately CEO at Herman Miller, a west Michigan manufacturing company as acclaimed for its employee-centered policies as for its high-style furniture. In books such as *Leadership is an Art* and *Leadership Jazz,* Max made simple but revolutionary statements about what it means to lead. (One of my favorites: "The first responsibility of a leader is to define reality. The last is to say thank you. In between, the leader is a servant and a debtor.")

He's an icon to people who study leadership, a world-renowned expert. And yet Max De Pree remains a man for whom celebrity is unimportant but integrity is huge. He's not a pitchman for his leadership philosophy, just a diligent, generous practitioner of it. He considers leaders worthy only insofar as they are serving followers, helping their organizations learn and create. Now eighty-four and retired from Herman Miller, Max doesn't grant many interviews. So when he agreed to a discussion about leadership and ATHENA, I was thrilled at the opportunity.

Outside his west-Michigan office, blue Lake Macatawa; inside, jammed bookshelves, playful art, family photos. Over two and a half hours, the conversation seemed to go everywhere. Reviewing the transcript later, I was struck by a subtle but definite pattern: a rhythm of teaching and learning. In response to a question, Max would offer a few thoughts, then a story . . . but "the moral of the story" was left to be discerned. Let me show you what I mean:

Question: Do you think women lead differently than men?
Max: Yes, I think they do, and I think a lot of my own
personal way of leadership has some feminine characteristics. I
wasn't always able to be a good listener. I wasn't always able to
worry about what's in the hearts of people. I learned that stuff
along the way . . .
One of my favorite stories: Driving home one Sunday evening
after church, I said to my wife Esther, 'Tomorrow's going to be
a really rough day because we're thinking of laying off forty
people'—a long time ago, we didn't just do that. Actually, what
I said was, 'We're going to lay off forty men.' And she said, 'You
know, that's not what you're doing: You're laying off forty families.'
And the next morning we were having breakfast together and she
said, 'You're having that meeting this morning? I'm going to be

praying during the meeting. I'm going to be praying it won't work.' So I'm sitting in the meeting and I know she's at home praying it isn't going to work.

Question: What traits does a leader have to have?

Max: I think a strong desire to lead—the need to lead. It isn't necessarily a desire for power, it's the joy of serving—and even the feeling that a lot of people need you to lead. That's in people, that's in a lot of people. . . .

When my granddaughter was born terribly prematurely, a baby I could hold in one hand, we had a nurse at the Grand Rapids hospital named Ruth. She said to me, 'You know, you're the father now'—she knew the biological dad had left—'you're the father now, and I want you here every day.' And she said, 'When you come to visit the baby, I want you to take your finger and rub it over her and all the time you're doing it, you keep saying I LOVE YOU, because she has to know your voice and your touch.' You don't always know who's a leader—that's one of the interesting things about leadership. You don't always have it; other people have it, too. In leadership, you're often the follower. And there was a case where Ruth knew who was the leader and who was the follower.

Question: How do people know what they know about leadership?

Max: I think some people who have leadership gifts need somebody to explain it to them. I think a lot of us need people to give us a clearer idea of who we are than we get by ourselves, people who love us enough to steer us in the direction of a combination of our gifts as leaders and the needs of followers. I know in my own life I had a couple of people who did that for me, who steered me and gave me a direction and explained some things I couldn't figure out by myself—which brings you to the whole idea of mentoring which, in my mind, is the best way to learn how to polish your gifts as a leader. . . .

One of the great women I worked with at Herman Miller was Michelle Hunt, an African-American woman who was our Vice President for People. She came into my office one day and said, 'Would you be willing to have a formal mentoring relationship with me?' And I said, 'Well, I do that with a lot of people but not with anybody who works for me, I don't know how that would work . . .' She said, 'I need a mentor—and you need one. You don't really have any idea of what's going on out in the company in terms of diversity. I can help you with that if you'll help me with my leadership.' So we formed an alliance and it was really good for both of us. She long ago left the company and has her own consulting firm in New York, and we still talk three times a year. And the wonderful thing is, when we hang up, we always say 'I love you.'

Of all the stories Max shared in that long, invaluable conversation, one of my favorites captured the ATHENA ideal of learning constantly, even if what you're learning is how wrong you can be. "No matter how good a leader you think you are," Max began, "you're not going to know what someone can do until you give them something to try . . . .

"We once hired a young woman to come work at Herman Miller, a handicapped young woman named Laurel, and every day her dad brought her to work. After about fifteen years, my wife and I were at home one evening and the doorbell rang. I went to the door and it was Laurel. I invited her in and she said, 'No, you come out.' We went outdoors and she showed us the car she had bought. She had learned to drive! For fifteen years I was saying to myself, Laurel will never drive. I'm a leader, I have the right to judge that. And there I am, standing in my own driveway, crying."

EIGHT

Advocate Fiercely

I AM ONLY ONE, BUT STILL I AM ONE. I CANNOT DO EVERY-
THING, BUT STILL I CAN DO SOMETHING.

—HELEN KELLER

I N FALL 1962 as the United States and Soviet Union raced to establish nuclear superiority, a Soviet physicist grew increasingly troubled. If the USSR went forward with a scheduled atmospheric test
of the bomb he had helped design, he believed it would accelerate
the arms race and shower deadly fallout on hundreds of thousands of
civilians. Desperate, the physicist called Soviet Prime Minister Nikita
Khrushchev and implored him to stop the test; Khrushchev said he'd
see about postponing. The next day, the test occurred as planned. When
he learned what had happened, physicist Andrei Sakharov later wrote, "I
dropped my face on the table and wept."

And then he acted. The onetime "father of the Soviet hydrogen bomb"
became a trailblazing political activist, advocating for nuclear disarma-
ment and human rights. In 1975, Sakharov's work earned him the Nobel
Peace Prize; in the early and mid-1980s, it earned him arrest and exile. By
the time he died in 1989, his impassioned dissent had sparked the democracy movement that brought down the Soviet Union two years later. In
his Nobel acceptance speech, Sakharov called others to the relentless

advocacy he had embraced. "We must fight for every individual person against injustice," he declared. "Our future depends on this."

ATHENA leaders become fierce advocates because they simply cannot do otherwise. They are that passionately and personally devoted to advancing what they believe. They refuse to be distracted by opponents or doubters; with their moral compass in one hand and their action plan in the other, they stay on the straight line toward their goal. That unswerving commitment to their beliefs drives their actions. More, it compels them to rally support, to fire up others to act along with them. Followers and partners are drawn to leaders for many reasons, but the magnetism and power of advocacy certainly is one of them. The ATHENA leader's strength as a nurturer, learner, creator, and relationship-builder is fortified with the steel of an advocate.

Fierce advocacy, when tempered by respect and compassion for others, generates a potent force for good. It is an inner fire, fed not just by the accomplishment of individual tasks or small victories but by a grander design. The ATHENA advocate dreams dreams that can transform, big enough to hold the fluidity of life, open enough to admit fallibility, yet unwavering in their drive toward a better world. Fierce advocates create and press toward fully-woven ideals; they go alone when they must, but more often are joined by those who appreciate their consensual thinking, their shared sense of ownership.

We chose, and I love, the word fierce because it's such a take-no-prisoners adjective. Imagine a mother bear whose cubs are in jeopardy. There is no stopping her. I believe ATHENA leaders develop that kind of ferocity for a cause that matters deeply to them. I also believe they are so effective because while their passion for their objectives is untamed, their march toward those objectives is methodical, well-plotted, respectful and wise. The goddess ATHENA has come through the centuries identified as a warrior; she certainly was dressed like one! But examine mythology and you'll find her finest talents to be those of a strategic thinker and advocate, one who takes the long view, one whose wisdom incorporates approaches to problems that remain flexible as situations unfold, but one who always holds strongly to her ultimate vision. At a leadership retreat a colleague and I led a few years ago in Dubai, here's what we concluded about ATHENA: "She provides a great lesson for us in choosing carefully the issues that we are willing to champion, and then showing up in full form and intention to accomplish what is necessary for the greater good." That, in a nutshell, is fierce advocacy.

SOMETIMES the most effective advocates start out as the quietest, the stealthiest. So it was with Marge Shelden, the woman who'd been a fixture at the Greater Lansing Chamber of Commerce for years when I arrived there. From the mid-1950s when Marge entered the workforce to 1993 when she left it—retiring from the ATHENA Foundation as its first executive director—women's access to leadership changed dramatically. Marge acted and advocated heroically to bring about that change.

From childhood, Marge was a keen observer of how gender colored opportunity in American society. Her mother Merle Landen set "a fabulous example" by ignoring the barriers and embracing the new, hard-won rights set before women in the early 1930s. "I'll never forget her passion for voting," Marge says. While her farmer father usually didn't vote—"he wouldn't take the time to change his clothes and unharness the horses"— Marge vividly recalls her mother bundling the four kids into the Model T Ford and driving herself (quite scandalous!) to town on election day. Her mother was her mentor before the term was coined. From her, Marge says, "I learned early on the value of having someone who believes in you support your growth and success."

Raised in eastern Michigan, Marge was just seventeen in 1942 when she took a summer job in an insurance company in "the big city of Lansing." The realities of the male-dominated workforce soon became clear to the pretty new mail clerk. "When you deliver the mail to the president, do not linger," Marge's supervisor told her. "He likes to hug young girls!" Exemplary work got her promoted to the "photostatting department" where she thought she'd learn new skills copying photos for insurance claims. "But it didn't take me long to realize that the manager was purposely brushing up against me in the darkroom, especially after he began fondling me," she recalls. "I moved out of his reach each time but he was the boss and I didn't know what action would be taken if I went to the supervisor and told the truth." Claiming she couldn't tolerate darkroom chemicals got her transferred down to the file room, where she "learned through the office grapevine that few girls lasted longer than I had in the photostatting department, and no wonder!"

While Marge was saving her insurance company earnings toward a college education, the United States entered World War II. "I had been writing to a sailor, a friend of my cousin, who was on the battleship Iowa. He came home on leave, we dated, and he asked me to marry him. I didn't hesitate. I was nineteen and my husband was twenty-three." Their church wedding in February 1945 was followed by a honeymoon in Chicago, and then a troop train carried Eugene Shelden back to his ship in San Francisco at leave's end. Marge went home alone to Lansing. Eugene finished his Navy tour in the fall, and their first child Katherine was born the next summer. The early 1950s found Eugene working as a mail carrier and Marge raising their three daughters but looking for other challenges. When an acquaintance from her insurance company days asked if she'd like to buy his small agency, she jumped at the chance. "I had to save up out of my grocery money" for the $50 insurance license exam, she recalls. She also had to get her mother to care for the girls during a week of agent training. Then for $300 down with $300 due in a year, Marge was in the insurance business.

The field agents for companies whose policies Marge sold "were polite," she recalls, but this is what they told her: While a man could establish his business in five years, "it would take me ten years to get people to believe I knew enough about insurance coverage" for them to do business with her. She would conclude later that the field agents were right (though she stuck with it and, she says now with pride, "did a good business for thirty-six years").

When Marge was forty-three years old, she was hired as part of the secretarial staff by the Lansing Chamber of Commerce. She immediately noticed the different standards for men and women there. "On payday, the men would take their checks to the bank and, we could tell, often return with fresh haircuts. Women were rarely even allowed to leave the office. We knew that the men sometimes went golfing when they had signed out for a meeting. It wouldn't have occurred to the women to do anything like that. When we did go out on a Chamber errand we were held to strict time standards. The director would actually clock us and compare the time it took to the amount of time he felt was appropriate." In our ATHENA work years later, Marge would recall these unequal ways of treating staff as "a perfect case of 'reverse role modeling,' exhibiting behaviors one would never like to adopt as a leader."

Getting up to speed on her new job, Marge reviewed the Chamber roster and saw no women listed as board members, committee chairs, or even as proposed board members. When she pointed out to her boss what she presumed was an oversight, she recalls, "his response was, 'I will never turn the Chamber into a ladies' aid society.' It was then and there that I had to make a decision. I asked myself: 'Do I want to stay here?' Ultimately, I decided to stay and do my best as an insider to make healthy changes."

Much as she wanted to make the Chamber more female-friendly, Marge knew any efforts to do so "couldn't be obvious or I would have lost my job." Her experience made her an invaluable resource for aspiring businesswomen, but her Chamber superiors hired her for office management, not "ladies' aid," so she could mentor only surreptitiously.

It was my great good fortune that Marge did decide to stay. Marge is a systems person, a researcher. By the time I arrived, she already had identified what we needed to learn about the Chamber's women members: How many were there, who were they, why had they joined, and what could we do to serve and involve them? Laboriously she sifted through the 1,200 names to find the forty-five women to whom we sent our meeting invitations. The rest, as she and I like to say with mock gravity, is history—ATHENA history.

When thirty-nine of those forty-five women came to meet with us, "we were delighted," Marge recalls, "and we learned a lot. From what we absorbed at that meeting, we began our plan to organize women members, bring them into leadership roles and guarantee a presence in the powerful inner circle of the Executive Committee. Our goal was that women would be empowered within the Chamber, a radical concept at that time." So radical that Marge had to sneak around to advance it, work on her own time, make calls on outside pay phones. She had to be, in essence, a stealth advocate. But make no mistake. Though discreet, she was fierce.

All the work was worth it, Marge says now, because ATHENA has fostered what she always believed it would. "Women who have attained positions of leadership are opening opportunities for others."

THE MID-1960S WORLD OF POLLY BUNTING—Harvard and Radcliffe campuses electric with demonstrations—was a life-changing place for Mary Bourke. She had come to Cambridge from County Mayo, Ireland, to get a graduate law degree. In the civil rights and anti-war movements, she witnessed the phenomenal power of people emerging to lead who'd never been seen as leaders before. Back at home, she questioned why "elderly male professors" so dominated the Irish Senate, so she ran for a seat and won. Two decades as a legislator, educator, and barrister burnished her reputation as a compassionate, innovative leader, and in 1990, Mary Bourke Robinson was elected president of Ireland.

I have watched with admiration as Mary Robinson moved across the world stage, both epitomizing and advocating for that step-out-and-lead philosophy. She helped found the Council of Women World Leaders, a network for women elected to top government posts once thought unattainable: president, prime minister. After seven years as her homeland's first woman president, she assumed one of the most prominent advocacy posts in world affairs, becoming the first woman United Nations High Commissioner on Human Rights. Leaving the United Nations in 2002,

The Honorable Mary Robinson, former president of Ireland. Photo courtesy of Mary Robinson.

she founded a group called Realizing Rights; it works with world leaders and organizations "to put human rights standards at the heart of global governance and policy-making, and to ensure that the needs of the poorest and most vulnerable are addressed." Today, she's a leader of such stature that when Nelson Mandela formed a select group called The Elders to share wisdom and forge alliances on issues of world importance, he invited the likes of Desmond Tutu, Kofi Annan, Jimmy Carter—and Mary Robinson.

Because HIV/AIDS cuts across so many other issues she cares about, Mary is active in several HIV/AIDS organizations including the UNAIDS Global Coalition on Women and AIDS. In an interview published on the UNAIDS Web site, she did what fierce advocates do best. She made the case for what she believes is important, and why. When she established Realizing Rights, she committed it to five goals she believes could benefit the planet, and one of them is "strengthening women's leadership." She addressed that in the interview.

"Leadership of women is particularly important because it brings different skills, experiences and ways of exercising power and influence," she said. As the first woman to lead Ireland and the UN High Commission, "I've thought a lot about it . . . and I was conscious that it was important to show that, as a woman, I was adding a new dimension that we had not seen enough of. Using a different kind of networking, the nurturing, the capacity of women to empathize more with the marginalized and the poor—all these skills are not necessarily present in the male, hierarchical holders of power who are not always listening very well to the grassroots."

While leadership is about rallying followers, it is "also about changing systems," Mary said in the UNAIDS interview. Women who ascend to influential positions of leadership and advocacy can use their standing literally to change how the world works, she believes. But it's critical to find "more contexts where women leaders can have access to and can contribute to visions of how to address global challenges." For example, international gatherings of women health ministers have surfaced new ways to address such issues as HIV/AIDS and maternal and infant mortality. And a "global security summit" of women leaders that Mary convened went beyond conventional topics such as weapons systems to consider broader security questions: how economic inequality breeds terrorism, how to protect civilians in conflict zones.

When asked what has formed her approach to leading, Mary Robinson often jokes that she had to become a champion of human rights "because I was the only sister wedged between four brothers." Whatever forces shaped her, she is surely an example of that ATHENA fierce advocate. Her call to action is clear. Women must use their status as leaders to bring attention to "issues that are important from the gender perspective," and to promote the ascendance of more women to leader roles.

I am deeply affected by the words Mary Robinson spoke to those who supported her after she was elected Ireland's president. She said, in part, "I was elected by men and women of all parties and none, by many with great moral courage who stepped out from the faded flags of Civil War . . . and above all by the women of Ireland . . . who instead of rocking the cradle rocked the system and who came out massively for a new Ireland."

NOBODY TELLS NELL MERLINO'S STORY better than Nell Merlino. It's a story about what inspires people to act, to lead and to follow; it starts in her childhood kitchen and spans the creation of high-profile advocacy campaigns such as Take Our Daughters to Work Day. I loved my recent, wild-ride interview with Nell; she's a red-haired, salty-tongued whirlwind. She knows from experience that fierce advocates may start as an army of one but that with grit, wit, and commitment, such leaders can rally followers and launch movements. It's a formula that worked for her, a story she's eager to share.

Nell Merlino, creator of advocacy campaigns including Take Our Daughters To Work Day and Count Me In for Women's Economic Independence. Photo by Linda Russell, courtesy of Nell Merlino.

"My mother Molly, who's still alive, is a painter. She had an easel set up in the kitchen and often boiled over dinner to make a painting because she would be absolutely transfixed .... And my father Joe, who died in 1998, was a politician, president of the New Jersey state senate, very influential in the state in the 1970s. I watched him in the legislature, listened to him when he came home so focused. ... I remember seeing my parents and thinking, 'I want to be that engaged.'" On summer evenings, Joe and Molly packed Nell and her four siblings into the car and went door-to-door registering voters. "My Italian-immigrant father thought this was just the most incredible country with great opportunities and you needed to participate," Nell says. From both parents, she absorbed "an interest in issues of fairness and equality."

"I came of age at some of the most interesting parts of the women's movement. And I was living it," as one of the few women doing advance work for presidential campaigns, in 1984 for Walter Mondale, in 1988 for Michael Dukakis, in 1992 for Bill Clinton. Nell doesn't hide her contempt for a campaign culture in which, she says, women staffers would do spadework and then male staffers "would go off and have closed-door meetings to decide what to do. Somehow what we knew needed to be filtered through them to make a decision? One day I got fed up and said something like, 'Oh, I know what's the matter, I left my blue suit and dick at home today.'" Despite the frustrations, Nell says the experience left her with valuable insights about leadership, about "why people did or didn't get listened to," and how important it is "to collectively focus and operate in a way where it isn't about who's going to get credit."

In the early 1990s, Nell got a request from the Ms. Foundation. "They wanted me to come up with something to help girls keep from losing their sense of self. Then I went to my dad's retirement dinner from the legislature and I saw all these people I'd met as a child, neighbors as well as people my dad had worked with . . . and I remember thinking, 'Those people also had an influence on me and the choices I made. What if all girls had the opportunity to see who their parents were interacting with outside the house, where they go every day, what they do? That's something so many children still don't know.' And I went home from that dinner and drafted Take Our Daughters to Work Day.

"If you remember, in the early '90s there was this realization dawning that by the year 2000, one of every three new workers was going to be a woman or a member of a minority group, in a workplace that had been majority white male . . . . I am fascinated by how we project into the future in terms of thinking about how we're going to handle different things, who's going to step into the lead roles . . . . So I said, 'What if we could help people visualize this change now, appreciate what their workplace was going to look like? You fill it with children representing the other gender and any number of ethnic and racial groups, and you have the future right there.'"

First marked in 1992 and now celebrated annually on the last Thursday in April, the event ultimately was expanded to include sons as well as daughters. A public opinion poll on the tenth anniversary of Take Our Daughters to Work Day found that the program had increased girls' interest in education, influenced their decision to go to college or professional school, and broadened their thinking about their goals, aspirations and work options. Take Our Daughters and Sons To Work Day now has its own sponsoring foundation; in 2008, more than 33 million Americans marked the day in more than three million workplaces.

Applaud Nell for hatching such a successful idea, and she shifts the credit to the collective. "For that many people to step out and do something doesn't mean I'm a genius; it means I'm in touch with things in myself that other people are as well, and they needed a way to let it out. I think millions of people knew their daughters weren't going to get a fair shake—were going to be left in the dust—if they didn't do something. So they embraced the idea of being able to take them to work to show them opportunity, to show them what happens if you stay in school and focus on what you want to do as opposed to what you look like. I think I see and understand things that are on a lot of people's minds; I articulate them and give people a way to do them."

Nell says her current advocacy project "has been a slower boil than Take Our Daughters to Work Day; it's a little more complex, but powerful." Called Count Me In for Women's Economic Independence, it's a non-profit organization that channels loans, mentorships and other resources to help women grow small businesses into million-dollar ones. Count Me In's most successful program, Make Mine a Million $ Business, awards packages of money, marketing, mentoring, technology and support to women entrepreneurs on the fast track to million-dollar growth. The program has been expanded into the Make Mine a Million $ Business RACE, a business growth "marathon" for tens of thousands of women entrepreneurs to race to their annual revenue goals; Count Me In supports them with resources online and live events. "Women go into business to help their families and because they're problem solvers," Nell says. "The RACE is a new movement of women building stability for their families, creating more jobs, and becoming their own solution to the national economic crisis."

Like her politician dad and her artist mom, Nell feels she's doing what she was meant to do. "I don't think it's any mistake that I'm running a business that's helping thousands of women step into leadership. I think people can step into leading; it's not necessarily something one is born with, but I can tell you I was. My kindergarten report card took me to task for being bossy! It was a naughty thing to be then, something the teacher wanted to get me out of doing . . . but I am fifty-five years old now, and I am a boss, and I knew it at age five."

The Count Me In project has struggled in the face of recent economic upheavals. But Nell also points to real achievements. "We already have a community of 70,000 women whose businesses have been responsible for creating 250,000 jobs. If we were a Fortune 500 company, we'd be number twenty on the list."

And if Nell were a Fortune 500–company CEO . . . well, she probably wouldn't be. When she ushered America's daughters into conventional workplaces, it wasn't so they'd see how to conform, but how to transform. When she set out to help women grow businesses, it wasn't just about making money but also about imbedding their values in those enterprises. Nell says she knows plenty of successful people who "are always trying to figure out what the rules are so that they can play by them." As a leader and a change agent, she goes at things from a different direction. "If you've been outside looking in—and I don't know a woman who hasn't been, whether they admit it or not—and you want to move people to action, then you need to create something that other people want to get into. That's what I think leadership really is. If you're not going to let me in, in a way that I can be myself, then I'm going to make my own."

Nell has her own book in the works and you can tell by the way she says it that she's crazy about the title: *Stepping Out of Line.* The book will have plenty to say about women emerging as leaders, including her sense that that phenomenon is "like everything I've worked on: the more people see it, the more comfortable they get with it. I think Hillary Clinton's presidential run was disappointing on the one hand and brilliant on the other, the fact that she didn't quit. All those things are important milestones, important in moving the boulder up the hill, and that's what you have to do if you're a woman and want to do this. It's a minefield, but I do think we have so many women governors, senators. They're all there, they're all pushing it forward, learning a lot of stuff. I think in my lifetime we will see a lot more women stepping into positions of leadership, because they're next. They're there, they have the skills and the contacts and the experience. I feel very positive about our chances and our ability to influence situations; I think that grows daily. "What difference will it make? We're different, so it will be different. If we are authentic, we will consider our purpose and our families, always. You cannot separate that in women, and I don't think we ever want to."

AT THE 2007 ATHENA International conference, we exultantly marked the organization's twenty-five years of advancing women's leadership. I felt vaguely embarrassed but deeply honored when "my" organization named me one of three ATHENA International Award recipients that year. And so it was that, in a gilded Chicago ballroom, I shared the conference dais with the other two honorees: Shinae Chun, director of the U.S. Department of Labor Women's Bureau, the federal agency that advocates for women in the workforce; and Karenna Gore Schiff.

In some circles, Karenna is best known for her political bloodlines. Her parents are Tipper Gore and Al Gore, longtime U.S. senator, two-term vice-president and now a Nobel-winning crusader against global warming. ATHENA, however, chose Karenna because of her own varied achievements. She's been a lawyer, a journalist, and an advocate for disadvantaged children; in 2005 she published her first book, *Lighting The Way: Nine Women Who Changed Modern America*. When Karenna came to Chicago for the award ceremony, ATHENA's then-president Yvonne Wood welcomed her. Yvonne remembers Karenna quipping that she felt like a bird out a cage as it was the first time in months that she had been away from her new baby. At the award presentation, where we hailed Karenna as "representing the next generation of ATHENA leader, who

Karenna Gore Schiff, recipient of the ATHENA Young Professional Award and author of *Lighting the Way: Nine Women Who Changed Modern America*. Photo by Tipper Gore, courtesy of Karenna Gore Schiff.

has chosen this new way and exemplifies all of its strength," Karenna also shared with Yvonne how impressed she was at the work ATHENA was doing on behalf of women worldwide.

Since she turned three on one of her dad's election nights and his entire campaign-rally crowd sang "Happy Birthday" to her, Karenna has lived much of her life on or near the political stage. From that "privileged vantage point," as she calls it, she could see all the marquee players, but also the many public servants and socially conscious citizens who work behind the scenes without fanfare. Put another way, she was seeing exactly the people ATHENA was created to acknowledge: people who demonstrated the best kinds of leadership even though they hadn't been given, or pointedly had been denied, official recognition as leaders.

Karenna had made that connection, too; it's the first thing she mentioned during our recent interview. "What you've done with ATHENA has really touched a chord with me and, I think, with a lot of women," she said, "because throughout United States and world history there have been women doing things behind the scenes and really not so much recognized for it." When she set out to write *Lighting the Way* about pivotal leaders in times of great change, she chose only women leaders because so many "have been overlooked because of the traditional bias toward male leadership."

But as she studied these women's histories, she concluded that the "circumscribed roles" society had assigned them might actually have worked to the advantage of their leadership. Being hemmed in by gender bias simply forced the women to find more "creative, innovative ways to influence the political agenda," she believes. And focusing more on doing the work than on getting credit for it, she says, ultimately "made their work more valuable and more effective."

"In my experience growing up in politics—not to take anything away from the great leaders who are men—I've seen that women have done a lot behind the scenes to bring people together, introduce ideas and coordinate efforts, " Karenna says. "And I think the fact that many of them have shelved their egos has been something that made their leadership more effective. But in retrospect, as we consider history, it may also have kind of blinded us to what their leadership really was. So in writing the book, I was exploring the unsung women in American history."

As Karenna spoke about the women she researched, every story echoed with the principles of ATHENA leadership, especially fierce advocacy. These leaders aimed for nothing less than significant social change: racial equality, worker rights, workplace safety, child welfare. Often they were "ridiculed and ostracized for arguing for the changes in national policy that are taken for granted today," Karenna says, and yet these leaders never stopped fighting for what they believed in.

Some of the women were relatively well known—for example, Frances Perkins, the first woman to serve in a presidential cabinet, and Dolores Huerta, a co-founder of the United Farm Workers movement. But as Labor Secretary to President Franklin Delano Roosevelt, Perkins probably has never been adequately credited for her pivotal role in crafting New Deal legislation, one of the FDR administration's signal achievements. And in the public eye, Huerta's considerable achievements were generally overshadowed by her higher-profile counterpart, Cesar Chavez.

Karenna clearly delights in bringing recognition to women leaders who moved, largely unheralded, through some of American history's most important chapters. She introduced me to one such figure: Septima Poinsette Clark (1898–1987). A passionate educator and advocate, in the 1950s Septima spearheaded "citizenship schools" that taught African Americans how to meet voter-registration requirements and, crucially, how to become organizers and desegregation activists in their communities. Karenna says that as she learned more about Clark (known to friends as "Miss Seppie") she was amazed that such an influential, catalytic figure in the civil rights movement was not more widely known. So she's eager to tell Septima's story, and I hung on every word.

In the segregated schools of the American South, Septima was first a gifted student and then a talented, devoted teacher. The inequality that surrounded her drew her to the civil rights movement; in 1953 she began teaching at the Highlander Folk School in southeastern Tennessee. Established in the 1930s as an adult education center where ordinary people could learn to effect social change, Highlander in the 1950s drew students from across the country to its integrated workshops on voter registration and community activism.

"Septima was a real moving force behind the civil rights movement because she pioneered these citizenship schools which were very much training the leaders," Karenna says. "It started as literacy class to get people registered to vote and it became about getting people engaged in the civil process, even to run for office." Though Septima is not well known, Karenna says her influence can be clearly seen in "two of her most famous students": John Lewis, now a u.s. House member from Georgia, and the late Rosa Parks.

"Septima really inspired John Lewis—he didn't get where he now is by accident," Karenna says. The son of a sharecropper, Lewis stuttered, didn't read well, and didn't look like leadership material to some at Highlander. Karenna says Septima "took him aside and said, 'It really doesn't matter if you have a problem speaking because the people you really need to speak to will not judge you on that and you can be very powerful among them.' He went on and became an activist and a Freedom Rider," orchestrating sit-ins to desegregate lunch counters and getting beaten unconscious by police on "Bloody Sunday" during a march from Selma to Montgomery. Lewis today is revered as a civil rights icon; in 2008 he was elected to his twelfth term as a congressman from Georgia.

Another of Septima's students at Highlander was Rosa Parks. Karenna observes that "while she's the person recognized as a prominent female figure in the civil changes, she actually was so much more a sophisticated activist than people realize." Long after she rose to fame for refusing to give up her seat on a bus in December 1955, Rosa Parks would say that her Highlander training was critical to her decision to take that stand, Karenna notes. Even Septima hadn't realized, at the time, that Rosa was capable of this world-changing act. Karenna's book quotes Septima's surprised, delighted reaction. "When I heard the news, I said, 'Rosa? Rosa?' She was so shy when she came to Highlander, but she got enough courage to do that."

Karenna is convinced that "There are moments in social change where there's a tipping point, and there are a lot of women who build up to that tipping point. I don't think it takes anything away from Rosa Parks to say she had this great teacher" in Septima Poinsette Clark.

Another leader Karenna came to admire through her research is Alice Hamilton. As the Industrial Revolution drew more Americans into factories in the early 1900s, Alice Hamilton was a tireless advocate for workplace safety regulations and workers' rights and compensation. Alice's mother inspired her advocacy, Karenna says, by telling her that in life she would encounter generally "two kinds of people: the ones who say, 'Somebody ought to do something about it, but why should it be me?' and those who say, 'Somebody must do something about it, why not me?'"

To Karenna, "That's the shocking thing. That happens a lot, people stand on the sidelines and say, 'This is really terrible, someone should do something about it.' But often it's women who—unrecognized—get in there and do something about it. That's one reason ATHENA is so important. You see how a little recognition can help keep these leaders going."

She carefully draws a distinction between acknowledging women leaders' achievements and focusing too much on a high-profile few. Throughout history, Karenna says, "women have been accustomed to barriers. And it's wonderful and important to break glass ceilings in various arenas, and I absolutely applaud people who do. But I also think it's really interesting to explore the ways women have been leaders behind the scenes and under the radar and have never been spotlighted so they don't get credit for being the major glass-ceiling breaker, yet they're the ones who really made it happen. I don't really like today's celebrity culture, and focusing only on these glass-ceiling breakers kind of plays into that. It's important to celebrate people who may not become famous but who are changing things for the better, and I think you're really on to something there with ATHENA."

I'm grateful to Karenna for reminding me, with her stories of history-making women and with her own example, of the power of heartfelt advocacy. And I'm happy to give the last word on this subject to one more of Karenna's research subjects, the firebrand labor activist known as Mother Jones. "Pray for the dead and fight like hell for the living," Mother Jones famously advised. And "whatever your fight, don't be ladylike."

NINE

Act Courageously

COURAGE DOESN'T ALWAYS ROAR.
SOMETIMES COURAGE IS THE LITTLE VOICE AT THE END
OF THE DAY THAT SAYS, "I'LL TRY AGAIN TOMORROW."
— MARY ANNE RADMACHER

I N OUR CULTURE, the word courage often evokes images of lion-hearted heroics in the face of daunting odds. There's the real-world courage demonstrated by military personnel, law enforcement officers, firefighters; there's the outsized, special-effects courage portrayed by movie stars on the screen and protagonists in literature. When our characterizations of courage run along those traditional lines, I believe two things happen. First, we see courage substantially as a male-dominated virtue. Second, we fail to recognize the broad range of subtle, profound human acts that can be described as courageous.

When the ATHENA Leadership Model encourages us to "act courageously," it's really giving us permission to own our acts of courage. You may not identify the difficult things you do in the course of daily existence as requiring courage, but perhaps you should think again. The showdown in your workplace did not call for a life-or-death show of bravery, but did it require you to stand alone and speak up? The dispute in your neighborhood didn't demand a dramatic act of valor, but did it mean following your heart's convictions instead of the status quo?

If we do not consider our actions to be of a special nature, we will not give ourselves a special kind of credit for them. When we recognize and credit our own courageousness, we nurture it; we bless ourselves with the knowledge that what we have done ennobles us and others. If we leave courage to the other guy, we miss out on one of the most empowering experiences of all.

ATHENA leaders affirm that the smallest everyday act—an ethical choice, a quietly kept promise—can be big in the bravery department. When I was a kid and smaller than all my playmates, I had a vested interest in claiming that courage came in small packages. Now that I'm grown, to all of five feet, four inches tall, I know it comes in all shapes and manifestations because I've met those who embody it.

A shade shorter than I am, Mary Fisher had to stand on a tall riser to see over the podium at the 1992 Republican National Convention. She was there to call for compassion and action on AIDS from a party that at that point hadn't shown much of either. Terrified as she should have been, she delivered a speech that hushed the crowd, moved many to tears, and spoke immortally of courage. An HIV-positive mother faced with the prospect of leaving her two young sons orphans, Mary told the audience she no longer believed "that courage is the absence of fear." Rather she said, she had come to believe "that courage is the strength to act wisely when most we are afraid."

"When most we are afraid." In the 1980s, as Chambers and other organizations around the country heard about the ATHENA Award program, they would contact our Lansing Chamber in search of someone to come speak about it. Increasingly, I was the go-to speaker for more and larger events. I hadn't seen this coming; I wasn't ready. I was a soul on fire about ATHENA, an able communicator in meetings and with clients, but a wimp when it came to public speaking. The prospect of addressing big audiences left me paralyzed with fear. Of what? Of pretty much everything. Fear of not doing justice to this message about which I cared so deeply, fear of not connecting with the audience, not drawing them into the circle of involvement that we sought. Giving speeches about ATH-ENA was the most explicit intersection of passion and fear that I had ever experienced.

When the invitations kept coming, I developed coping mechanisms. One was the art of procrastination: Refusing to face zero hour was my stab at avoiding the fear that accompanied it. Before many engagements, I would be madly assembling a speech outline, decipherable only by me, on my way to the venue. Sometimes I was actually jotting notes as I drove (a tactic I'm admitting, not encouraging). Once I had prepared nothing at all and, as a good friend and mentor was introducing me to an audience, I realized with alarm that the only thing going through my head, over and over, like words on a ticker tape, was "It was a dark and stormy night." Trying to conceal my panic, I walked to the podium—and proceeded to tell the audience of the recent death of my mother. Somewhere I found threads to weave into a talk about leadership; somehow I connected with my listeners, who seemed to have no idea how fearful I had been. By not preparing, I had sabotaged myself. By getting up there anyway, I had also planted seeds of courage.

I kept taking speaking engagements, suffering the dread. I kept trying to defuse the fear by skirting the reality, not formally preparing, making it a high-wire act every time. I chastised myself repeatedly for this deny-and-avoid approach to speaking. But for the longest time, I never gave myself credit for summoning the courage to do that which I so feared.

When finally I did admit it (I guess that did take guts) I drew more courage from the admission. Gradually, the terror lessened to stage fright . . . the stage fright melted to jitters . . . and now, before most speeches, I just feel excitement and gratitude for the chance to share the ATHENA precepts and spirit. Facing that problem, and in doing so summoning and honoring my courage, allowed me to transform my life.

In a bracing little book called *Courage: The Heart and Spirit of Every*

Woman, author Sandra Ford Walston writes this: "All women have had debilitating experiences that compel self-examination and reinvention. Many emotional, physical, and psychological crises are common to women cross-culturally; fear, loss, illness, abuse, betrayal, and low self-esteem. Yet the courage to face and conquer these obstacles is available" to all of us.

Fears arise when one's sense of oneself is distorted or unfinished. Attempting to rise above fear, even haltingly, with baby steps, can be a great act of personal courage. Having had that mountain to climb, I've become more aware of other people's struggles. I can see them in a context with which I deeply empathize; I can recognize others' small, brave successes just as I learned to appreciate mine.

ATHENA encourages leaders to act courageously. To do that, we must know courage when we see it, in all its faces and forms. I am grateful to have learned that, with wisdom like Walston's to guide me. "Make yourself aware of courage as a force and a virtue," she counsels. "Then practice it, and choose it as a way of life."

CARLOTTA WALLS LANIER AND I have a few things in common. We're about the same age and we both went to college at Michigan State University. We both made careers in real estate. She's a broker now in the Denver, Colorado, area. But in 1957, I was watching on television as nine black students entered segregated Little Rock Central High School. Carlotta was one of those nine. When we spoke recently, Carlotta told me that in adult life she has shied away from the spotlight that was trained on the "Little Rock Nine." But she agreed to a conversation about leadership and courage because, she said, many of the ATHENA principles—especially "fostering collaboration, respecting diversity and celebrating the achievements of others"—resonate with her beliefs and experiences.

Before she walked into Central High School and, later, into the

Carlotta Walls LaNier in her 1960 graduation photo from Little Rock Central High School. Photo courtesy of Carlotta Walls LaNier.

history books, Carlotta would have called herself "a quiet person, quietly involved but very active." In the community, she participated in YWCA, Girl Scouts, and the Methodist church; at her all-black school she was basketball team captain, cheerleader, student council officer. The discrimination there wasn't about race. "When you ran for student council office, the assumption was for the males to be president. I don't know whether I bought into it or not; more accepted it, I guess. I was elected as the vice president." In hindsight, Carlotta sees a pattern. "Some of us acquiesced, worked within the system, in an environment where you knew eventually it was going to change."

Starting with the Supreme Court's *Brown v. Board of Education* decision when Carlotta was in seventh grade, she imagined the opportunities to come: "It was talked about at home, school and church, and we knew positive changes were going to take place." The Little Rock school board's grudging plan, which took three years to work out, offered integration in phases, with the black high school remaining open but a few black students being admitted to Central.

Though Carlotta remembers having doubts about the piecemeal approach, she still believed integrating the high school could be "an easy transition. You have to understand, at that time Little Rock was considered a moderate southern city. I lived on a block that was all black, the next block was all white, and when school was out, all summer long we'd play softball together." She jumped at the chance to apply to Central High School and was one of seventeen accepted. As the first day of school neared and tensions rose, the number dwindled to nine, with Carlotta the youngest at fourteen.

Carlotta blames "foolishness and politicization" for Governor Orval Faubus's decision to side with segregationists and block the black students' entry. Faubus ordered the state's National Guard to surround the high school, claiming it was to prevent mob violence. When Carlotta and the eight others tried to enter, they were turned back by guardsmen and threatened by furious crowds.

After almost three weeks, under court order, Faubus withdrew the Guard that had blocked the students' entry. Carlotta remembers the "extremely frightening" scene outside the school on September 23, 1957. "The only thing the city could do to hold back the mob was to send out the police, and there were only seventeen policemen on the ground when we got into school that particular day. By noon it was doubtful they could control the people gathered across the street. There were black people there that they had chased and beaten, there were effigies of hanging people . . . . So the policeman had to remove us, and it was scary. We were brought out of class and taken down into the bowels of the building, three stories underground, and put into police cars and told to duck our heads. We drove out of there fast—it was dark and then all of a sudden light, and if anyone had been on the sidewalk, they would have been killed . . . . "

In Washington, President Eisenhower had had enough. He sent in troops of the 101st Airborne Division to patrol outside the school and escort the Nine in. "Two days later, we went back into the high school under their protection and they took us through every day and walked the halls," Carlotta says. "But even with them being there, and even with the mentality of Governor Faubus and others being rejected by the president of the United States, it didn't stop the little groups from wanting to get to you."

Carlotta didn't want her parents to worry so she never told them much of what she and the other eight endured: being spat upon, slammed against lockers, pelted with burning paper wads. "One person would walk on the back of my heels until they would bleed," Carlotta recalls. "So I figured if she was going to walk on the back of my heels, I'd walk fast. They called me a roadrunner. I had a different 101st Airborne bodyguard every week because I walked so fast I was wearing them out." Every day as the Nine were driven home, they'd compare notes on the day's indignities. Of that ritual, Carlotta says now, "We learned a great deal about people's fears, in thinking that the color of someone's skin would justify that treatment."

I asked Carlotta if she grasped at the time both the history-making nature of her own actions, and the indefensibility of her tormentors' behavior. Her reply: "Yes and no. I realized there were people defying what we lived by: the law, the Supreme Court's decision. As a fourteen-year-old, I thought they'd be put in their place, shown that this was the law and they'd have to abide by it. People were saying to me, 'You're making history' and all that kind of stuff. None of that meant anything to me; I was going to school to get the best education, my father paid taxes just like everybody else, that meant I could go to school—and I was going."

Carlotta finished her sophomore year and in spring 1958 saw her comrade Ernest Green become the first black student to graduate from Central High School. Still fighting desegregation, Faubus invoked a state law to close Little Rock's public schools for what would have been Carlotta's junior year; she kept up her studies through University of Arkansas correspondence courses. When Central High School reopened in fall 1959 for her senior year, Carlotta returned; in February 1960, her family's home was bombed, "probably in hopes that I wouldn't graduate." But she did, at age seventeen, and was the only female member of the Nine to participate in Central's formal graduation ceremony.

"When I got that diploma," she says now, "that just sealed everything for me. It validated all the things that I knew were right, all I had gone through, that I had done the right thing. When I graduated, that was a chapter of my life done. I got on a train the very next day to St. Louis, I left Little Rock for good."

In the ensuing years, as Carlotta built a family and business, she held onto lessons from Central High School, that "nothing worthwhile happens without some adversity or obstacle" and that "when something like that is embedded, it gives you the strength to do other things." She still thinks of herself as a fighter, "but, as my college roommate says, 'You're one of those fighters behind closed doors.' I'm not the one who goes out and walks in marches; I find there are other ways to achieve my goals. I'm not looking to be a poster child for anything. I've had that already, and I don't like it."

Carlotta and her comrades have formed a non-profit organization, The Little Rock Nine Foundation; it offers scholarships and mentoring for youngsters, especially young people of color, who might otherwise lack educational opportunity. Carlotta, the foundation's president, notes with pride that in September 2007, the foundation chose nine college-bound students to receive $10,000 scholarships as well as leadership training and one-on-one mentoring. "Each of us had one young person to mentor through the first year, and then the next year they will mentor others," she says. "In this way, we're hoping to teach them to do well in school and meanwhile to be helping someone else."

Of the nine brave students who demanded their rights at Central High School, six were young women. "I think women are very strong leaders," Carlotta says. "We believe in strong leaders, that's what we've been taught in this country, but you don't have to be a heavy-handed person to get the job done. Leaders are not necessarily the ones that are talking all the time. They may just be do-ers."

WHENEVER my friend and collaborator Dutch Landen found something he thought relevant to an ATHENA principle, he'd send it along to me. And so one day a few years ago, I found in my mail box eight short free-verse lines on the subject of courage. The title of Christopher Logue's poem is the same as its first line: "Come to the Edge."

> *Come to the edge.*
> We might fall.
> *Come to the edge.*
> It's too high!
> *COME TO THE EDGE!*
> And they came
> and he pushed
> and they flew . . .

IT'S THE KIND OF APHORISM that a Texan would appreciate: "Courage is being scared to death, but saddling up anyway." John Wayne is supposed to have said it. Sarah Weddington did it.

As a Methodist preacher's kid, Sarah moved every few years among towns "so small that most Texans have never heard of them" and learned to land on her feet. As a teen, she joined "the kinds of organizations that allowed young women to be leaders," and wound up as drum major of her school band, president of her church's youth fellowship and president of the local Future Homemakers of America. At little McMurry College

Sarah Weddington, ATHENA International Award recipient who argued *Roe v. Wade* before the U.S. Supreme Court. Photo courtesy of Sarah Weddington.

in Abilene, an English professor named Selma made her a better writer, and a speech coach named Carolyn sharpened a full range of speaking skills. But as Sarah considered career paths, "my generation of women basically were told, 'You can be teachers, secretaries and nurses.' People still were saying, 'Women don't,' 'women can't,' 'women shouldn't.' But I and a good many others were saying, 'That makes no sense.'"

A McMurry dean warned Sarah that, since his son found law school challenging, it would surely be too hard for her—"so of course, that was the moment I thought, 'I am going to law school.'" In her University of Texas law school class of about 150, there were five women. As she prepared to graduate in 1967, law firms came to UT's Austin campus and interviewed both men and women but for follow-up interviews at the firms, would only pay travel expenses for men. In her first run at advocacy as an almost-lawyer, Sarah convinced the placement office to mandate that interviewing firms pay travel costs for both genders; she was "the first woman ever to have her way paid to interview, from Austin to Dallas, 187 whole miles."

Like other women graduating law school and going on job interviews, Sarah heard variations on the same excuse—"we've never had a woman lawyer in this firm and we don't think our wives would be comfortable with it"—and got no offers. She was working as a research assistant to a UT law professor when a group of grad students sought her out for legal advice on a birth control counseling service they ran. The university's health center would provide birth control only to women who signed a statement saying they would be married within six weeks and would need it for their wedding night. As a result, the grad students said, young women were asking them for referrals for birth control or, more desperately, abortion. The grad students asked Sarah if providing such information could get them arrested under Texas's anti-abortion law.

Researching the question in UT's law library, Sarah found two U.S. Supreme Court cases that seemed relevant. In *Griswold v. Connecticut,* a case in which Planned Parenthood professionals had been prosecuted for giving a contraceptive device to a married couple, the Supreme Court had ruled that people had the right to privacy in their decisions about childbearing. And in *Eisenstadt v. Baird,* a case where a contraceptive was given to an unmarried woman, the high court went further, asserting every individual's right to privacy in choices about birth control. Those precedents, Sarah told the grad students, would surely protect their birth control counseling service, and probably could be used to challenge Texas's anti-abortion statute.

"Now, if somebody had said to me, 'Would you mind trying a case about abortion in the Supreme Court?' I would have said, 'No way!'" Weddington says now. "At that point in my law career I had done a few uncontested divorces, wills for people with no money and one adoption for my uncle. But I think courage often is doing something in spite of fear, knowing the odds might be against you. I certainly did have that sense, but there wasn't any other woman I knew of who was willing to give the time, or who had the time to give. So you just do that thing that gives you a possibility of having an impact." The class-action case filed on March 3, 1970, in Dallas was *Roe v. Wade,* named for "Jane Roe"—a pseudonym to represent all women who were pregnant and didn't want to be—and Henry Wade, the district attorney responsible for enforcing the state statute.

Across the United States, numerous challenges to anti-abortion statutes were moving through federal courts. Some fell away for procedural reasons, or when the money for lawyers ran out—but Sarah was working pro bono. On May 21, 1971, the Supreme Court published notice that it would hear *Roe v. Wade.* At age twenty-six, Sarah would do something unnerving for any lawyer, arguing her first contested case before the highest court in the land.

"The night before, I couldn't sleep," she recalls. "I would think, 'What if they ask such-and-such?' so I was up and down all night, checking points." Arriving at the Supreme Court, she went to the lounge area provided for lawyers waiting to argue, and discovered it had no ladies' room. Leaving the court after oral arguments, she says, "I had no idea if we had won or lost." On January 22, 1973, the answer came. In a 7–2 decision, the court ruled that the constitutional right to privacy "is broad enough to encompass a woman's decision to terminate her pregnancy."

More than thirty-six years after the decision, abortion remains one of the most polarizing issues in America; advocates of equal conviction argue that *Roe v. Wade* should be upheld, revisited, struck down. Sarah knows well the passionate divisions on the issue. She did what she did, she says, from a deep belief "that women were not being treated fairly, that this was not right, and that we needed to change it."

While working on the case, Sarah pursued other means to change things she thought were wrong. She ran for a seat in the Texas legislature in 1972 and won. Through three terms in the Texas House of Representatives, she fought to reform laws she felt were unfair to women, including credit laws that dealt inequitably with male and female breadwinners, and rape laws that "put women on trial for past sexual conduct more than they put men on trial for unconsented sexual contact." She later served as a White House assistant to President Jimmy Carter, and now is a law professor, author, and speaker on issues including, not surprisingly, leadership.

In 2006, when Sarah was named a recipient of the ATHENA International Award, the presentation noted "that as a young woman and freshly minted attorney . . . she brought a legal challenge to a law of the land she held to be untenable for women and families." Sarah has observed, dryly but with good humor, that it is rather "unnatural to have done what will define your life when you're twenty-six." That's one way to look at it; I might offer another. Whatever else Sarah has done, and whatever one's opinion on *Roe v. Wade*, in that politically-charged, pressure-cooker situation, she lived out her convictions. Such moments not only define lives, they define leaders. Courageous ATHENA leaders follow their beliefs, even when that means challenging the status quo.

WHEN NPR LEGAL AFFAIRS CORRESPONDENT NINA TOTENBERG accepted our first ATHENA International Award in 1994, she spoke of the importance of calling leaders to account, even when they're as prominent as a Supreme Court justice nominee or as powerful as the senators responsible for vetting that nominee.

In 1991 as she reported on Anita Hill's harassment charges against Clarence Thomas and whether senators had duly investigated them, "I didn't perceive it as courageous," Nina says now. "At the time, it was like being in the middle of a storm or a war. It's really unpleasant and you didn't bargain for it, but you really didn't have options, once there. I may not have completely understood I was going to get that big target on my head, but I didn't have any choice other than to stand up. I thought it was a good story; I thought I reported it the right way." For her coverage, Totenberg won some of the most prestigious awards in journalism (although, she says, the ATHENA Award sculpture remains "the prettiest award I have").

In the years since Nina was ATHENA's honoree, much has changed for women in the world she covers. "There are many more judges, federal judges, state judges, who are women—close to half," she says. "And in many cases, it's more women than men in law schools. But having said that, to have a Supreme Court that now has only one woman on it is very discouraging to Justice O'Connor"—Sandra Day O'Connor, the first woman appointed to the high court, in 1981—"not to mention Justice Ginsburg who's made no secret of the fact that she's lonely up there." (Justice Ruth Bader Ginsburg, appointed to the court in 1993, was the 1995 recipient of the ATHENA International Award.)

When Nina thinks of courage, she says, "I see it in all of these women who were pioneers: Ruth Ginsburg, Sandra Day O'Connor. The second time Ruth Ginsburg was pregnant, she was at Rutgers and she hid her pregnancy because she was afraid she would lose her professorship. And

Two recipients of the National ATHENA Award: above, Supreme Court Justice Ruth Bader Ginsburg, with Martha; at right, NPR Legal Affairs Correspondent Nina Totenberg. Photos courtesy of ATHENA International.

O'Connor, after she graduated third in her law school class at Stanford, she couldn't get a job, she was being offered receptionist jobs. So she finally convinced the district attorney in Alameda County to give her a job without pay, to let her work for free at a desk next to his secretary's, so she could prove herself.... These women had remarkable guts."

By sticking it out, proving their mettle and rising to the top of their profession, these women changed the playing field for everyone, Nina contends. "Today, I don't think, by and large, that a really first-rate female officeholder or judge or whatever is taken less seriously than a male counterpart. I think sometimes you have something to prove; you probably have to prove it more than a man would. But do I think for a second that Justice Ginsburg is taken less seriously on the Supreme Court because she's a woman? Absolutely not."

I DO LOVE THE STORY of how ATHENA made her entrance: bursting fully formed and armed from the skull of Zeus, ready to take on the world. It's important to note, though, that for most of us, coming forth as leaders is nothing like that. We find our voice little by little, in all different settings, speaking with more confidence each time. We build up courage by trying to act bravely when we are most afraid, trying, even if we fail. For ATHENA leaders, there's no such thing as fully formed because as long as we're on life's path, the journey constantly forms us.

In the old ways of thinking, would-be leaders pushed (or were pushed) to accumulate titles and training, to get their ticket punched at the requisite corporate stops. With that accomplished, they would arrive, as if landing a playing piece on the final square of a board game, at the corner office, a completed leader. For the twenty-first century, and for ATHENA leaders, that notion is not just obsolete, it's unappealing. How much more vitality and possibility there is in seeing ourselves, and our leadership, as perpetual works in progress.

Kathleen Cravero, director of the United Nations Development Program's Bureau for Crisis Prevention and Recovery. Photo courtesy of UNDP Sierra Leone.

ATHENA leaders do not obsess about being perfected, established, done. Rather, they focus on doing, on rising to a challenge even if they're not sure they can meet it. Leading this way takes courage; it is, in every sense, braving the unknown.

As a teenaged drama student, Kathleen Cravero played everything from the wicked witch in *The Wizard of Oz* to leading roles in *The Lottery* and *The Women*. It was fun, she recalls, to capture people's attention just to entertain them. But more, it gave her a sense of "my ability to move people. Later, when I was giving speeches and advocating for things I believed in, I realized that it was a very similar feeling. I had an ability to take people along with me."

For more than two decades, Kathleen has traveled the world for the United Nations. In more than fifty nations on five continents, she has worked with UNICEF, the UN's children's program; WHO, its health program; UNAIDS, its HIV/AIDS program; and UNDP, its development program. Since 2005, she has directed UNDP's Bureau for Crisis Prevention and Recovery, which leads relief and redevelopment efforts in nations devastated by natural disaster or violent conflict.

Wherever acts of war or "acts of god" leave people in need and in danger, Kathleen and colleagues intercede. One day when we spoke, she had just returned from a trip to Myanmar as part of the UN team struggling to get humanitarian aid into the military-ruled country after a devastating cyclone. When I marveled at the pace and demands of her work, all Kathleen said was: "When you go to places where the circumstances are difficult and see people coping with them on a daily basis, you gather your courage from their determination and resilience."

In a long, generous chat, Kathleen shared insights she has gained from her years of observing and working with leaders around the world. In addition to what does work, she has seen plenty of what doesn't, and ticks off a list: "Failure to listen makes it impossible to understand opposing views. Instilling fear prevents bad news from filtering up, which is dangerous in conflict situations. Lying or saying things differently to different people undermines credibility. And being too much in the weeds of a problem or an issue disempowers others whose job it is to untangle those weeds.

What people need from a leader is to keep their heads up and the vision clear, not to be down there doing what they could do as well or better."

In her own quest to become a leader who inspires trust and confidence, Kathleen says, "the principles you identify in the ATHENA model resonate with me, all eight of them. If I were to describe the traits of a leader, I would come up with those. The only one I might add would be vision. If you're going to advocate fiercely or act courageously or foster collaboration, it's got to be toward something and you have to be able to communicate what that something is."

Before we met through mutual friends, I already admired Kathleen for what I knew of her leadership on global women's issues. While at UNAIDS, she launched its Global Coalition on Women and AIDS, a network of organizations that work to blunt the impact of AIDS on women and girls worldwide. She is a leading force behind Stop Rape Now: UN Action to End Sexual Violence in Conflict, a campaign uniting twelve UN entities around the goal of eliminating sexual violence as a weapon of war. "I've tried to use every position of influence that I have had to do something significant for women," she says. When Kathleen says our ATHENA ideals ring true with her, I take that as high praise because she so obviously embodies what I esteem in leaders.

There is one episode in Kathleen's life that speaks with exceptional power about leadership and courage. It had been shared with me only privately by our mutual friends. Kathleen did not mention it until I asked. Her voice was even but quiet.

"I was Humanitarian Coordinator and Resident Coordinator in Burundi, the leader of the UN team, from September 1997 to December 1999. During that time, Burundi was ruled by a minority group, with a long history of ethnic violence and grinding poverty. About a year after I arrived, the government adopted a strategy of clearing the hills in the countryside—mostly populated by small-scale farmers of the opposing ethnic group—and driving entire villages into the valleys below. In most cases, their houses and fields were pillaged by the army that was supposedly protecting them. I would then get a call from the President's Office or the Ministry of Interior, requesting international support for these 'displaced' populations. This obviously posed a dilemma for the UN: if we didn't help, they would die of starvation and cold; if we did help, we were aiding and abetting gross violations of human rights . . . .

"So the humanitarian entities in Burundi developed a joint policy in response. Every time this happened, we would visit the place where people were driven and, depending on the circumstances, we would provide lifesaving support but nothing of a permanent nature. For example, we would provide water bladders but no wells, food but no seed—because we needed to make the point that these people should go home. We were clear with the government that we could not and would not support their resettlement in these valleys so that the army could control the hills. This went on for some months. Extremist elements of the minority ruling group were furious that the UN was not providing enough to settle people in these valleys, and the rebels from the other group were adamant that nothing should be provided, in order to force the issue.

"On October 11, 1999, I got a call saying 25,000 people were in a valley in the southern province of Rutana and needed UN support. The next day I led a mission to Rutana to verify the claims. As we drove up, we were ambushed by armed men, who seemed to come out from everywhere.

"I was up against a wall with a security guard and five colleagues. We began negotiating with a young man who appeared to be in charge and who looked, at most, eighteen years old. We explained that we were from the UN and there to help keep people alive, and it seemed to be working. And then he turned around to deal with something else and a young kid—couldn't have been more than fifteen—started blowing our heads off, one by one. He murdered the UNICEF representative and the logistics officer from the World Food Programme, the first two against the wall.

I was third, but before he could shoot me, the security guard reached for his pistol and shot the boy in the leg, at which point he stumbled off in the other direction.

"There was so much confusion that we managed to run away with about 100 people who were fleeing from a neighboring village. We spent three hours running through the fields before we found shelter .... I remember thinking that, while this was the worst day of my life, it was a regular occurrence for these villagers—always running from violence, with no idea from whom, to where, or for what reason."

Kathleen stopped speaking. I had heard more of that story, and it was this: that after the four survivors had gotten safely away, Kathleen insisted that the bodies of her colleagues be retrieved lest they be lost or forgotten. I asked if that were so.

"Yes," she said. "We had faced the absolute worst thing that could have happened, literally it couldn't get any worse, and at that point we weren't sure whether it was better to be dead, or to be alive and going home with two dead colleagues. We would have preferred to be dead ourselves rather than to go back without them." With help from the aid group Doctors Without Borders, the bodies were reclaimed and returned to the slain workers' families.

These were her last words about that day: "When you witness a horrible demonstration of evil, you never forget that moment. You never 'get over it.' It changes you and becomes part of who you are. The challenge is not to let evil defeat you. The tragedy of that day—and the loss of my colleagues—strengthened my resolve to work for peace and to stand up for the world's most vulnerable."

TEN

Foster Collaboration

WE WILL SURELY GET TO OUR DESTINATION IF WE JOIN HANDS.
—AUNG SAN SUU KYI

WHEN BURMA'S PRO-DEMOCRACY PARTY won a landslide victory in 1990, the ruling military junta voided the vote. To maintain the power it seized in 1962, the military has used intimidation, detention, torture and murder. But against its single most powerful foe, opposition leader Aung San Suu Kyi, the junta employs a devastating weapon: isolation. For nearly fourteen of the past twenty years, she has lived under house arrest, deprived of most human contact, her communication and movements strictly limited. Despite punishing economic sanctions and relentless international pressure, the junta has kept Suu Kyi confined so she cannot do one thing: work with others. What more proof do we need of the formidable power of collaboration?

Like most who admire Aung San Suu Kyi, I have seen her only in still pictures, except for one very memorable time. In September 1995, I was one of thousands of people from around the world who went to China for the UN's Fourth World Conference for Women. At a forum for non-governmental organizations, in a packed meeting hall, we waited for keynote speaker Suu Kyi to "arrive" via a tape smuggled out from her confinement. And then, on the towering video screen, there she was: dark hair, delicate features, the face of Audrey Hepburn with the force of Dr. King.

It was time, Suu Kyi exhorted us, for women "to apply in the arena of the world the wisdom and experience . . . gained in activities of peace over so many thousands of years." She spoke of the "triumphant demonstration of female solidarity" that is unleashed when strong, principled women come together. And she called listeners to "the common hopes that unite us: that as the shackles of prejudice and intolerance fall from our own limbs, we can together strive to identify and remove the impediments to human development everywhere." Though her voice was not loud and her oratory not grand, her address was riveting because of the ethical, intellectual and spiritual strength she projected, the soulful depth of her being. Everyone in that auditorium, filled beyond capacity, was silent, motionless, transfixed as I was.

Aung San Suu Kyi was just two years old in 1947 when assassins killed her father, General Aung San, a national hero who led Burma's successful fight against British colonial rulers. She accompanied her mother to India for a diplomatic posting, then studied at Oxford; in 1972 she married British scholar Michael Aris, and soon was raising two young sons, Alexander and Kim.

She returned to Burma in 1988 to visit her ailing mother just as the pro-democracy movement ignited, and answered the call to lead. She has not seen England since. Through nearly two decades of arrest, release and re-arrest, she's been absent when the Nobel committee awarded her its 1991 Peace Prize; absent for most of her sons' lives (they're now in their thirties), and absent when her husband died in 1999.

And still she remains a light in the world, a beacon for all who face oppression. Despite the junta's walls and wiretaps, she inspires, she rallies, she leads. The Nobel presentation said it well: "In the good fight for peace and reconciliation, we are dependent on persons who . . . mobilize the best in us. Aung San Suu Kyi is just such a person."

Fostering collaboration, in ATHENA terms, is about being a mobilizer, a catalyst. It's about drawing in those who've been shut out, soliciting input from those who've gone unheard, valuing the gifts each individual brings. It is also about modeling collaboration ourselves by sharing the reins of leadership. Remember MSU president Lou Anna Simon's point about promoting "the *we* as opposed to the *I*"? That is what ATHENA leaders aim to do, secure in the knowledge that sharing leadership does not mean relinquishing it, and that helping others find their power doesn't diminish our own. ATHENA leaders welcome others to the work of leadership.

Though all the ATHENA principles are rooted in women's time-honored ways of working together, I feel that connection particularly strongly in this principle. Our mothers and their mothers probably never talked about collaboration, but everywhere they practiced it: at quilting bees, charity functions and suffragists' marches; by helping each other raise children or bring in crops, network for jobs or nurse ailing loved ones. That willingness to join forces is a noble human impulse—and, Margaret Mead would say, as old as civilization itself.

As the story goes, a student of Mead's once asked the famed anthropologist what, in any given culture, is the earliest sign of civilization. The student imagined that Mead's answer would be some object, a particular sort of vessel or grindstone, a primitive tool or weapon. The student was not prepared for Mead's three-word answer: "a healed femur."

So Mead explained. She said that no healed femurs—that is, broken leg bones that were tended until the break healed—have been found in ancient, survival-of-the-fittest cultures where the weak were on their own. Discovery of a healed femur meant that people cared for an injured party, that they did the hunting and gathering in her stead, protected her while she was immobilized, fed and nursed her until she recovered. The earliest sign of civilization, Mead concluded, was the compassionate, collaborative effort signified by that healed bone.

Collaboration encourages people to believe in each other. ATHENA leaders create conditions that help individuals develop their own ideas and gifts and to weave them together with the ideas and gifts of others. The result? A breadth of perspectives that expands potential.

"IT BECAME CLEAR TO ME early on that people saw me in ways that I did not see myself." I certainly could have made this statement in the years before ATHENA, when I perceived myself as strong and capable, an emerging leader—but others, because of my gender, saw me differently. That quote isn't from me, though; it's from Dinah Eng, a gifted journalist who has spent much of her life helping open eyes and dismantle stereotypes.

Dinah is the first Asian-American columnist whose commentary is available nationwide, in a weekly newspaper column distributed by the Gannett News Service. In her profession, she has tirelessly championed diversity in the workforce and cultural sensitivity in media coverage. But more broadly, Dinah is devoted to what ATHENA calls collaboration: that truly communal state where we value and bond with each other because of our rich differences, not just in spite of them.

Growing up in a Chinese-American family in Houston, Dinah experienced how "in the Chinese culture as in many cultures, men are considered more worthy than women." As the eldest of seven daughters whose father always wanted a son, Dinah grew up determined "to always be out in front and prove that a woman is just as good as a man." Early aspirations to be a doctor yielded to her growing love of writing; she went from high school newspaper editor to journalism studies in college and grad school. After stints at *The Detroit News* and USA TODAY, Dinah landed at Gannett News Service (GNS), the wire service for what is today the nation's largest newspaper publisher. As she rose through the ranks at GNS to become editor of the college wire service division of Gannett New Media she experienced more than once what she described in that earlier quote: People not seeing her as she was but through their own, distorting preconceptions.

An example: "When I first started at GNS, I was a features editor and someone who was a graphic artist came up to me one day and gave me a graphic they were working on. It had something to do with a Chinese event and they were trying to put some Chinese characters in it. The person asked me, 'So, what does this character say?' I said, 'I don't know, I don't read or write Chinese.' And the person looked at me and said, 'But what does this character say?!'"

To define herself in the face of such assumptions, Dinah says, "I realized in some ways I was on my own—and in other ways I could never be on my own, because I couldn't accomplish what I wanted by myself. I think a lesson that anybody who is a leader learns early on is: You can't do anything alone."

Dinah Eng, creator and director of a leadership training program for the Asian American Journalists Association. Photo courtesy of Dinah Eng.

Dinah became a leader of minority journalism groups and a bridge to mainstream journalism groups. She was president first of the Asian American Journalists Association (AAJA), and then of UNITY, an umbrella group for African-American, Native American, and Hispanic as well as Asian-American journalists. In 1995, Dinah created an AAJA leadership training program that embodies what ATHENA means by collaboration: valuing the gifts each individual brings and insuring that disparate voices are heard.

In the program (which Dinah still directs) Asian-American trainees explore their culturally influenced values and how to integrate them in the corporate setting. "We help people identify what it is they value and believe, we look at how their beliefs get expressed in the workplace, and we help them see the flipside, how that is received by others from a different culture," Dinah says. "We look at white, American, male, corporate values and we pose the question: Where do we fit? And as we explore that, the question then becomes: If you want to succeed in this environment, how much are you willing to stretch? How much are you hurting yourself if you do not stay true to your own values?"

For example, Dinah says, when it comes to communication style, "some Asian-American people may sit in meetings and not speak up because in the Asian culture, it's understood that if you agree, you don't need to say anything . . . . But in a white, male corporate culture, if you don't speak up in a meeting, you can be thought of as disengaged, not sociable and able to work with others, not leadership material. On the other hand, there are Asian-American journalists who have gone through our program and are extremely talkative, right in your face because they're used to asking questions—and they get the flipside of being seen as too aggressive, chip on their shoulder, by those who don't expect that an Asian person is going to speak like that." The situation, Eng agreed, is strikingly similar to the damned-if-you-do, damned-if-you-don't choices many women experience in traditional corporate settings.

While the program ultimately can't give trainees all the answers, Dinah hopes it "leads them to question and explore, to grow in the wholeness of who they are." Dinah notes with pride that when program graduates were surveyed, more than half said they earned one or more promotions after taking the training. But she's even prouder, she says, when many graduates tell her the program was a life-changing experience.

In 2007 when the National Association of Multicultural Media Executives honored Dinah for her achievements in fostering diversity, a colleague described her this way: "There are leaders who inspire us to follow—and then there are people like Dinah Eng who inspire us to lead." At the podium to receive her award, Dinah told the audience, "Breakthroughs in diversity happen every day, but we don't always recognize them, and we don't always remember them." Then she led the audience through "a little exercise: I'm going to call out some categories, and if this applies to you, stand up." How many, she asked, were born east of the Mississippi? Were the oldest sibling in their family? Drive a sports car? Practice yoga?

"These are the kinds of things we would never know about people unless we took the time to talk to them," Dinah went on. "Our family origins, our interests, the things that are important to us: They all point to our values and who we are. If you stood up for any of those categories, you have something in common with me. But we all have something in common that's even greater, in that every one of us wants to feel valued and appreciated for who we are." For that to happen, she said, "takes action. It requires taking a risk. So I'm going to ask you to do one last thing. If everybody would please stand up and join hands with the person next to you? Now repeat after me: 'I can never be separate . . . . I live in the consciousness of peace . . . . In my heart, there is only love.' If we remember these things, we will have breakthroughs constantly."

After the exercise, Dinah says, "People came up to me and said it was the most connected they had ever felt to the ideas a speaker was talking about, and that, while they would feel and hope such things in their own heart, they had not experienced saying it aloud." Dinah says she frequently leads audiences through similar exercises "because I believe diversity is something that we have to share outwardly and that it's not just sharing who we are, it's listening and learning who other people are and finding the places in which we connect."

She also believes that in the final analysis "diversity happens one person at a time. That's the only way to move an individual from fearing another who is different, to understanding that there are common bonds. Doing that one person at a time is why it takes so long—but some of us will spend our whole lives struggling to get there."

BEFORE BILL GEORGE BECAME A PROFESSOR of management practice at the Harvard Business School, he was chairman and CEO of Medtronic, one of the world's leading medical technology companies. Through roughly a decade under George's leadership starting in 1991, Medtronic's market capitalization grew from $1.1 billion to $60 billion. But George now says flatly that he never could have achieved such success had he not made one critical shift. He calls it "the transformation from 'I' to 'We'" and it is a central element in his 2007 book about leadership, *True North*. In George's description of that transformation, I hear echoes of the ATHENA commitment to fostering collaboration.

For many of us, George observes, "early success in life depends upon our individual efforts, from the grades we earn in school to our performance in individual sports to our initial jobs." But success as a leader isn't about what we can accomplish on our own, he contends. Rather, it's about what we can inspire, encourage and enable others to accomplish. It is only through that transition—that shift from "I" to "We"—that leaders find their true purpose and power by empowering others.

Early in his own career, George notes, "I saw myself on an unbroken sprint to the top of a major corporation." He was so fixed on that goal, that individual achievement, that he took one pressure-cooker corporate job after another until he finally realized his unhappiness at work was spilling over to damage his relationships with his wife, sons and friends. "I was so focused on becoming CEO that I had lost sight of the purpose of my leadership, to benefit the lives of others," he writes in *True North*. Determined to find his way back to collaborative, enabling leadership, he became president of a company he once considered too small for his big, personal ambitions: Medtronic. "My thirteen years there became the best professional experience of my life," he says now. "By embracing the Medtronic mission of restoring people to full life and health, and discovering the purpose of my leadership in serving patients and empowering 30,000 employees, I was finally on the right side of the transformation from 'I' to "We.'"

WHEN RITA SINGH was growing up in New Delhi, India, her parents impressed on her and her three older brothers the importance of a good education. Though Rita had hoped to study medicine, her father's untimely death left her mother unable to afford the cost of medical school. "I thought, 'Since my dream of becoming a doctor isn't coming true, I might as well do the best I can,'" Rita recalls. To prepare herself for a range of possible careers, Rita got a bachelor's degree in liberal arts, and then a master's degree in English literature.

Because India in the 1970s offered fewer opportunities for professionals, Rita recalls, "all our doctors, scientists and engineers were coming to America. Everybody was attracted, including me. I wanted to go to America, people went there to fulfill their dreams." In 1979 Rita married Nipendra Singh and they moved to the United States, settling in Cleveland. While the United States today is accustomed to foreign-born

Rita Singh, recipient of the ATHENA Award in Cleveland who envisioned and inaugurated the presentation of the first ATHENA Award in her native India.

hoto courtesy of Rita Singh.

students, "thirty years ago it was a big struggle for me," she says. "I had to go from university to university" seeking one that would credit her Indian coursework. Though it meant repeating many courses while raising two young daughters, Rita persevered, earned a business management degree and completed studies to be a certified public accountant. In a new country and community where she had no networks of friends or business contacts, Rita set out methodically to create them. She joined civic groups, women's groups, professional organizations; she offered herself as a hard-working, hands-on collaborator. By 1989 when she and her husband started their own business, a management consulting firm, clients arose naturally from her deep and wide network of associates.

An avid online researcher, Rita regularly travels the Web in search of new ideas for her business, and for the women's and professional groups with which she works. She already knew about ATHENA International and had drawn inspiration from its Web site's resources for women leaders when Cleveland launched its own ATHENA Award program in 2003.

The next year when Cleveland's ATHENA organizers began their confidential award deliberations, Rita knew several associates had nominated her. But her mind was half a world away, with her ailing mother in New Delhi. As the ceremony neared when the Award recipient would be announced, Rita booked her flight to India. The day before she left, not knowing when she might return, organizers called to tell her privately that she was the 2004 Award recipient. "I can't tell you the feeling," Rita says now, "I can't describe it. This was one of the best things that ever happened to me!"

After a week in India stabilizing her mother's health, Rita brought her mother back to the United States, the day before the ATHENA Award ceremony. "My mother was in her eighties, in a wheelchair, with jetlag and all, but I said, 'Please, you have to go with me to this award, it's all due to the things you taught me.'" It meant so much to Rita that her mother was in the hall as she was commended for her professional excellence, her community involvement and her dedication to promoting opportunity for women. In August 2004 Rita N. Singh became the first Indian recipient of an ATHENA Award.

Collaborative leader that Rita is, here's what she was thinking as they handed her that ATHENA Award: "The first thing that crossed my mind was taking this to my native country, where women still are struggling."

THERE IS SOMETHING MAGICALLY SPECIAL about a relationship between a mother and her daughter. So it hit me hard in the late 1980s when my twenty-something daughter Michelle came to me and, in a very authoritative yet compassionate way, told me that my efforts through ATHENA were, essentially, obsolete. The work of championing women leaders had been very useful once, she said, but the world had changed. There wasn't an issue any longer for women who wanted to achieve. There weren't barriers to confront. Everything that had needed to happen, had happened.

I didn't defend my position. I simply listened to her, registered the comment, told her I appreciated the thoughts and would consider them. Then I went right on doing exactly the same things I had been doing, but I didn't forget what she'd said.

It was therefore amazing to me when she revisited that conversation nearly ten years later. She remembered what she said before, and wanted to tell me she had been wrong then—that all sorts of barriers, attitudes, exclusions affecting women remained, but that they just were less visible. In the entry-level and even middle-level positions, women were plentiful and, by all appearances, welcomed. However, she and her friends had begun to understand that, in sometimes subtle, sometimes not-so-subtle ways, the old boys' network was still operational. It just took a more elevated view to see it.

Michelle had recently finished her undergraduate degree in business from Michigan State University and was trying to find her footing in a number of ways. She was leaving a relationship and a lackluster job; she didn't like her present surroundings, and her immediate future wasn't clear. Feeling a bit like Mom To The Rescue, I told Michelle about two options. At Mayhood/Mertz, Inc., my executive assistant Debbie Arnold hired her to work part-time on a range of office tasks. At the same time, the young ATHENA Foundation needed a part-time office assistant, a job that paid the royal sum of $6.50 an hour. I didn't intervene on her behalf, and I don't recall her expressing much enthusiasm for it initially, but Michelle got that job, too.

Michelle Mertz-Stoneham, director of development for the College of Education, Michigan State University, began her career in resource development in the early days at ATHENA. Photo courtesy of Michigan State University.

At ATHENA, we both felt it important to respect the professional distance. We were mother and daughter but in the office, we were founder and clerk. Michelle did all the required menial jobs with a very good attitude. Over time she found additional ways to pitch in and began to become more invested in the organization's mission. After she'd been there about eighteen months, ATHENA was hiring a director of development and she was chosen, again without my intervention.

Once Michelle became a full-time professional staff member, she and I worked in tandem, and I discovered how proficient and reliable she was. Always prepared and armed with research, she was articulate, warm-hearted, and able to build rapport with a wide range of people, most of

Above, the highlight of the 1997 National ATHENA Conference was an onstage "intimate conversation" between Maya Angelou and Harry Belafonte, before a rapt crowd of more than 2,000. Photo courtesy of ATHENA International.

Celebrating backstage at the 1997 conference, from left: former ATHENA president Mary Lou Bessette, Maya Angelou, Martha and daughter Michelle. Photo courtesy of ATHENA International.

them significantly older than she. On top of that she had a tremendous sense of humor and was fun to be around.

It wasn't all roses, though. During one particularly difficult time, ATHENA lost its executive director and other key staff shortly before we were to host a national conference on the home turf of two key underwriters. It was crucial that the conference be uplifting and top quality. It also was clear the ATHENA staff lacked the hands to pull that off. Michelle and I and the few others who were left began recruiting volunteers from wherever we could find them. Then we set out to handle every detail of conference organization: planning, registration, venue selection,

Harry Belafonte, Martha Mertz, Edward Ingraham. Photo courtesy of ATHENA International.

contracts, speakers. All kinds of things went right but a lot didn't. As those of us in the core group only confessed to each other later, we'd go home many nights near tears, weary to our bones and overwhelmed by the mountains of tasks yet to tackle. The stress was beyond anything any of us had ever dealt with, but we waded through.

Our reward was witnessing one of the best conferences ATHENA ever produced. The highlight: an onstage "intimate living room" conversation between Maya Angelou and Harry Belafonte, with an audience of 2,500 people listening raptly and then treating our stars to an eight-minute standing ovation. Michelle was assigned to escort Maya and Harry to and from their performance. It was a special moment she'll always remember.

I also treasure memories of those times, for personal as well as professional reasons. Though I had seen sons follow fathers into the "family business" to work side by side, I had never known of or anticipated the daughter/mother combo Michelle and I formed. It was such a privilege to be in professional collaboration with her, with neither more nor less weight accorded for her ideas (or mine) because of our family ties. We were respectful, respected colleagues—until Saturday mornings, when we'd grab coffee and revert to our "normal" relationship, laughing and relaxing with each other. After a few short years with ATHENA, Michelle Mertz-Stoneham went on to greater professional challenges and has established herself as a true star in her field. As I write this, she's the top development official at Michigan State University's College of Education.

I am exceedingly grateful to have shared that brief part of our life journey, to have had the chance to know each other in that collegial way. The experience remains one of the great blessings of my life.

WHOEVER COINED THE PHRASE "DRESSES LIKE A BANKER" never met Linda Stevenson, a senior vice-president for National City Bank. To her boardroom meetings, Linda carries chic little purses fit for the club scene. Curvy silver earrings peek from under her mane of pale, wavy hair. For fifteen-plus years she's been a bank executive and community leader in Erie, Pennsylvania, a town built on tough-guy industries such as steel and shipbuilding. Yet to be taken seriously by her male counterparts, she has never tried to act or dress as they do. She just does her work with excellence, treats everyone as respectfully as she expects to be treated, and burnishes her exacting professionalism with a wicked wit and easy laugh.

When Linda describes women's underrepresentation in leadership circles as "one pink jacket in a roomful of pinstriped ones," she knows from experience. Her whole working life, literally and figuratively, Linda

Erie, Pennsylvania, bank executive Linda Stevenson, a driving force behind the ATHENA PowerLink program. Photo courtesy of Linda Stevenson.

has made a point of being the pink jacket in those pinstriped-jacket rooms—and holding open the door to those rooms, so other women can enter. At one of the nation's largest financial holding companies, she oversees business banking for small businesses and women-owned businesses. And as an ATHENA International board member, she has been a driving force behind a program called ATHENA PowerLink.

The PowerLink program was launched in Pittsburgh, Pennsylvania, by Barbara Moore and Ilana Diamond, two businesswomen concerned that female entrepreneurs often lacked access to advisors and mentors. Their idea was simple: Identify a woman business owner with the potential for greater success and link her with a panel of coaches, seasoned experts from her community, who could help her take her business to the next level. The panel and business owner work together for one year to meet the owner's objectives. The business owner receives invaluable help with networking, accessing capital, implementing best practices, and all of it at no cost.

In each PowerLink community, a governing board sifts through many business-owner applicants to choose those who would benefit most from the program. "You're going to be giving this owner an advisory panel that, over the year, will provide services worth anywhere from $40,000 to $80,000, so you want to give that to an enterprise with a substantial ability to stay in business," Linda explains. "This is not for start-ups; it's for women with businesses in the growth mode. The standards are two years in business, minimum two employees, and doing business annually of at least $250,000 for a manufacturing or retail operation, or $100,000 annually for a service-related business." Once the business owner is selected, she is linked with a panel of advisors who meet with her regularly and serve as on-call resources. Generally, says Linda, "every panel has three members we call the ABCs: the attorney, the banker and the CPA. Beyond that, panels are formed around a given business' objectives: Do you need marketing? Do you need technology help?"

Since 1999, ATHENA PowerLink has expanded its programs city by city from Anchorage to Orlando. Some programs sponsor just a few business owners in a year, while larger programs may have many more. To date, Linda says, hundreds of women CEOs of companies of all sizes, involved in every area of business, have been beneficiaries of a Power-Link advisory panel. Almost to a person, the business owners emerge with stories of how the experience enhanced their knowledge, confidence and success. In Akron, a dentist whose practice had changed little in seventeen years took her panel's advice on raising efficiency and visibility, and in the next year her business grew 25 percent. In Erie, in the four years since an employment agency owner worked with her panel, she has tripled her revenues.

"The problem we women have growing businesses is that we often don't have the same high level of professional contacts as our male peers," Linda says. "ATHENA PowerLink breaks that wall down. For example, in Erie, our first woman business owner had a home interiors and window treatment business, and one of the men sitting on her panel was a partner at a top local law firm. At the end of the year, on his personal stationery, this lawyer sent out a letter to his clients recommending that they utilize her services. Now what was that worth, to have that man on that panel? There was not a woman in Erie who could have done that for her."

Linda recalls sitting in on an ATHENA PowerLink meeting with a business owner and her panel, "and at one point my eyes were tearing up. I was thinking, 'Does this woman know what she's getting here?' And the women do get it. They are so appreciative, they are so in love with what has happened to them, they all want to give back." After the year working together, Linda says, panelists often continue to support business owners, and owners take their turns on the next wave of PowerLink panels, mentoring others. Those who have been "PowerLinked" even have formed an offshoot program, the ATHENA Bridge, that uses peer-to-peer mentoring to more widely share ideas and expertise garnered from expert panels.

"I think all the ATHENA principles fit into ATHENA PowerLink," Linda concludes. "It's about collaboration, relationship-building, giving back... it's about leadership."

WHEN THE WESTERN OREGON University Wolves and the Central Washington University Wildcats met in a softball doubleheader in April 2008, Western Oregon senior Sara Tucholsky knew she was running out of chances. As long as she'd been playing, including four years of college ball, Sara never had hit a home run. Then in the second inning of the second game, with two runners on base, she drove a pitch over the center-field fence of the Ellensburg, Washington, field. Ecstatically rounding first base, Sarah failed to touch the bag. As she doubled back to tag it, her right knee gave out and she crumpled to the ground.

In such pain she could barely drag herself back to first base, Sarah was, under the rules of play, still an active runner. If anyone on her team tried to assist her, umpires would call an out. Western Oregon coach Pam Knox's only option seemed to be to put in a pinch runner—but then Sarah's hit would be recorded not as that dreamt-of three-run homer but only as a two-run single, As Knox would later remember the moment, she was about to make the painful call when she heard a voice asking the umpire: "Excuse me, would it be okay if we carried her around and she touched each bag?"

The person asking was Mallory Holtman, a Central Washington star who holds her athletic conference's all-time record for home runs. Holtman, also a senior, was playing her last home game; she knew its outcome could determine whether her team advanced to the NCAA playoffs. But when the umpires confirmed there was no rule against opposing team members assisting an injured player, Mallory and teammate Liz Wallace gently lifted Sara and carried her along the base path. They stopped at each base and lowered Sara just enough for her left foot to tap the bag.

Sarah Tucholsky is carried around the bases by opposing team members Liz Wallace and Mallory Holtman.
Photo by Blake Wolf.

Despite Sara's pain, Liz said the three young women couldn't help giggling as they rounded the bases, thinking what an odd sight they must have presented to onlookers. But when Mallory looked up into the stands, she later told ESPN, "I didn't see giant smiles and screaming, I saw emotion and tears." Borne by her opponents, Sara tagged home plate to a standing ovation.

In the end, Mallory and Liz's team lost the game 4–2. Though the torn knee ligament ended Sara's softball career, her team went on to the first conference championship in Wildcat history, and to the NCAA playoffs. But ultimately, as coach Pam Knox observed, the episode was a reminder that some things matter more than winning. Sportsmanship, the newscasters called it, and certainly that's part of it. Character, as well. And that reflexive, unselfish choice to help others do what they could not do alone—collaboration, in the best sense of the word.

ELEVEN

Build Relationships

IN THE COLDEST FEBRUARY, AS IN EVERY OTHER MONTH
IN EVERY OTHER YEAR, THE BEST THING TO HOLD
ON TO IN THIS WORLD IS EACH OTHER.

— LINDA ELLERBEE

O F THE ALM'S EIGHT PRINCIPLES, I sometimes think this one, "build relationships," is most subject to fraud in contemporary life. Management manuals espouse it, and self-help gurus preach it; the highest scorn is reserved for those we say "just can't relate." Like flossing, saving, and wearing sunscreen, "tending relationships" has won a spot on our societal must-do list. But that doesn't mean it is easy, or that, even if we attempt it, we'll succeed. And what we cannot achieve, we are sometimes tempted to fake.

In our small-world-getting-smaller, every day brings more opportunities to relate to more people across what once were barriers: distance, language, culture. But too often in this warp-speed, tech-driven existence, the connections we make seem perishable, synthetic, superficial. In the booming business of soul-baring, bonding instantly with strangers is considered well-adjusted.

We've got countless facile ways to connect with each other. Can U say TXT MSG? Or better yet, meet me at Twitter.com where relationships are rationed, 140 typed characters at a time. Against this backdrop, crafting person-to-person relationships can seem frightfully low-bandwidth.

The challenge for ATHENA leaders, though, is to take this principle at its word—specifically, at its verb. We are not called to simulate relationships, YouTube style, nor to profess relationships, with no walk behind the talk. We are not called to approximate relationships, going through the motions at a distance, safe from entanglement or risk. We are called to build them, and I draw my sense of that word both from the leaders I've known through ATHENA and from construction sites I've walked in my career. Good builders are exacting, patient, and in it for the long haul. They earn the callouses on their hands. They stand by what they create. ATHENA summons leaders to the brawny, demanding work of building relationships, work that, at its best, overflows with potential and changes the landscape forever.

Consider your vocations and avocations so far. Has relationship-building been central to satisfaction, to achievement? It certainly has been for me. In two central professional pursuits of my life, real estate and ATHENA, creating and maintaining productive relationships with others is invaluable. I became a broker to help inexperienced, first-time home buyers, and because they felt I extended myself for them they came back to me repeatedly as clients. As I've traveled for ATHENA, invariably the richest aspect of any event is getting to know new friends and strengthening bonds with existing ones.

"If real estate were just a logical field, everyone could do it and make money," a male colleague once said to me. He attributed my success in the profession to reliance on two things: relationships and intuition. I knew what he meant about the former, but he got me thinking when he said this about the latter: "Martha, you have this tremendous confidence in intuition, which has been beaten or ironed out of most of us." I've always loved that women are strongly intuitive, and that we tend to trust that kind of "knowing/thinking" that defines intuition for me. It's one of those sixth senses that develop from need, like the bone-deep need to know the condition or whereabouts of one's children or one's mate.

I wondered if my colleague meant that intuition had been beaten out of most men, notwithstanding all the admiring talk about male leaders who "go with their gut." I know from years of experience that we women often are criticized for being willing to trust our intuition in professional settings. And yet I've known so many ATHENA leaders who swear by intuition's value, not least when deciding how, when, and with whom to build the relationships that are bedrock in their lives.

Maybe my sixty-something colleague meant that intuition gets ironed out of most adults, unless we are actively, purposefully about the business of heeding it. I find that when I'm most openly listening to my intuition, most willing to hear and learn from it, I tap into all kinds of insights, opportunities and relationships that might otherwise slip past.

Claire, who'll turn fourteen soon, blazes around the Internet collecting words and images that fire her imagination. One day not long ago, she found this colorfully lettered quotation: "There is an unseen life that dreams us; it knows our true direction and destiny. We can trust ourselves more than we realize, and we need have no fear of change."

This idea spoke to Claire's heart as if it had been written just for her. Who wrote it? John O'Donohue, an eloquent Irish poet and philosopher who died at age fifty-two, within days, or even hours, of when Claire discovered his words. So of course, to Claire it's manifestly true that she was meant to have these words, almost to receive them from O'Donohue on his way from this life to that "unseen" one he envisioned.

Claire's mother is a friend who knew I'd love the quote and the story and so shared them both with me. Only then did I learn more about John O'Donohue and how his passions in life intersected with my own. A bestselling author of books on beauty, creativity and spirituality, he had begun sharing his insights in the corporate world as a speaker on vision, change and ... leadership.

One of O'Donohue's best-known books is titled *Anam Cara*, from the Gaelic words for soul (*anam*) and friend (*cara*). In the ancient Celtic belief system, an *anam cara* is that person with whom you relate so strongly and trustingly that they become your teacher, guide, companion. Not a bad model, when you think of it, for a relationship-building leader.

Like Claire, I feel a little sad to have discovered O'Donohue only after he's no longer among us. But he's still quite present, able to lead and teach, in the words he left behind.

Consider this passage about relationship, from an interview with O'Dohonue published on his Web site. "The creator of the universe loves circles: time and space are circles, the day is a circle, the year is a circle, the earth is a circle. But when creating and fashioning the human heart, the creator only created a half-circle, so that there is something ontologically unfinished in human nature. That is why you can't enter your own life or inhabit your full presence without a vital and real relationship with some other person. Your awakening and the fulfillment of your identity requires that you belong together with others . . . The Celtic tradition sensed that no one lives for herself alone. Your call to discover who you are and to bring your soul into birth is also a great act of creativity toward everyone else."

IN THIS WHOLE CHAPTER on building relationships, I may still not approach the wisdom that Max De Pree delivered in just eight sentences on the topic in his landmark *Leadership Is An Art*. Here are those sentences: "Leadership is more tribal than scientific, more a weaving of relationships than an amassing of information . . . . A good family, a good institution, or a good corporation can be a place of healing. It can be a place where work becomes redemptive, where every person is included on her own terms. We know in our hearts that to be included is both beautiful and right. Leaders have to find a way to work that out, to contribute toward that vision. When we think about the people with whom we work, people on whom we depend, we can see that without each individual, we are not going to go very far as a group. By ourselves, we suffer serious limitations. Together we can be something wonderful."

WHEN TAMARA WOODBURY received her ATHENA Award, the Greater Phoenix Chamber of Commerce called her "the epitome of what ATHENA represents: she is strong, wise, courageous and very, very humble. She gives her time and energy to so many terrific causes, yet has not sought accolades or attention for her efforts."

Tamara calls herself "the reluctant ATHENA recipient." She is thrilled at the honor, but uncomfortable being singled out. "I'm not saying this to sound humble, or because it's the right thing to say," she insists. "Maybe ten years ago when I first was nominated, my ego was hungrier. But now I really feel I shouldn't stand out above other nominees; there are so many unbelievable women who've been nominated."

Tamara's reluctance aside, the more I learned about her, the more I saw to admire, and the more I felt her profound commitment to leading by building relationships.

Girl Scouts programs that Tamara piloted in Arizona have become national models. One serves girls whose mothers are incarcerated. Another works with girls along the Mexican border. A third assists girls who are in, or at risk of entering, the juvenile justice system. In every case, the emphasis is on building edifying relationships—"a knitting-together," as Tamara calls it. "I don't care if a girl earns one badge; if she feels loved and she feels seen, she feels absolutely legitimated for who she is, then you have been successful, as far as I'm concerned."

Another program Tamara founded was inspired by a conversation in the early 1990s with ATHENA recipient Mary Lou Bessette, a leader in Phoenix's business community and my immediate successor as president of our organization. As Tamara describes it, "We looked at the data about women who were successful business owners. In Arizona, one in three women who started businesses were successful, a dramatically higher success rate than for men. And yet, most of these women didn't try to start their first business until they were in their early forties and none of them had that as a goal in high school or college. So we asked, what would happen if we got girls interested in actually seeing themselves as business owners, making that a goal, when they were teens? Then by the time they were forty-two they'd be veterans, their businesses would be coming to scale, going multinational . . . . "

And so was born Camp CEO, a Girl Scout camping experience that inspires and prepares girls for future business ownership, in part by building relationships between young women and established women business leaders.

Remember that earlier story about Tamara, spending two years preparing her climbing team for an assault on Mt. Rainier? You sense the same commitment, the same zeal, when she speaks of the journey she's on now, "to question and examine what leadership really is." Because she questions so diligently, I am eager to hear her answer. "It may be way too pollyannaish," she says. "But for me, it's coming down to what builds relationships, the quality of relationships . . . what contributes to improved outcomes, and not at the expense of others . . . really, what promotes and sustains life for all."

GENERAL MOTORS executive Lynn Myers lent critical support to ATHENA twenty-some years ago, when we were securing our first national sponsorship (from Oldsmobile). In the years since, Lynn has brought her clear thinking and enthusiasm to a variety of ATHENA efforts, and in 2007-08, she served with distinction as ATHENA International president. If Lynn tells me that someone fits the ATHENA criteria for leadership, I believe her—but, Lynn being Lynn, she always has data to make her case. So when I asked her to suggest colleagues who would have insights for this book, she gave me Maureen Kempston Darkes's name and also her statistics. As a General Motors group vice president and president of Latin America, Africa and the Middle East (one of the highest-ranking women in one of the world's largest industries) Maureen's areas of responsibility encompass eighty-four countries on three continents, four major languages and many more dialects, most major religions, fifteen currencies, and nine time zones.

Ask Maureen the key to thriving in this twenty-first-century global environment, and she brings it down to three words. "Relationships are critical."

Maureen Kempston Darkes, GM group vice president over Latin America, the Middle East, and Africa. Photo courtesy of Maureen Kempston Darkes.

"There's very little you do in business or in the world generally that isn't about relationships," she declared when we spoke recently. "It's always about understanding what matters to people. In our business, we sell cars and trucks and we sell to the consumer, so it's critically important that we have a relationship with the consumer, that we and our dealers step up together as a team to make a difference for the consumer. It's critically important that we relate to governments as to what their needs are and how they see the transportation industry, the role we play in the development of their economies. So at every level you work in, relationships matter. They matter in how you envision your goal, how you engage and empower people to work for those goals. I work with people every single day in that kind of a model."

Lynn had told me what to expect from Maureen: That despite both the pressures and the prestige of her corporate position, she relates to people in a very down-to-earth, collegial way. Our conversation was relaxed; she responded thoughtfully to all my questions, despite her pressing schedule. She shared not only what she believed about leadership—"it's about helping people go further and farther than they ever expected they could"—but how that belief was planted during her childhood in Toronto.

"My father died when I was twelve; my parents were Irish immigrants, and we didn't have a lot of money. Yet the most optimistic person I ever knew in the world, and the greatest leader, was my mother Vera Kempston, and I'll tell you why. She said, 'Life handed us this—but we know life will go on and we can make ourselves whatever we wish.' She had to bring up three young children on a limited income, but she always taught us, 'Set your goals high.'" Maureen's brothers became a doctor and a dentist. She earned a law degree, joined General Motors Canada in 1975 and held a wide range of positions within GM before assuming her current post in 2002.

Having risen for three-plus decades through one of the world's top corporations, Maureen surely is a seasoned, credentialed executive. But what makes her a leader is something more. It's the way she lives out the ATHENA principle of building relationships: Connecting genuinely with those around you, regardless of status. A willingness to bond with others, profoundly and productively, to reach beyond self-interest in search of common ground.

Maureen believes one key to leading is constructing and maintaining strong relationships. "I run operations for a big part of the world and I'm not under any illusion that I run it solely from my desk in Florida," she says. "I have managing directors in each of the countries that I'm responsible for, who are empowered and engaged to run their countries .... What do I do? I'm there with support. I give direction when needed but I always spend a lot of time listening, helping people create, removing roadblocks and hoping that I'm opening doors for them to continuously expand the opportunities as they become available.

"I am directive when I need to be, but for me, my best leadership style is more listening, supporting, really developing the people. As you get up in business and have larger and larger operations to run, you are paid for a couple of things. One is your judgment; two is your ability to develop other people—motivated people who have a line of sight on what matters. That's what gets results. It's not about being 'The Great I Am' and saying, 'I do this, I do that.' It's not about that. It's about people coming together in a common purpose to develop, to lead, to pursue ideas.

"Make no mistake, I focus on results and I am paid to get results—that's fundamental," she emphasized. "How I go about getting results may be a little different than some others .... It has been my experience that the really great things that get accomplished happen because a team of people came together to work on a broad vision, and you invest in that team."

To build a team and strong relationships with its members, she said, "you have to be patient and listen to people. For example: In many countries I visit, the role of women is very much changing. They've become more independent, they're going to universities in large numbers, and, guess what, that means we need to spend time listening to them, thinking about their aspirations and needs . . . . Today as we go global, you have to see the world from so many different perspectives, and you have to invest time in understanding those perspectives. How else will you relate to the world, how will you know about it? In all of the countries in which I do business, I need to have relationships and a workforce that reflect that society. I don't think you can get along in the world with a few people at the top thinking they know what the world looks like."

One of Maureen's favorite examples of the importance of relating across cultural differences comes from an encounter she had with a dinner companion. "I remember sitting at dinner in the Middle East one night and an Arab sheikh asking me whether I had a husband. I said I did. Then he asked, did my husband have other wives?" Because Maureen had studied her host country, she knew the sheikh's small talk reflected the norms of his culture and that his question was well-meaning. And so I simply said to him, 'Not that I know of.'" Thriving and leading in the twenty-first century, Maureen believes, "is not about just accepting diversity. I think over time you can get people to accept it, but it's more about truly valuing it."

Maureen expressly credits her success to the values instilled by her mother Vera, who died in 1996. "Her philosophy was that success is measured by going as far as you can using everything you've got, and always being there to make a difference," she says. "That's how I lead my life." The most effective leaders, she believes "put most everything but themselves first. It's not because they don't have egos and don't care about their welfare. They do. But they see a bigger picture.

"When it all comes together, it's kind of like the conductor with the orchestra. It's the orchestra that makes the event, plays the music. The conductor is leading it, but at the end, the applause is for the orchestra. Those are the kinds of leaders that I think inspire people."

THERE IS AN ART TO RELATIONSHIPS. Building them requires sensitivity, creativity, attention to detail, and time. There is also a science to relationships, actually a scientific field where mathematicians, physicists and sociologists study relationships in what they call network theory. You may not know that term, but you know the concept if you can finish this phrase: *Six Degrees of . . .*

If you said *Separation,* you named the play by American playwright John Guare (and the 1993 movie based on the play). If you said *Kevin Bacon,* you named the parlor game that traced actor Bacon's connections to demonstrate Guare's theme: that any two people on earth can be linked to each other by a chain of acquaintances that has, at most, five intermediaries.

Here's how one of Guare's characters described it: "I read somewhere that everybody on this planet is separated by only six other people. Six degrees of separation between us and everyone else on this planet. The President of the United States, a gondolier in Venice, just fill in the names. I find it (a) extremely comforting that we're so close, and (b) like Chinese water torture that we're so close because you have to find the right six people to make the right connection . . . . I am bound to everyone on this planet by a trail of six people."

That six-degrees notion has gripped imaginations since the late 1920s, when a Hungarian writer posited it in a short story called "Chain Links." Many Americans first heard of it in the late 1960s when sociologist Stanley Milgram tested the theory through the U.S. mail. Milgram asked 400 randomly-chosen midwesterners to try to get a package to a stranger in Massachusetts by sending it to one friend, who'd send it to another, who'd send it to another ... while Milgram tracked how many intermediaries it took for the package to reach its intended recipient. Then in 2001, Columbia University Professor Duncan Watts took the six-degrees experiment into cyberspace. His Small World Project recruited thousands of people worldwide—"searchers"—who each received an email address for one of eighteen to twenty-one people around the globe, "targets." Searchers could not email targets directly but were to try reaching them by emailing someone they knew, who'd then email someone they knew . . . and on and on, to complete the connection. Over six years Watts ran two rounds of the experiment involving more than 184,000 people from more than 160 countries.

Four decades ago Milgram found that getting each package delivered took, on average, five to seven intermediaries. In 2007, Watts's research report concluded that most searchers never reached their targets, but in the few hundred chains that were completed, the median number of links was either seven or . . . six.

What, if anything, does this prove? Among scientists, there's no consensus. Is there intrinsic worth to that number, six links in the chain, six nodes in a network? That seems unlikely. And yet, there's something compelling about the idea of such potential, universal interconnectedness. At least there is if we do something positive with it.

Kevin Bacon did. He launched a Web site where volunteers and donors can connect to charitable causes (including the favorite charities of Bacon's famous friends), and corporate grants match many donations. The project, Bacon says, is about using relationships "to accomplish something good. It's social networking with a social conscience." The site spurred more than $2.5million in giving in its first two years of operation.

There is much of the ATHENA spirit in how Bacon parlayed the six-degrees idea. Ideally, ATHENA leaders are open to relationships from all points of origin. We don't seek solely to "relate up," to connect only with people who share, or can raise, our status. Nor do ATHENA leaders instigate relationships just to rack 'em up: more names in a contact file, more friends on a Facebook page. ATHENA leaders seek relationships with others that are genuine, empowering and productive.

I can't begin to count the rewarding, edifying connections I've made in the course of my work with ATHENA. For a classic example of how these kinds of relationships arise and intertwine, consider Mary Schnack.

Raised on a farm in Iowa, Mary knew early that she wanted to live somewhere more international, more diverse. Armed with a journalism degree and a year of newspaper experience in Charleston, West Virginia, she flipped a coin: Los Angeles or New York City? On the flight to California, she sat next to the man that, two years later, she would marry. Journalism jobs led her into public relations; soon, she was PR director at two Los Angeles hospitals. There she handled media during high-profile events, including the 1992 riots after a jury acquitted police in the videotaped beating of Rodney King. Having built a résumé as a crisis communications expert, she started her own PR firm.

In April 1993 when an armed standoff in Waco, Texas, ended with the Branch Davidian compound in flames, the Seventh Day Adventist Church (of which the Davidians were an offshoot) hired Mary to handle media. A year later, the crisis was in Rwanda, a civil war and genocide that claimed 800,000 lives, and the Adventists again sent Mary. "That was my life-changing moment," she says now. Seeing the poverty and desperation of Rwandans in refugee camps "really created a calling for me to help." She resolved to use her communications skills to work more in Africa, or wherever in the world she could make a difference.

Assignments for the Adventists took her to Russia, then West Africa, then South America. In 1996 she moved to Sedona and, a few years later, started a local chapter of the National Association of Women Business Owners, with which she'd been involved in Los Angeles. NAWBO tapped

Mary Schnack, an international media and public relations expert who helped bring ATHENA to Sedona, Arizona, to Bermuda and to Kenya. Photo courtesy of Mary Schnack.

her to help start an international forum to open global opportunities for U.S. businesswomen. Now, Mary is so plugged in to helping women develop entrepreneurial and communications skills that one opening leads to another.

For example: "Speaking at the African Women Entrepreneurship Venture Capital Forum in Brussels in 1994, I met Amanda Ellis from the International Finance Corporation of the World Bank," she recalls. "Then a few months later at the World Association of Women Entrepreneurs meeting in Scotland, I met Bola Olabisi of the Global Women Inventors and Innovators Network. A few months after that, Bola, Amanda and I all were at the Global Summit of Women in Mexico City. Bola was putting on an International Finance Corporation meeting in Ghana and Bola and Amanda asked me to do a communications seminar there. At that Ghana conference, I met Eva Muraya of Kenya and she connected me to Vital Voices, a women's leadership organization that has sent me to Kenya, South Africa and the Ukraine . . . . "

Where do I enter the Mary Schnack chain? At just about that point in Mary's narrative. While serving on a corporate women's advisory board, I became friends with Barbara Litrell, then head of the company that published *Working Woman* magazine. When I moved to Sedona, Barbara already was living there and made a point of helping me settle in. About two years ago, Barbara insisted I had to meet this other immigrant to Sedona with whom I would have so much in common . . . .

And so Mary Schnack and I connected. Since then, we've worked together on all kinds of projects, from local and national NAWBO efforts to a Washington, D. C., forum of the businesswomen's group Women Impacting Public Policy. And the circles of relationship just keep widening. As Mary recalls, "After I met Eva Muraya in Kenya, I met Martha. Then when I went back to Kenya I talked to Eva about bringing the ATHENA Award to Kenya . . . and three days later Eva says to me, 'I had lunch today with an ATHENA Award recipient from Phoenix, Arizona!'" Over dinner in Nairobi, Mary met that Phoenix ATHENA recipient, Eileen Rogers, Mary introduced me to Eileen, and late 2008 found Eileen in Nepal, suggesting an ATHENA Awards program there! By the time you read this, who knows where the connections will extend.

Being a four-time cancer survivor, Mary says, has helped her focus on two things: going full-throttle after what she wants, and taking every opportunity to build productive, life-giving relationships. When friends kept coveting the beautiful foreign-made objects she brought back from world travels, Mary saw an opportunity. So in 2006 she founded Up From The Dust, an online and home-party business that supports women entrepreneurs around the globe by selling the jewelry, scarves and home products they make.

What results does Mary see from spinning all these webs of relationship? "I see that I'm living my dream," she says. "Being able to do international work and help empower people around the world."

IT WAS, IN A WAY, like showing off a new baby to a big extended family. In 1999, at the ATHENA International annual conference, we introduced the newly minted ATHENA Leadership Model to about 250 conference participants. We wanted to present the Model in a way that would give participants maximum freedom and encouragement to explore its eight principles, but guidance and structure as well. Good fortune led us to an organization that specialized in "facilitated conversation," and in tailoring that conversation process to the issues being addressed.

We loved what we heard in conversations that day. Participants were enthusiastic about the ALM principles. They savored the chance to think together in an idea-rich, liberating setting that combined creative thinking and respectful listening, serious discussions and artful expression. We call it ATHENA World Café.

In the decade since, the ATHENA World Café process has become a tradition for us, an activity that epitomizes the creative power of relationships. A World Café in September 2008 was a perfect example—and in an exotically beautiful locale for good measure.

Thanks to connections made through (who else?) my friend Mary Schnack, Bermuda's first ATHENA Award was to be presented in that United Kingdom territory. In Arizona, Mary had introduced me to the Women's Leadership Exchange (WLE), a social entrepreneurship and networking organization for professional women. When Mary began helping WLE organize an international retreat in Bermuda in conjunction with a first-ever Bermudan Business Women's conference, she asked me about incorporating an ATHENA Award program. The pieces fit together exquisitely. The ATHENA World Café conversation would form a bridge, giving participants in the women entrepreneurs' meeting a chance to connect with participants in the Bermudan Business Women's event.

Arriving in Bermuda was like entering a dream. The twenty-six-mile-long island is narrow enough that the bluest blue ocean is nearly always in view (as you look past the astonishing flowers). A lovely mixture of British and Caribbean influences has produced colorful island architecture, distinctive cuisine, an intriguing lilt to the language, and a warm, welcoming atmosphere.

The local event, called Navigating Business Success, was a powerhouse conference of workshops and panel discussions, with prominent speakers who included Bermuda's deputy premier and finance minister. The aim was to inspire and empower Bermuda's professional women, and a throng of them attended—public officials, tourism experts, meeting planners, importers, retailers. Bermuda's inaugural ATHENA Award recipient, Emilygail Dill, was honored for her energy and excellence in a wide range of activities, from patron of the performing arts to ordained minister to advocate and fundraiser for struggling college-bound youth. When Reverend Dill was described with that phrase I've heard applied to so many ATHENA honorees—"an unsung hero"—I couldn't help but smile. There it was again. That focus on service more than self, truly a hallmark of ATHENA leaders.

Meanwhile, the international WLE event, billed as a retreat, had a working-spa feel. High-powered, busy women from around the globe were departing from their daily routines to enjoy some personal time along with thought-provoking discussions and networking dinners. Professionally, the participants were a rainbow: experts in e-commerce, philanthropy and media; a certified life coach and a professional photographer; the owner of a construction company, and the former owner of an airline. The stories shared were personal and fascinating, tales of strength and intelligence, tragedy and achievement.

The World Café provided an ideal opportunity for participants from both events to interact. As is World Café tradition, we began by sorting participants into small working groups, shaking friends apart so people are seated with others they've never met, to encourage fresh and independent thinking. (We try to find creative ways to do this. On occasion, we have handed each arriving participant a semi-precious stone, directing her to find others who have that same kind of stone, and encouraging that group to break the ice by discussing the properties that legend attributes to their stone—e.g., carnelian is associated with confidence, citrine with optimism, jade with serenity.)

In a spacious conference room of the Fairmont Hamilton Princess hotel, participants settled into their small groups. Each table was covered with butcher paper and set with fistfuls of color markers, encouraging participants to illustrate their thoughts with vivid notations and artistic flourishes. With Mary Schnack and her Bermudan collaborator Keetha Lowe, I provided a quick welcome and a brief explanation of the ATHENA Leadership Model.

Then we gave participants a starting statement and set them loose to explore it. The topic for this Café was, appropriately, big and global and full of potential: "Describe a future that is vastly different from our world today and talk about what leadership you would bring to make that possible." Though the topic statements (and the responses they prompt) differ from event to event, the intention of a World Café conversation is always the same: to use ALM principles to help participants consider strengths and gifts they have, attributes they may never have identified with leadership.

At this World Café event as at so many before it, I was amazed by the speed at which newly-met groups of women coalesce into highly effective teams. As explorers must in facing a new frontier, right away they treated each other with trust, confidence and camaraderie. They received each others' ideas with respect; each made it safe for the other to say what she really thought and felt. After fifteen to twenty minutes in conversation, one member of each team presented the results of its discussions to the assembly. Invariably these reports were offered with conviction, even passion; frequently they were laced with laughter and, on occasion, tears. Then we repeated the process with several more questions. At the end of the Café it was clear from their comments that many participants had come to realize that they possessed, already, the qualities needed to be leaders. When these women spoke about the leadership they would bring to animate a brighter future, they spoke with not just great wisdom and ambition but with great heart. My own modest contribution was to say at the conclusion—with a catch in my throat that I hoped no one detected—how proud I was to have been part of this groundbreaking event.

But mostly, in Bermuda, I just breathed it all in. I appreciated again how this World Café process is so aligned and all-of-one-piece with the principles of ATHENA leadership. Every person who left that conference room—distributing handshakes, hugs and business cards on the way out—had begun building promising new relationships. And I'd go so far as to say that everyone also left that event with a new appreciation of what we call ATHENA principles, those "women's ways" of acting collectively on the challenges of today and the opportunities of tomorrow.

GAYLE AND DUTCH LANDEN embraced the World Café process from its inception and spent the last decade helping expand and refine it. We lost Dutch on February 20, 2008, at age eighty-five. During the World Café in Bermuda, I could not help thinking how much he would have loved the event. It really did represent what Dutch envisioned and what he wrote about to me, in notes I kept and cherish. "Leadership is sharing. It is sharing what we believe, what we value, what we dream. The world needs ATHENA leaders, their special brand of leadership and their special skills in sharing their views and working with others to bring them to fruition. The journey that ATHENA embarked on more than twenty-five years ago is still in its beginning stages. We welcome with open arms all who would join us. The beauty of our journey is that there is no fixed destination; the greatest joy is in the pursuit and the discovery. It is during the journey that we find our voice, make our mark, and define our legacy."

Dutch and Gayle Landen, longtime ATHENA collaborators whose professional lives were centered on leadership. Photo courtesy of Gayle Landen.

TWELVE

Give Back

IN HELPING OTHERS, WE SHALL HELP
OURSELVES, FOR WHATEVER GOOD WE GIVE OUT
COMPLETES THE CIRCLE AND COMES BACK TO US.

— FLORA EDWARDS

O
NE DAY *a man was walking along the beach* . . . . Perhaps this moral fable has been forwarded to you in email, or tucked into a speech at some event you attended. Variants of it have been liberally shared in cyberspace and widely quoted by motivational speakers. A popular version goes like this:

One day a man was walking along the beach when he noticed a boy picking something up and gently throwing it into the ocean. Approaching the boy, the man asked, "What are you doing?"

The youngster replied, "Throwing starfish back into the ocean. The surf is up and the tide is going out. If I don't throw them back, they'll die."

"Son," the man said, "don't you realize there are miles and miles of beach and hundreds or thousands of starfish? You can't make a difference!" After listening politely, the boy bent down, picked up another starfish, and threw it back into the surf.

Smiling at the man, he said: "I made a difference for that one."

Hearing the uplifting little tale made me curious to known more about its origins. And what I learned, after a bit of research, lent a whole new depth and power to this parable.

That simplified version—popularly known as "the starfish story"—was adapted from a more complex essay called "The Star Thrower." Its author, Loren Eiseley (1907–1977), was both a man of science, an anthropologist, archaeologist and naturalist, and a man of letters, a poet. As he moved through the natural world much of what he wrote about it was perceptive, vivid, and bleak. The poet W. H. Auden called Eiseley "a wanderer who is often in danger of being shipwrecked on the shores of Dejection."

In "The Star Thrower," Eiseley describes a beach grimly littered with dying sea creatures, washed up too high to return to the surf. Out beyond the collectors greedily hunting for shells, Eiseley encounters a lone man throwing barely-alive creatures back into the water:

> "There are not many come this far," I said, groping in a sudden embarrassment for words. "Do you collect?"
>
> "Only like this," he said softly, gesturing amidst the wreckage of the shore. "And only for the living." He stooped again, oblivious of my curiosity, and skipped another star neatly across the water. "The stars," he said, "throw well. One can help them." He looked full at me with a faint question kindling in his eyes, which seemed to take on the far depths of the sea.
>
> "I do not collect," I said uncomfortably, the wind beating at my garments. "Neither the living nor the dead. I gave it up a long time ago. Death is the only successful collector."

The scientist in Eiseley finds this pursuit insignificant, futile. He turns away—but he cannot forget the scene. The more he reflects, the more his detachment crumbles and his heart opens. Against the inevitability of death, he chooses to do what he can. He returns to the beach to find the star thrower:

> Silently I sought and picked up a still-living star, spinning it
> far out into the waves. I spoke once briefly. "I understand," I said.
> "Call me another thrower." Only then I allowed myself to think,
> He is not alone any longer. After us there will be others.... I flung
> and flung again while all about us roared the insatiable waters of
> death.

ATHENA urges leaders to give back, to offer committed service to our colleagues, community and world. Sometimes giving is as simple and untroubled as it was in the first starfish story. We can say, as the child did, "I made a difference for that one" and feel satisfied. Knowing that our actions mattered, at least in some small way, gives us fuel to carry on.

But at other times, as leaders, we may find ourselves with Eiseley, veering toward those shores of dejection. When needs are great and solutions are elusive, even our best efforts seem a drop in the bucket, insufficient, pointless. In gratitude for all we've received, we try to give back, and yet we may wind up frustrated, unacknowledged, or even criticized.

As you've surely noticed, this ATHENA principle comes without footnotes. It does not say, "Give back[1] ([1]and your success is assured)." It does not say "Give back[2] ([2]then bask in the applause)." The ideal for ATHENA leaders is this: Give back because it's the right thing to do, and then work like hell to make your efforts as successful as they are sincere. ATHENA leaders give back to create a worthy and enduring contribution, not a monument to self. ATHENA leaders strive for success not just for its own sake, but because success gives us more traction in advancing the greater good.

DURING THAT LONG LEARNING INTERVIEW with leadership pioneer Max De Pree, he made a book recommendation. "Have you ever read the book *Three Cups of Tea*? It's about an American guy who was a mountain climber, ran into trouble, got rescued by a Pakistani family that saved his life so he figured out what he could do to show his thanks . . . . "

A short time later a friend in Sedona pressed a copy of *Three Cups of Tea* into my hands and I knew I had to read it. It is a wonderful story, told by that mountain climber, Greg Mortenson, with help from veteran journalist David Oliver Relin. I won't spoil the book, which is a *New York Times* bestseller, by telling you too much of the story. But in one poignant moment where Mortenson embraced the principle of giving back, he set forces in motion that changed not only his own life but the lives of countless others.

A nursing student and former Army medic, Mortenson set out in 1993 to climb Pakistan's K2, the world's second-highest mountain, in memory of Christa, his beloved sister who died at age twenty-three. Attempting the treacherous trek, Mortenson became ill and weak, lost his way, and might not have survived had he not stumbled upon the mountain village of Korphe. Its chief, Haji Ali, took him in, and its villagers nursed him back to health, sharing with him what little they had. In gratitude, Mortenson provided basic medical care with his first aid kit, gave away his trekking gear, and then looked for more he could do. When Mortenson asked to visit Korphe's school, the chief led him up a path to a frigid mountain ledge. Here's how Relin described the scene: "Eighty-two children—78 boys, and four girls who had the pluck to join them—were kneeling on the frosty ground. Haji Ali, avoiding Mortenson's eyes, said that the village had no school"—only a teacher who came three days a week, which was all the village could afford as the teacher cost the equivalent of one dollar a day. The children stood to sing their national anthem, then sat on the ground "in a neat circle and began copying their multiplication tables. Most scratched in the dirt with sticks they'd brought for that purpose. The more fortunate . . . had slate boards they wrote on with sticks dipped in a mixture of mud and water." Mortenson knew he had only enough money to travel back to the United States, where his work prospects were uncertain and most of what he owned fit in his old Buick. But watching Korphe's children bend over their studies, he said, "I felt like my heart was being torn out. There was a fierceness in their desire to learn, despite how mightily everything was stacked against them . . . . I knew I had to do something." Turning to Haji Ali, he made a promise: "I'm going to build you a school.

In the fifteen years since making that impulsive promise, Mortenson has devoted his life to bringing education to remote areas of Pakistan and Afghanistan, opening a future especially for girls who previously were denied schooling, and for boys who otherwise might be swept into extremist, Taliban-influenced madrassahs. Through the non-profit Central Asian Institute he founded, Mortenson established nearly eighty schools and provided education for some 28,000 children, about two-thirds of them girls.

Though it hasn't become a best-selling book (yet), I've been privileged to learn another inspiring story from that part of the world. It's a story of generous, courageous leadership; of quiet but important progress, sheltered behind veils and in family compounds. It's the story of Rangina Hamidi who, like Mortenson, is making a difference in Afghanistan by giving back, in her case, to her homeland.

In August 1977 when Rangina was born in Kandahar, the reception was decidedly mixed. Her parents had three daughters already, and the extended family was rooting for a son. An aunt had brought the traditional sweets to welcome a male child; learning of Rangina's birth, she packed them up and left. But Rangina's father Ghulam Haider and his father Ghulam Sarwar refused to treat this as a second-class occasion. On the Thursday after the birth as was traditional for sons, they held a big celebration for the tiny daughter. By now, Rangina has heard the

Greg Mortenson, whose book *Three Cups of Tea* tells how he has promoted education, especially for girls, in Afghanistan and Pakistan. Photo courtesy of Greg Mortenson.

story countless times but still loves to tell it: "My grandfather held me up in his arms and gave me my name and told the people he had invited, 'She is going to grow up to become someone special for our country.'"

In 1981 when the Soviets occupied Afghanistan, Haider refused to join the Communist party and his life was threatened, so the family fled as refugees to Pakistan. To supplement her father's income, Rangina's mother and sisters worked in their home, making and tailoring clothes. Haider scrimped and borrowed to put the girls in private schools. Rangina was about ten years old when a new element moved into their community. "Predecessors of the Taliban," she calls them now. "Ultra-conservative, uneducated thugs, many of them involved in illegal businesses like drugs or weapons" and outraged that girls were being given an education.

"Then one day in the middle of third grade for me, my father came in the morning and said, 'You are not going to school any more.' A man in the community had come and warned my father that these newcomers were going to throw acid in our faces because we were going to school. That was the punishment to give to people who didn't obey their laws."

A few months after the girls were forced to leave school, the family's immigration request was approved; in February 1988, they settled in a Washington, D. C., suburb. Rangina thrived in American schools, was her high school's valedictorian and was accepted by all four top-notch universities to which she applied. She chose the nearby University of Virginia so her parents could visit every weekend. She had thought she might become a doctor but felt much more drawn to women's studies and religion so she changed her major. She graduated in 2000 with a thesis on the Taliban movement's treatment of women, treatment so harsh that though she wanted to return to her homeland, she hesitated. Then came the destruction of 9/11 and the American-led invasion of Afghanistan, and Rangina became convinced "there was nothing better for me to do in my life than to go back" to see how she could contribute.

In December 2001 she flew to Pakistan with $10,000 in donations from Central Asians living in the United States and became a one-woman war relief operation, purchasing clothing, food and firewood for Afghan refugees crossing the border. She returned to the United States,

Rangina Hamidi, who has brought opportunities to the women of her native Afghanistan. Photo by Paula Lerner, courtesy of Rangina Hamidi.

determined to find a more substantial and long-term way to help, and was offered a job she considered "a gift from God"—helping women in Kandahar make a living doing Khamak, the intricate, centuries-old style of embroidery native to the region. In 2003, she became manager of the women's income generation project of Afghans for Civil Society, a development organization founded by the brother of Afghanistan's President Hamid Karzai.

By strict patriarchal, tribal, and traditional customs, most women in the Kandahar region are confined to family compounds "so it is very difficult to ask women to come out and work," Rangina says now. "But we knew so many women needed a source of income and opportunity, so we decided we would go to their homes. We started with twenty women, giving them raw materials, patterns, and eyeglasses, showing them samples of what to do, then going back to collect what they made. The women loved it, they told their neighbors, and in two years we went from twenty women to more than 300 women making home-décor items, clothing, and accessories." Though Rangina and her project colleagues faced risk, both from random acts of war and from people who disliked what they were doing, they persevered.

They also began offering the women of Kandahar more than just embroidery work. Roughly 90 percent of Kandahar's women are illiterate. Rangina's program teaches them to write and sign their names, and to read easy texts. Most of the women also have little or no education about health and hygiene so they and their children are frequently ill. Rangina's program promotes sanitary habits and arranges medical care when needed.

By 2006, Rangina was frustrated with the limitations of the nonprofit operation, including the constant hunt for grant money. "I knew that for this to survive and grow, it needed to be a well-run, for-profit business," she says now. And then, just when she needed it, another blessing. She learned about Thunderbird School of Global Management which every year brings fifteen aspiring Afghan businesswomen to its Arizona campus for business training and mentorship. Thunderbird gave Rangina help writing a business plan, exposure to successful businesses, and extensive, personalized coaching. That opportunity led to another: two weeks at New York City's Fashion Institute of Technology learning how to improve her handmade products with support from the Business Council for Peace, a group that helps women entrepreneurs in conflict-ridden countries build businesses and create jobs.

Armed with new skills and confidence, in late 2006 Rangina launched a for-profit company, Kandahar Treasure. "This is the perfect name," she says, "because women have been creating this embroidery for centuries but it never was particularly valued as the beautiful, skilled work of women. The women feel such pride when we call their work a treasure."

Today, Kandahar Treasure employs nearly 500 women, many of them destitute, widowed mothers whose lives have been transformed by the income. Wares can be seen online; they are sold mostly in the United States at arts fairs and small shops or through specially-arranged events. Rangina works fulltime (and unpaid) for the little company, which is selling four times the merchandise that it sold two years ago and made $50,000 in 2008 (up from $10,000 three years earlier).

And yet, Rangina says, "I almost feel guilty saying I run a business, because this is not about the money. It is literacy education and medical assistance and counseling. It's advocacy for the women, and encouraging them to fight for their rights."

I was fortunate to meet Rangina through Arizona friends on one of her follow-up visits to Thunderbird. She told her life's story in her simple, modest way. I told her she wasn't crediting herself enough for the tremendous ways in which she leads and gives back. With a bashful laugh, she admitted I was not the first to make that observation.

"I don't do this to make myself look good," she explained. "I went back to Afghanistan because if my father had not made the choice to leave with us when he did, I might have become one of the women with whom I'm now working. So what better for me to do than to serve and work with women who have this potential? It may not happen in my lifetime, but if we can just give them that spark, that encouragement, maybe these women can become leaders for tomorrow. If that happens, then I've done my job."

ON THE 200-ACRE FARM near Clovis, New Mexico, young Tim Sanders lived alone with Billye, the grandmother who was raising him. Though Tim was no more than eight, he vividly remembers a visit from a poorly-dressed man, "walking through our wheat field like something out of a dream." How the man said he'd lost his livelihood in Oklahoma and was walking to find a future in California, seeking odd jobs on the way. How his grandmother Billye gave the man a half-dozen chores and, as Tim tagged along, the man demonstrated how to do every job well and with pride. How Billye carried out lunch for the two of them, plates of ranch beans and canned Vienna sausages that the man savored "like he was at the Ritz eating lobster." And how, when the man was about to walk on in his badly-worn shoes, Billye pulled out a pair of wingtips, a keepsake from her late father, and insisted he take them. "You've got an angel there," the man told Tim. "You should study what she does."

The experience was Tim's first object lesson in the power of doing good. He carried it through life, as a debate star in high school and college, reggae musician, dotcom innovator who rose to oracle status. Yahoo! Inc. made him its Chief Solutions Officer, charged with developing next-generation business strategies, and later its leadership coach. For the past decade Tim has written and given speeches prolifically, capturing the digital zeitgeist, but while some techies sound like they have circuits where hearts should be, Tim is quite the opposite. To futuristic discussions of business and leadership, he brings Billye's fine old ethos of giving.

Tim's first book, in 2002, declared that *Love Is the Killer App*. By "killer app," he meant an amazing new business idea or application that supersedes all that came before it. And by love, he broadly meant compassion, empathy, trust, generosity, all essential building blocks of business success, he says. His 2005 book *The Likeability Factor* reinforced that message. By the time we spoke in late 2008, Tim had written a third book taking the notion of benevolent business behavior to its broadest possible "app." He called the book *Saving the World at Work: What Companies and Individuals Can Do to Go Beyond Making A Profit to Making a Difference*. In it, he gathered stories of givers like his grandmother, except these people apply their values at work to benefit their colleagues, their communities and the planet as well as their company's bottom line.

A successful, sustainable business plan for giving back must have three elements, Tim says. It must make a contribution to the community, improve conditions for the business and give those who participate a sense of purpose and satisfaction. His example: a company that rounds up donated computers and gives them to a school. The donation helps the school deliver a higher-quality education, and the company gains, too, from a better-trained future workforce. Tim says that when companies create such giving opportunities for their employees, they derive one more benefit. Employees feel more positive about work, their willingness to collaborate increases, and their productivity soars.

In the twenty-first century, Tim contends, a brand or company's greatest attribute won't be its uniqueness, its high profile, or even its relevance, but its reputation as a socially responsible enterprise. Increasingly, he says, young jobseekers research the ethical, environmental, and philanthropic records of prospective employers and won't consider a firm "that they'd be embarrassed to put on their Facebook page." Two-thirds of American consumers say they would change to brands associated with a good cause if price and quality were comparable. And between 1995 and 2005, assets in so-called socially responsible investments—mutual funds that screen companies for their contributions to society—ballooned from $235 billion to $2.3 trillion. When it comes to what makes a great company, Tim says, "good is the new great." And a good company, he says, "is one whose mission is to improve the lives of everyone in its footprint: employees, suppliers, customers, supporting communities, and the planet."

To chronicle this "responsibility revolution" in business, "I've gone out in the world in search of stories about generosity and leadership—and more often than not, I find that they start with women," Tim said during our recent interview. "One of the things I've learned over time is that the difference between a male-influenced style of leadership and a female-influenced style of leadership is the difference between independence and interdependence. What we're learning is, independently you are an island and islands do poorly during hurricanes, they don't fare well. So you have to string a bunch of islands together, because survival depends on it.

"The reason I see so much generosity right now with respect to work is that interdependence is being taught to us by current events at such a rapid pace," Tim went on. "In a single era, multiple generations are all realizing that everything connects to everything. That's breeding a really strong sense of responsibility and accountability, and bringing out that female tendency to nurture and to grow... I think we have entered the age of female-influenced leadership principles because interdependence is a reality, and that demands strategies where we behave less like motivators and machinists and more like gardeners and farmers." Farmers like his grandmother Billye, now in her mid-nineties.

Tim says Billye fretted recently that when economic times are tough, "a lot of people stop trying to help others because they're so worried about themselves." Through lean and fat times, Billye told Tim, she holds to the same creed: "You give until you notice something's missing and then give a little more until it hurts." In Tim's view, "it's important for

Americans to take up those give-until-it-hurts values because otherwise, in the tough years, we'll all be gripped with this scarcity mindset and panic... But if we take a deep breath and go out and continue giving even during tough times, we'll see: There will still be enough to go around."

MARY FISHER grew up in a prominent, affluent Detroit family where she was taught, by example, the importance of giving back. Her father, industrialist-turned-philanthropist Max Fisher, was a generous supporter of Detroit, of Israel, and of Republican groups and candidates. Her mother, Marjorie, was a patron of the arts and special social causes.

As Mary moved through adult life, as a successful television producer, a White House assistant to President Gerald R. Ford, a promising artist, she continued the family legacy. Even as a mother busy with two young sons, she helped with charity events and served her community, especially women in need, orphans, and recovering substance abusers.

Then came the phone call that forever changed not only how Mary would live but how she would give.

In July 1991, less than a year after they'd divorced, Mary's ex-husband called to say he had tested positive for the AIDS virus. Dazed and disbelieving, Mary got tested; her results were the same. To her great relief, tests showed that sons Max, three, and Zachary, one (who was adopted), were not infected. Her gratitude that the boys would live collided with the realization that she would not. "At that time, everyone infected with the virus was headed for the grave. We knew it. Our doctors knew it. We were pilgrims on the road to AIDS, marching to our deaths."

Keeping news of the illness within a close circle of loved ones, Mary "proceeded to take on dying as I took on everything, as a project," she says now. "I accepted it, organized it and planned for it." She wrote journals for Max and Zachary so they could know her when she was gone. She wrote and rewrote wills; she agonized over guardianships. She ached at

Mary Fisher, an artist, author, activist and ambassador for the United Nations' HIV/AIDS program, at an African clinic with some of the HIV-positive people to whom she brings encouragement and hope. Photo courtesy of Mary Fisher.

the frustration of her father, accustomed to moving fortunes and nations yet powerless to save his daughter. But through her own pain and dread, Mary never forgot "what Daddy always told us: That we need to give back in life, to have as much impact as we can wherever we are. And since I had only a short while to live, I figured I needed to make an impact fast." Mary sought guidance from her dear friend and mentor, former first lady Betty Ford, whose own candor had shattered the silence around

breast cancer and substance-abuse treatment. She pressed the question with AIDS experts and activists. What could she, just one woman, do to make a difference? The answer, time and again, was the same. "Just tell your story." And so she did. To a world that generally chalked off AIDS as a plague on promiscuous gay men and destitute drug abusers, Mary presented herself: a white, affluent, straight woman who contracted the virus in marriage. She went public with her illness, gave several speeches, and on a steamy August night she took the stage at the 1992 Republican National Convention. In a primetime speech that moved conventioneers to silence and tears, and stunned millions around the world watching on TV, she called for action and compassion in the fight against AIDS. "The AIDS virus is not a political creature," she told the hushed hall. "It does not care whether you are Democrat or Republican. It does not ask whether you are black or white, male or female, gay or straight, young or old ... HIV asks only one thing of those it attacks: Are you human? And this is the right question: Are you human?"

The convention speech put Mary in the headlines and pushed her to the forefront of HIV/AIDS advocacy. As she traveled the country giving speeches, she recalls seeing "tremendous amounts of stigma and homophobia. As discrimination mounted against the AIDS community, fear took root within that community and silence stifled those who already felt vulnerable and knew they were dying. The more I saw it happening, the more I felt the need to speak out."

"At first," Mary admits, "I was speaking out for a very personal reason: basically, for my children, to remove the stigma around HIV/AIDS so that when I was gone, they would not have to live with shame. But over time, the reasons for speaking out grew. The message wasn't any longer just about my children, but about everybody's children."

Contracting the virus was "not anything that I would have chosen or could have planned," she says. "But AIDS came, and made my community much larger." It became the ultimate vehicle for that which her late father, especially, had raised her to do: give back.

An accomplished artist as well as a writer and public speaker, Mary has woven together her life in such a way that everything she does makes a difference. Her speeches move people not only to tears, but to action. Her five books speak of truth and justice in language that persuades more than it angers. Her artwork—from handmade paper and sculpture to jewelry, prints, and quilts—incorporates themes from her life on the road to AIDS: images and materials from Africa, words from testimony to Congress, photos of her children.

The late 1990s brought antiretroviral medications (ARVs), miracle drugs that eventually, in combinations, began extending the lives of people with HIV. Though they are not a cure and can have troubling side effects, they offer years of life beyond what Mary and many other HIV-positive people had ever expected.

With that reprieve of sorts, Mary didn't pause in her advocacy but entered a new phase, a "life inseparable from the moral imperative of fighting AIDS," as Margaret Talbot wrote in a MORE *Magazine* profile of Mary. Knowing most people in Africa and Asia lacked the ARVs that were sustaining her, Mary began traveling to the hardest hit regions, working to broaden access to the drugs and bringing information and hope to her fellow AIDS pilgrims. She accepted an appointment as an ambassador of the Joint United Nations Programme on HIV/AIDS (UNAIDS); she spoke out about the suffering of at-risk populations such as the millions of women and girls who are trafficked every year, mostly in forced sex trades. With her family's support, Mary established a non-profit organization to fund AIDS research, education and advocacy: The Mary Fisher Clinical AIDS Research and Education (CARE) Fund, based at the University of Alabama at Birmingham and led by Dr. Michael Saag, an internationally recognized AIDS researcher and physician.

I first met Mary a couple of years ago when she began spending time in Sedona; we bonded instantly over our shared commitment to helping women thrive. I had watched her give the riveting 1992 speech and I knew about some of her contributions: the books, the art, the UNAIDS work. But what I came to see more clearly, over time, is Mary's almost magical way of inspiring others to join her in giving back.

For example, in the summer of 2007 she took two dozen friends and relatives on a fact-finding trip through Zambia so they could see both the breathtaking beauty (Victoria Falls, bush camps full of wildlife) and the extraordinary challenges—compounds where people live on pennies per day, clinics treating the one in six Zambians who have the virus, orphans scrounging for food in the garbage heaps of Lusaka, Zambia's capital. Of those who accompanied Mary to Zambia, virtually all have found their own ways to give back. A Long Island doctor rounded up medical equipment donations for the Lusaka clinics; an Arizona mother "adopted" two impoverished Zambian girls by paying their school costs; a Michigan college student returned in summer 2008 to work with a Lusaka program that teaches job skills to widowed and orphaned women and girls. "People come with me to Africa wishing to learn and they come back wishing to give," Mary says. "They see the need and the value. They see ways they can contribute. That's the satisfaction."

In spring 2008, I joined Mary at a gathering she once could not have dared to imagine, her sixtieth birthday party! If milestone birthdays are complained about at many such parties, Mary's was celebrated for what it was, a triumph. Scores of friends came to rejoice with her. But even there, Mary was giving. At each place at the table sat a tiny, hand-woven basket, made by an HIV-positive African artisan whose work Mary has championed. "As often as I have grieved AIDS," says Mary, "I've also known that it came into my life for a purpose. Maybe it was God's way of enabling me to be one with the impoverished woman in Kansas City, the imprisoned women at Riker's Island, and the wasting women in Zambia. Perhaps it was what balanced my life. The White House taught one set of lessons and the morgues of Kenya taught me another. I don't know why I have AIDS. But, having it, I know what I need to do: use it to serve others, to make a difference. To keep faith with my late father, and give back."

EARLY 1950S, RURAL LOUISIANA. She was a wisp of a girl but there she was, in the steaming cotton fields with her mother, trudging along the rows doing the work of a person twice her size. Before that part of her life was over, Sherian Grace Cadoria could carry 100 pounds of cotton. She didn't even weigh that much herself; she must have figured out how to balance it just right.

When I met Sherian she was still a wisp, ninety-five pounds of finely honed person, body and soul. ATHENA International chose her as its 1998 Award recipient in tribute to her remarkable achievements. She had just retired as a U.S. Army brigadier general, the highest position the Army had to that point conferred on a black woman. I remember being struck by the stories she had to tell, stories of trials and obstacles but also of altruism and vision. A decade after we first met, I asked her to tell those stories again, so I could record them here.

My mother Bernice was both mom and dad to her three children, of whom I am the youngest. My father was hospitalized when I was three months old and remained there until his death in 1994. Though she only had an eighth-grade education, my mother instilled in us the importance of a good education . . . . Before we could talk, she was teaching us the Ten Commandments, and how it was so important to learn math because we must never cheat anyone or allow anyone to cheat us. We were extremely poor, but each week my mom gave us an allowance of ten cents. She made us put one nickel in the basket at church and the other was ours to do with what we wanted. She taught us, 'Give to God first, and He will multiply your blessings.' With that strong confidence, we knew we could face the difficulties and stumbling blocks that would confront us.

That outlook carried Sherian through college (she graduated in 1961) and a tough Women's Army Corps recruiting program. It sustained the young WAC when, to enter Alabama's Fort McClellan, she had to pass robed Ku Klux Klan members at the gate. Racism, sexism and nearly three years in Vietnam took their toll and Sherian considered leaving the Army, but Bernice urged her daughter to keep going, so she did. By 1969, Sherian was a major.

"In the military, I learned that sometimes even though you give 200 percent effort, if you are female and black, you would not even get 90 percent credit. But I also learned that I should always be optimistic and positive. While I had no idea that senior people were observing me, it turned out they were taking note that no matter what job I was assigned, no matter how menial or difficult, it was accomplished in an outstanding manner."

As a young officer Sherian watched her white colleagues go off to get graduate degrees, while she was given excuses about why she could not. "I knew that when all my colleagues had that extra degree and I didn't, I

Brigadier General Sherian Cadoria, who made history during her career in the U.S. Army then returned to her Louisiana hometown to give back. Photo courtesy of ATHENA International.

would not succeed," she says now. Working by day as WAC branch executive officer in Washington, D. C., she took classes at night. As the Army prepared to integrate WACs into the full corps in 1978, a superior took her aside, praised her record of service, but told her that to compete with the male peers in the combined forces she needed an advanced degree.

"The colonel advised me that the University of Oklahoma had an intensified program which would allow me to go to school eight hours on Saturday and eight hours on Sunday. I couldn't tell the colonel he was out of his mind, but I said, 'Sir, have you forgotten how far Washington, D. C., is from Oklahoma?' He said, 'Major, get enrolled now.' So I did. I traveled every Friday evening to Oklahoma, returned to Washington every Sunday night, and was at work at my usual time of 0500 hours on Monday morning. And the rest is history!"

History indeed. During her twenty-nine-year Army career, Sherian was the first woman to command an all-male battalion, the first woman to lead a criminal investigation brigade, and among the first women to serve as a military police officer. She was the first black woman admitted in residence to the U.S. Army War College, and the first black female director for the Joint Chiefs of Staff. When she retired in 1990, she was one of only four female generals on active duty in the U. S. Army, and, say those who know her, an exemplary leader: ethical and fair, compassionate and selfless.

On those strengths alone, ATHENA surely chose well in naming Sherian an award recipient. But it's her life's second act—what she has done since the Army—that speaks to me so powerfully about the principle of giving back.

In 1991 I started my own business as a public speaker, to fill
in for the times I was not at the nursing homes with my mother
and father. Within a year, I was receiving requests to speak
throughout the United States and internationally—success beyond

my wildest imagination! Then in 1997, I received a call from the pastor of the parochial school in Marksville, Louisiana, that I had attended as a child. He said the sister-principal had to return to the motherhouse, there was no replacement, and the church had no funds to hire a civilian principal. I said, 'Father, what can an old general do?' I contacted three men I knew, any of whom would have made an outstanding principal—but with families to care for and educate, they could not work without pay.

After praying about this, I called the pastor and told him I would close my business for one year and serve as principal.

Not only was Sherian working gratis, but the church had no funds to pay teachers or operating expenses, to make much-needed repairs or to cover $8,000 in old debts. Sherian dipped into her personal savings to meet payroll and keep the Holy Ghost Catholic School open. Then she began publicizing the school's plight and raising funds, squeezing in speaking engagements so she could donate her fees.

From across the United States and beyond, people pitched in to help. One man traveled from Canada to spend two weeks supervising volunteers who built a school playground. Others donated enough cash to buy two school buses.

The "one year" Sherian promised turned into three. She gave up the job only when her doctor insisted, so she could have a long-postponed surgery. Though Sherian had left the school on as solid a footing as she could, within two years of her departure the pastor was forced to close it. Her legacy at the school lives on, though, in the lives of the many students she helped.

Zachary Augustine, valedictorian of Holy Ghost's eighth-grade graduating class in 2002, says that "Other than my parents, General Cadoria has been my greatest inspiration in my younger years of learning. I was privileged to be guided by the moral, intellectual and disciplinary standards she instilled while she was principal. She took me under her wing in the summer construction of the playground and remodeling of the school. I will never forget the opportunity she gave me to meet former Secretary of State Colin Powell! But the most gracious gift she shared was establishing a program with Benedictine University to offer a four-year, fully-paid, academic scholarship to the top three students of each eighth-grade graduating class of Holy Ghost." When Zachary graduated from high school in 2006, Sherian came to the ceremony to present him with that scholarship: $120,000 to study at the Lisle, Illinois, Catholic university.

When I caught up with Zachary, he was well into his junior year at Benedictine, majoring in political science with a concentration in pre-law. Armed with the standards and the inspiration he got from Sherian, Zachary says, "I will one day become a renowned lawyer and political figure. Notice that I said 'I will' rather than 'I hope to'—because if there is one thing that I have learned from the general, it is that all things are possible through the Lord Jesus Christ. I will forever be indebted to her."

Sherian is retired now, struggling with health issues and living modestly on her military pension. "Truthfully, I was scared to death when I used most of my savings to help save the school," she told me. "But my life was so enriched by being able to share the gifts God has given to me. And some 500 children's lives were, I hope, enriched during my tenure." When she speaks of those students, Sherian slips into a motherly possessive. "Several of my children have gone into the military, several have become registered nurses, and several are studying to be teachers. Two are in the process of becoming lawyers, one is studying to be a therapist, and one is studying to be a pharmacist. One wants to be a WNBA star and started college on an athletic scholarship, after graduating high school with a 4.0 average. Proud? You bet I am! I am so grateful that God sent me on the mission to positively impact children's lives."

To give back, our ATHENA principle says, is to leave a worthy legacy, and to serve. Sherian has done that, and more. "For me," she says, "leading is giving everything of self. It is putting my heart, soul, spirit, humor, tears, compassion, time and effort to ensure that a positive environment is created so that those whom I lead can reach higher, run faster, speak better, walk straighter and drop the word *never* from their vocabulary. It is seeing myself in each person and praying that I never lose sight of the fact that God blessed me. Leading is knowing that if I can inspire and motivate others they too may go on and attain the best that life has to offer."

Celebrate

STOP WORRYING ABOUT THE POTHOLES
IN THE ROAD AND CELEBRATE THE JOURNEY!
— BARBARA HOFFMAN

I T WAS 1999 and many from the ATHENA family had gathered in Pittsburgh for our annual conference. This was the time that I had chosen to pass the leadership of the organization to a successor, lest the whole concept become too closely associated with me.

It had been seventeen years since the first intentions for this project were articulated. We were now attending our fifth annual national conference. There were award programs in more than 250 cities and counting; some of the programs had been honoring ATHENA recipients for more than a decade. We had started several other significant initiatives that furthered our mission, including the ATHENA PowerLink mentoring systems and the ATHENA World Café forums. Ours was a strong and committed board of directors, women and men from all over the United States bringing their talents and vision to the table. Our reputation was solid, our finances were professionally managed, our underwriters were pleased with the association and we had a healthy and growing fund reserve. It was time.

The last evening of my long tenure, after all the board business was finished, I invited a few of my colleagues to share a little time and a glass of wine. I hardly understood how much this "end of an era" was affecting me until I started talking about it, surprisingly with quite a lot of sadness.

Then something amazing happened. Someone suggested that we needed to memorialize the moment, and asked me to remove the red jacket I was wearing. One by one, each person claimed some part of the jacket—a sleeve, a lapel, a pocket—and stated some heartfelt wish for me or for the organization. This spontaneous laying on of hands, imbuing my jacket with hopes and blessings, was both serious and light hearted, and most certainly caring and loving.

When the jacket had been passed all around and returned, I slipped it back on. As my colleagues prepared to depart, one of them, a high-level manager from a Fortune 50 corporation, mentioned she was concerned about a meeting she would have the next day with a group of women from her organization. They were suffering unusually low morale due to some company circumstance now long forgotten. She was dreading that meeting. After hearing her, I stood up, again removed my jacket and handed it to her, saying she needed to take it to the meeting. With all the blessings on that jacket, surely something good would happen.

In the middle of the next day, a crowd of excited people suddenly surrounded me, handing back the (quite rumpled) jacket and telling me what had happened. The corporate executive had opened her meeting by sharing the red-jacket story, with my jacket as her prop. One meeting participant had asked to hold it and then began to speak candidly about what was troubling her. Someone else then took the jacket and did the same. One by one, the women confided their frustrations, difficulties, anguish. There were torrents of words, candid talk.

Before they were finished, the jacket circulated to every person there, empowering them to talk, even to cry, about what their issues really were.

The exercise opened hearts and built a new sense of togetherness and purpose among them. Everyone left with a sense of resolve to hold onto the spirit of that meeting. With that outpouring of authentic feelings, the women had created a foundation of support and encouragement on which each of them could rely, for that day and into the future. (I don't think that kind of thing happens frequently in large organizations, and that's too bad.)

The original descriptions of this final ATHENA tenet spoke about "celebration and joy," and ATHENA leaders unquestionably value both. But I've never thought this tenet was simply about happy occasions; that would be too shallow, too narrow. Celebration is also about gathering people together when they have something sad, painful or final to commemorate. It's about being actively together in marking something profound and, from that action, forging lasting bonds. It's about taking the time to share and perhaps even elevating that sharing into a ritual, as with the passed-around red jacket.

In that meeting led by my executive friend, the impromptu red-jacket ritual changed a very negative dynamic. It allowed meeting participants to dig beneath the stream of business problems and reveal how those problems affected them not just professionally, but personally. Perhaps for the first time, they really trusted the group with their honest perspectives. They established and deepened relationships. They created a way to collectively face matters of great difficulty, a way that contained layers of reward and renewal.

That, to me, is the essence of the ATHENA principle of celebration. Leaders, particularly women, use celebration and ritual to promote a shared sense of purpose, and to express their commitment to transforming what is into what might be. They take pleasure in shared work and accomplishments, and they express that, sometimes in creative forms such as music, dance, art or poetry, for the celebration of life and the restoration of their own energies.

ATHENA celebration isn't chiefly about happiness or hoopla, though. It is simply about being together, in genuine and even vulnerable ways, to mark something important to the group. Sometimes what we celebrate is a triumph, other times a disaster, but it's all the stuff of indelible, meaningful human experience. In celebrating, we confirm our capacity to deal with all life's possibilities. In celebrating, we re-plant our feet in the circle of our humanity.

I still have that red jacket, and I still love to wear it.

HOW are we to celebrate in the buttoned-down confines of work life?

You may know Ray Bradbury as one of America's most popular writers, a National Medal of Arts winner, and author of more than 500 published works including *The Martian Chronicles, The Illustrated Man* and *Fahrenheit 451*. But based on a quote from Bradbury in an essay he wrote in 1984, I'd say he was also one seriously celebratory leader. Here is Bradbury's vision of the model work environment:

> If your meeting room, your board room, or your office (take your pick) isn't a nursery for ideas, a rumpus room where seals frolic, forget it. Burn the table, lock the room, fire the clerks. You will rarely come up with any ideas worth entertaining. The full room with the heavy people trudging in with long faces to solve problems by beating them to death is very death itself. Serious confrontations rarely arrive at serious ends. Unless the people you meet with are fun-loving kids out for a romp, tossing ideas like confetti, and letting the damn bits fall where they may, no spirit will ever rouse, no notion will ever birth, no love will be mentioned, no climax reached. You must swim at your meetings, you must jump for baskets, you must take hefty swings for great or missed drives, you must run and dive, you must fall and roll, and when the fun stops, get the hell out.

An original artwork by Barbara Hranilovich, commissioned for the 2000 ATHENA Conference in Denver, captured the spirit of the ATHENA principles including joyful celebration.

IN 1981 when we created the ATHENA Awards, here's the problem I saw: too little attention being paid to women leaders. In 1995 when China hosted the UN's Fourth World Conference on Women, here's the problem Beijing bureaucrats saw: too much attention being paid to women leaders.

Of course, that wasn't the stated reason Chinese officials relocated the event I attended, a gathering of 30,000 representatives of nongovernmental organizations (NGOs) on the eve of the UN Conference. The Chinese government's official explanation was that NGOs could not be accommodated as well in Beijing as in Huairou, a rural community 60 kilometers away. But many who attended believed, as I did, that the Chinese government was keeping the NGOs away from Beijing to curb political speech and activity. Just how alarmed were Beijing officials at the prospect of militant women flooding city streets? Our delegation was told, though it was impossible to confirm, that Beijing police officers had been issued cloth sheets, in case they needed them to cover naked women protesters.

Because most of us booked lodgings in Beijing before the August 30–September 8 forum was relocated, we commuted to Huairou by crowded, unreliable buses, ninety minutes or more each way. In Huairou, forum activities were held in schools, arenas, libraries, and even tents. The morning plenary session that started each day was booked in an elementary school auditorium that held 1,500, although thousands of us wanted in. People had spent years planning for this event, to gather visibly and freely in Beijing. Here, the facilities were so inadequate that a speech by Betty Friedan, that "founding mother" of feminism, was assigned to a small tent with no public address system, near a garbage dump.

On the forum's first day, there was angry rumbling: *Oh my goodness, we've been had.* But by the second day, frustration was turning to resolve. Participants in the event had decided. We were not going to let conditions get in the way of making this gathering wonderful. Instead of griping, we started celebrating. Every night there were rounds of cultural events, people from nearly 180 different countries meeting in a riot of colorful attire. Some brought musical instruments, and we danced and sang in all different tongues and voices. Even those who never had met knew how to be together, and to rejoice. Instead of the forum becoming a morass of angry people, it became a gathering of what is possible.

When America's First Lady, Hillary Rodham Clinton, was scheduled to address the forum at Huairou, we boarded buses from Beijing early in hopes of getting into the auditorium to hear her. By the time we arrived, the jammed building was locked; we stood outside in the rain, listening to her remarks on crackling speakers. But when she had addressed the formal UN Conference earlier, she had spoken for us as well as to us, and the whole world heard her. Lines of her speech still ring in my memory. "The voices of this conference and of the women at Huairou must be heard loud and clear," she said. "If there is one message that echoes forth from this conference, it is that human rights are women's rights—and women's rights are human rights . . . . Women must enjoy the right to participate fully in the social and political lives of their countries if we want freedom and democracy to thrive and endure."

"A LONG TIME AGO, we decided we wanted to do something to celebrate people." Max De Pree was telling another story from his days as CEO at Herman Miller, Inc., the furniture company that frequently makes the list of *Fortune* magazine's Best Companies to Work For.

"I was in this gallery of Native American art, talking to the owner, and I said, 'I'm looking for something that we can use to celebrate people in a manufacturing company, that acknowledges when they've been there twenty years.' He said, 'You need to talk to the gentleman over there in the corner.' I asked, 'Who is he?' And the owner said, 'Well, he's an Indian chief, he knows about this, go tell him what you need.' And the chief told me, 'What you need is a water carrier.'" In Native American Indian tribes, Max explained, the water carrier was an important, respected figure because without what he brought, the tribe could not live.

"So," Max continued, "I bought this six-feet-tall, bronze statue," *Water Carrier,* by acclaimed Chiricahua Apache artist Allan Houser. The statue was placed in a Herman Miller courtyard and surrounded by a low granite plinth on which every twenty-year employee's name is engraved. "Whenever there is a celebration of people who've been there twenty years," Max says, "we get hundreds of people in the courtyard to come out for that event. Celebration is one of the skills of leadership, no doubt about it. That's what the watercarrier does. It's a beautiful thing."

Ever since Linda Ackley cast our first bronze award sculpture, with its curving spars like arms raised in triumph, ATHENA has encouraged public, purposeful celebration of those we identify as leaders. Celebrating ATHENA leaders for all to see, we reasoned, would not only give these individuals their due; it also would inspire and embolden more leaders like them.

That's certainly how it has worked out in Stockton, California. To put that community's ATHENA history in perspective, the year Stockton named its first ATHENA Award recipient was the same year IBM introduced the first laptop computer—and "The Oprah Winfrey Show" premiered! Its 1986 launch means Stockton has one of the longest-running ATHENA Award programs. So I was deeply honored when Stockton asked me to speak at the November 2008 event honoring its twenty-second ATHENA Award recipient.

The Stockton event's invitation was both elegant and eloquent. It read in part:

There is a new kind of leader
lighting the way in the twenty-first century—
one who leads with the head and heart,
blending a keen intellect with the
intuitive wisdom that comes
from rich life experience.

This new leader is a nurturer,
a learner, a teacher and a creator
who takes risks and advocates fiercely
for change, for justice, and
above all, for others.

The way ATHENA Award recipients are celebrated has changed a lot in Stockton since university administrator Judith Chambers received the honor in 1986. Back then, Judy was invited to a dinner, introduced from the podium and handed her award sculpture, and that was pretty much the extent of it. How different things were for 2008 recipient Mary Bava, a political consultant and longtime advocate for women and families. I joined Stockton's ATHENA community in toasting Mary not just at its traditional luncheon, but also the night before at a grand reception in a previous ATHENA Award recipient's beautiful home.

After more than two decades, Stockton has a small army of past recipients, and they are on the march. Several of them have begun meeting regularly, calling themselves Team ATHENA, to see how they can support and expand the movement. Their goal in 2009 is to help Stockton establish an offshoot program that is gaining momentum in other cities: The Young Professional ATHENA Award (fondly called "Baby ATHENA") which specifically honors promising leaders ages twenty to forty. Kristen Spracher-Birtwhistle, Stockton's ATHENA Award recipient in 2002 and a Team ATHENA organizer, personifies the spirit of leaders for whom being honored is not a crowning achievement but a launch pad. "This community has a limitless talent pool of women leaders," she told me. "We need to showcase and share that."

Heading home after addressing a crowd of 300 at Stockton's ATHENA Award luncheon, I found myself thinking back over all the years and the many places I'd been privileged to go, participating in this very same kind of celebration. Each reflects the flavor of its host community; each honors someone who made extraordinary contributions to that community, and who accepts the community's thanks with disarming grace and humility. Such celebrations aren't just breathtaking for recipients but affirming for us all.

STUDIES ON THE EFFECTS of birth order speak of a "middle child syndrome," a sibling shortchanged by being neither the eagerly-awaited firstborn nor the doted-upon baby in the family. If my son Michael suffered from being the middle child of three, it hasn't been apparent. In Michael, I see someone who makes the most of any place he lands. Some places have been charmed and others have been challenging, as in any life. Michael's gift is finding something in each place to celebrate.

From the age of four when we moved to a suburb of East Lansing, Michigan, Michael was raised in a community crazy for basketball. He religiously followed the hometown Michigan State Spartans and the Everett High School team, where one guard was so skilled that people replaced his given name, Earvin, with a nickname: "Magic." Though Michael never was the biggest player on the court, he had an uncanny court awareness, was quick, intense and determined. Practicing was never work for him, whether in the gym or on the driveway until well after dark.

The sound of a bouncing basketball and voices of the neighborhood boys became background music at our house. Michael's athletic gifts and hard work as a starting guard helped his high school team win the state finals two years in a row, a feat that hasn't been repeated. He was also a top student, earning an academic scholarship to a small liberal arts college where he continued to play basketball until he graduated. In short, he has been able to excel at whatever he attempted.

After earning advanced degrees in psychology, he took a job with a particularly challenging clientele, children whose lives had been as traumatic as his had been smooth. As the clinical director at a California residential school, Michael works with youngsters at the end of their ropes, those shattered by abuse or neglect, cut off from family, bounced around the juvenile justice system, scarred by illiteracy and substance abuse. Working in a facility with about 700 staff and twice that many kids, he nonetheless relates to each person in his charge with extraordinary patience, listening skills and understanding. Though the bleak truth is that many of these kids may never fully heal, he manages to help them believe in themselves, sort through their difficulties and, perhaps for the first time, see positive options for their lives.

Michael seems always to find something in each of these youngsters to celebrate, some way to keep their dreams alive. He has bucked many of the working assumptions in his field about how to help people through difficult times. He approaches people's problems and therapies as inseparable from what has marginalized them in life, including issues of race, gender, poverty and sexual orientation. He rejects the idea that it's his job to find deficits in people and try to fix them; rather, he helps people find the means within themselves to pursue success and healing. Once, Michael's determination led his basketball teams to championships. Now, his determination leads his colleagues to more respectful modes of treatment, and his patients toward healthier futures.

Of all the places Michael's gifts could take him, here's where he chooses to be: steadfast for the youngsters at his school, loving and devoted to his children Cameron, Ryan, and Angelo, caring more about making a difference than about making a fortune. In my journey with ATHENA, as women have been "becoming," there's a new kind of man that has been becoming as well. Michael, I'm proud to say, is one of them.

EVERY ROOM in Cheryl and Mike Haggard's suburban-Denver home is decorated with their children's pictures, handmade art projects, team photos, school portraits, baby pictures. Chase, the firstborn, is a ninth grader who plays baseball and loves the online fantasy game World of Warcraft. Seventh-grader Anna spends hours every week on tumbling and gymnastics, and competes with a nationally-ranked cheerleading team. Third-grader Natalie is also a cheerleader, and a budding rock star who makes "concert videos" in the family's garage.

And then there is the lastborn, Maddux. Throughout her fourth pregnancy, Cheryl could not shake the feeling that something was wrong; she felt so few stirrings. On February 4, 2005, Maddux Achilles Haggard was born with myotubular myopathy, a rare genetic condition that kept him from breathing, swallowing, or moving on his own. In a hospital maternity ward hung with exquisite photos of infants, doctors told Cheryl and Mike their baby would not survive.

After six days of agony and prayer, the couple prepared for Maddux to be taken off life support. Cheryl could not bear the thought that his image would not hang in their home alongside his siblings'. Mike found the name of the photographer whose work the hospital displayed, Sandy Puc'. Mike called. Sandy came. Quietly, sensitively, Sandy photographed Cheryl and Mike cradling Maddux. She made images before he was removed from life support and after, when he was free from the tubes and wires.

"I didn't care that we were crying hysterically or how we appeared," Cheryl recalls. "I didn't think about whether I would share the images

Cheryl Haggard with her son Maddux Achilles Haggard. Photo by Sandy Puc', courtesy of Cheryl and Mike Haggard.

with my family or other people. I just remember thinking I wanted something of him to take home, to be able to look back and see him." Sandy retouched the digital photos and gave a disc of them to the Haggards, to reproduce as they wished. When they offered to pay, she declined. As they wrestled with their grief, Cheryl says, it helped enormously to have the images, to let others see Maddux and to display his tiny, peaceful face among the family photos.

In the days after Maddux's death, Cheryl thought about how such images could help other grieving families, and Sandy was summoned to the hospital again, to photograph another infant. After a few weeks, Cheryl phoned Sandy. "I remember the conversation vividly," she says now. "We started talking about the other families that this happens to, and what if they knew they could have these pictures . . . and Sandy said, 'By sharing your story, we might be able to help.'" Sandy could enlist photographer friends who would donate their time and talent. Cheryl could publicize the service to hospitals, clergy, genetic counselors and others serving parents whose babies might not live. "And as soon as we thought of creating an organization to do this," Cheryl says, "everything fell into our laps—people to help us file papers for the IRS and build a Web site, a reporter to do a story on it. It seemed like every person in my life at that time was there for this purpose."

In April 2005, Cheryl and Sandy launched a non-profit foundation and named it Now I Lay Me Down to Sleep. At first, they and a few volunteers ran the organization from the Haggards' home, working in what would have been Maddux's bedroom. As word spread, demand grew and more photographers signed on, they hired a director and rented an office. By early 2009—when Maddux Haggard would have turned four—Now I Lay Me Down to Sleep had arranged free, professional photos for thousands of bereaved families, through a network of more than 5,000 photographers in the United States and nineteen other countries. "The honor that these photographers bring to these short lives helps the families heal," Cheryl said when we spoke recently. "It's about healing through remembrance."

Raised in modest means in Missouri's Lake of the Ozarks region, Cheryl finished high school, skipped college, and found work as a travel agent. Once she and Mike started their family, she became a stay-at-home mom. "Before Maddux, I would never have called myself creative or a professional; I never thought of myself as a leader," she told me. "If you had asked me ten years ago what I was going to do with the rest of my life, I just expected to be a mom and raise my children the best I could. And now it's like, I've gone a little above what I thought was the best I could do."

In my years with ATHENA, I have heard this refrain repeatedly. Committed, dynamic people who give of themselves, accomplish important things—and yet don't see themselves as leaders. At the same time, they generously credit leadership in others. Cheryl, for example, says that if she had known more about Sandy when she proposed joining forces, "I think I would have been intimidated by her." A master photographer and successful entrepreneur, Sandy is in her second decade running a flourishing studio; she's an internationally-known lecturer and author who travels the country teaching photography.

And yet, in founding and nurturing Now I Lay Me Down to Sleep, Cheryl and Sandy are equally remarkable ATHENA leaders, in my estimation. They are not focused on building a kingdom. They saw a need and acted to meet it. They have led with their hearts, even hearts that are breaking. Surrounded by scalding grief, they seize on celebration.

For Sandy, "If I had thought of this idea myself, it probably would have gone on a shelf of good ideas I'm going to do someday. But Cheryl took all of her grief and pain and turned it into this incredible energy to do this, and now it has touched all these people."

For Cheryl, it all comes back to the family pictures on the wall—Chase, Anna, Natalie. "I look at my children and the siblings of these other babies, and I think we are forming a new generation's ideas about bereavement," she says. "We are shaping how the death of a loved one affects them—that it should not be hidden, that even the briefest life can be celebrated."

And, always, Maddux. "Look what he accomplished with just his short time on Earth. How many people can say they've done anything like that?"

"OUR DEEPEST FEAR is not that we are inadequate. Our deepest fear is that we are powerful beyond measure. It is our light, not our darkness that most frightens us. We ask ourselves, Who am I to be brilliant, gorgeous, talented, fabulous? Actually, who are you not to be?"

I love those lines from author and spiritual teacher Marianne Williamson. What a bracing affirmation of self! I tucked that thought into my backpack in March 2007 as I embarked on a once-in-a-lifetime journey. With a dozen other women, I would celebrate the beauty of life, friends, and the eighth wonder of the world, the magnificent Grand Canyon, by hiking deep into the canyon and back.

It's the kind of adventure that sounds like a good idea when it first is mentioned, in this case after a glass or two of wine at a birthday gathering. I considered it entirely likely that after that evening and a few passing references, the notion would be shelved for the all the usual reasons. But that didn't happen. This idea stuck.

Through years of shared social events and volunteer projects, a group of women had become fast friends, carving out time to come together regularly. When I moved to Sedona, they kindly welcomed me. Several times a year we'd gather for a multi-person birthday celebration; everyone would bring a tasty treat and silly, witty birthday cards, some of them handmade. In early 2007, when we met to toast several members of the group, someone proposed marking these occasions with a little more than a potluck. How about a guided Canyon trek? As my friend and fellow hiker Meredith recalls it, the next thing we knew, "we were planning the trip of a lifetime. How would we do this? Who would be fit enough to go? If we all got together once a week and hiked, would we be in good enough shape? 'Yes, we can do this!' It was our new goal."

Because Sedona is a hiking mecca with more than 250 miles of hiking trails, most of us were at least weekend walkers and several among us were real trail blazers. Over several months, a dozen of us committed to the trip. The veteran hikers became our teachers, setting up weekly forays over gradually more difficult terrain to toughen us up. We came from all walks of life and some fairly long walks at that. None of us was under fifty and most were well past it, with the oldest then age seventy-two. Meredith, one of the most seasoned hikers, is a former flight attendant; through family ties in Palm Springs, California, she knows lots of golden-era movie stars. Spirited Sandy, who worked in real estate marketing, defied her fear of heights to join the expedition. Helen, a former attorney who's more than six feet tall, made up in grit what she lacked in hiking experience. Jessica, relatively new to the group, is a tango dancer, petite and frail-looking but determined.

Jawn, a former actress, haunts garage and estate sales every weekend and loves to show off her finds. Barbara, appealingly vivacious, missed sharing the pre-trek excitement with her husband, who died several years ago. Maura is a renowned Sedona yoga teacher. Vicki, the editor/publisher of *Scottsdale Magazine,* came along to chronicle the trip, entering our circle of friends but managing also to observe from just outside it. As she noted, our expedition "had all the spiritual and medical support we needed" thanks to Pam, a masseuse; Karen, a retired pediatrician; and Marilyn, a former nun who once worked in Mother Teresa's facility in Calcutta. At the heart of the group is Dottie, a specialist in stress and anxiety management whose work has taken her to Rwanda to help people scarred by the 1994 genocide.

The plan was for the thirteen of us, plus three veteran guides, to spend a day descending ten miles to a base camp 2,000 feet down in the canyon. Pack horses would transport all the supplies; we would arrive in time for guides to set up camp near Havasu Falls and cook us a restorative hot dinner. We'd have the next full day to explore and, if we dared, to make our way along 1,000-feet-tall cliffs that were the spillway for Mooney Falls, then down to the canyon floor. The third day, we'd make the challenging hike back out.

It was dark and chilly when we left Sedona and still nippy upon

The triumphant trekkers on the floor of the canyon: In front, Barbara Randall and Jessica Sierra; in the middle row, Dottie Webster, Meredith Greenleaf, Marilyn Thaden Dexter, Helen Knoll; in the back, Victoria Collins, Karen Dansby, Maura Marks, Sandy Brandvold, Jawn McKinley, Pam Clark, Martha. Photo courtesy of Martha Mayhood Mertz.

our arrival at the Hualapai Hilltop trail head on Hualapai Reservation land. Our backpacks were filled with the suggested essentials, including lip gloss, sunscreen, trail snacks and band-aids. Dressed in layers, our broken-in boots laced snugly, we embarked down the side wall of the canyon, two by two or single file as the trail allowed. "I was assured this was to be a slow, leisurely paced hike to allow ample time to take in the sights," Vicki later wrote in a vivid, humor-laced article for her magazine. "What I experienced was, as Helen aptly described, a 'death march' led by Meredith . . . stopping only long enough for those of us lagging behind to snap a picture or two to catch up." Thanks to our training, we generally fared well on the descent (though as the trail grew steeper, Jessica was rethinking her choice of footgear). We stopped for lunch along a rock ledge with a world class view, then stopped again in the village of Supai, reputed to have the last U.S. Post Office that moves mail by Pony Express. Finally, toward dusk we arrived at our campsite where the tents were already sprouting thanks to the guides. We slept gratefully under a sky blazing with stars.

Day two began with perhaps the most formidable challenge of the trip: the spillway for Mooney Falls, where we'd have to climb 300 feet down to reach the wooded canyon floor. Trekkers long before us had installed a few climbing aids, stubs of rebar embedded in the sheer cliff. But the descent still involved some heart-pounding maneuvers: hanging on heavy chains, climbing though rock formations and dropping farther than legs could reach. As Vicki reported in her article, "Dennis told me later that he expected only five or six of us to actually make the climb down. Instead, all thirteen of us did." Marilyn, an avid hiker and the expedition's wise elder, had what was later diagnosed as 95 percent–torn rotator cuff and so made the dizzying descent using just one arm (and lots of help from trek mates). Given her fear of heights, Sandy summoned enormous courage just to begin, as guides had warned we would not be able to change our minds once we started down. At the end of the descent, the scene was pure exhilaration. As each woman touched down, those already on the canyon floor roared with joy, celebrating what we had dared and achieved together. Departing meant retracing our steps to the Mooney Falls cliff, only this time our guides chose a path that was 200 feet almost straight up. From the trek down we had drawn confidence and, from our time on the canyon floor, a kind of tranquility. Reaching out as needed to help each other, we made our way back to camp, for another hearty dinner and starlit night.

On day three, the journey back out proved grueling even for our seasoned hikers. Climbing steep, dusty trails in the hot afternoon sun, we ran very low on water. We walked slowly, stopping with increasing frequency just to catch our breath. With about one mile still to go, we realized one trekker was in trouble, having a great deal of difficulty just walking. Two guides spent the next hour half-carrying her up to the rim where she fell into the back of a jeep, seriously dehydrated, barely conscious, legs swollen and bleeding under the skin. Others of us suffered to lesser degrees, nauseated and weak, but this woman needed medical attention, and we were hours away from the nearest medical facility.

I ended the day in the car, racing this sick friend back to Sedona as Dr. Karen tended to her. By the time we got her to care, our friend had revived enough to feel embarrassed for causing so much concern. Later, doctors discovered one probable source of her distress, a congenital heart problem that never had troubled her before. She has not let it defeat her, though, or take away what she gained from our trek. Today she organizes and leads weekly hikes for our group among the Sedona red rocks.

After our adventure, Meredith wrote something that really captured it. "For each of us the experience was exactly what was meant to be," she wrote. "We did yoga, we walked in silence, we ate wonderful food (cooked by the men!) . . . We sang, we told stories by the camp fire, we talked about other adventures. We were a community. We all became one, helping each other accomplish whatever secret or quiet goal we had set for ourselves."

Our group has a name for itself: The Que Sera Sera Women. As that Spanish phrase says, "Whatever will be, will be." Much in life—perhaps most of life—is beyond our power to control. But what we can control is how we live into things: what we risk, whom we embrace, how we celebrate. Meredith says that whenever the Que Sera Sera women gather, we create "that blissful place of now." If that's not worth celebrating, I don't know what is.

FOURTEEN

Into the World . . .

I T HAD LONG BEEN OUR HOPE that the ATHENA philosophy would step beyond U.S. borders, eventually to encircle the globe. We knew that the voices of leadership were as out of balance, in gender terms, in other countries as in our own. The first chance to remedy that came just across Michigan's border. Loretta Stoyka, barrister by profession and volunteer leader of the Windsor, Ontario Chamber of Commerce, invited us to make an ATHENA Award presentation to her board. We leapt at the opportunity and, in 1995, the first ATHENA Award was presented in Windsor. Several years later Loretta was serving on our now international board of directors, helping in the efforts to inspire women as leaders across Canada. Since then, as ATHENA programs continue to grow and spin off through the United States, they also are finding footing in other countries. In some cases, recipients now living in the United States reach back to plant ATHENA in their countries of origin. In other cases, visitors from abroad see the programs' potential and take ATHENA home with them.

Much as goddesses in myth took on different guises in different situations, ATHENA becomes something new, and yet remains, at heart, the same, as it advances around the world in this new century.

WELL INTO THE TWENTIETH CENTURY, seven emirates on the southeastern Arabian Peninsula were plagued by poverty, illiteracy, and malnutrition. Then oil was discovered and, in 1971, Sheikh Zayed bin Sultan Al Nahyan led the states in forming a federation, the United Arab Emirates. As UAE's president (until his death in 2004), Sheikh Zayed used oil revenues to build infrastructure and institutions that transformed his people's existence. He also recognized the potential lost because half the Emirati population—the female half—lacked the training and opportunity to contribute fully to society. So in 1998 he helped establish Zayed University to educate Emirati women and prepare them for leadership.

Because a U.S. provost working at Zayed University was familiar with ATHENA, a colleague and I were invited to participate in training these new students. In 2000, we visited the university's two campuses, in Dubai and Abu Dhabi, to stage two-and-a-half day sessions we called ATHENA Leadership Institutes. We worked with the administration and professors so they could continue to teach ALM principles once we were gone, and with a select group of juniors and seniors, young women who would be the first graduates from the fledgling university. Our sessions were as much an education for me and my colleague as for the young women. I never will forget what I learned there, particularly what I learned about a view of ATHENA beyond my own.

In one exercise, we asked the young women to identify various characteristics they associated with leadership. They came up with forty or fifty, wrote each on a card, and posted the cards on a wall. Then we asked the students to group the cards together, organizing them around themes. My colleague and I had used this technique before and we knew

Fatima receives Athena Award

'Her life, work has had a powerful, positive impact on women'

By A Staff Reporter

Abu Dhabi

Her Highness Sheikha Fatima bint Mubarak, Wife of President His Highness Sheikh Zayed bin Sultan Al Nahyan and Chairperson of the General Women's Union, received the international Athena Award yesterday for her role in supporting women's education.

The award, which was founded in the U.S. in 1982, is given to female personalities who have contributed in the development and empowerment of women. It is the highest award presented by the International Athena Foundation.

Sheikha Fatima is the first eminent personality in the Middle East to receive the award and the 11th in the world.

She was honoured by Marth Mertz, founder of the Athena Foundation, on the occasion of the first graduation ceremony of the Zayed University held at the Abu Dhabi National Theatre.

Marth Mertz in her speech congratulated Sheikha Fatima for her contribution towards women's education in the UAE and praised her role.

"I am honoured and deeply moved to thank Sheikha Fatima on behalf of the girls and women around the globe for exemplifying the highest model of leadership and to present her with this award for her quiet yet powerful contribution to positively change all of us."

Mertz said the award is pre-

The Athena Award

sented to an outstanding recipient who has met three criteria. She is a person who has achieved the highest level of professional excellence, who has given her time and talent back to her entire community and, most especially, her life and work has had a powerful and positive impact upon women and girls throughout the land and beyond.

She said in the 20 years history of the Athena Foundation,

only 10 such awards have been presented. This is a historic occasion because for the first time such an award is being given in the UAE.

"This award highlights the valued partnership between Zayed University and the International Athena Foundation and it underscores the value of their shared missions, opening leadership opportunities for women. This award emphasises the importance of expanding leadership roles in the 21st century for women and girls."

In a video speech transmitted on the occasion, Sheikh Nahyan bin Mubarak Al Nahyan, Minister of Higher Education and Scientific Research and Chancellor of the university, praised the role of Sheikha Fatima in supporting women's education and congratulated her on receiving the award.

"The distinctive role of Sheikha Fatima in leading women's progress in the UAE is highly appreciated and admired by everyone. Recognising this role the Athena Foundation has given her this international award, an award provided to prominent women leaders who make great and tremendous efforts in serving women issues all over the world."

Sheikh Nahyan added: "I invite you all to share with me this glorious moment in giving her this honour in appreciation of her great accomplishments and pioneer achievements in all fields."

The first Middle East recipient of the ATHENA International Award was the United Arab Emirates' Sheikha Fatima bint Mubarak, who with her husband Sheikh Zayed bin Sultan Al Nahyan helped establish higher education and leadership training opportunities for girls and women in their country.

from experience that, with some prompting, the characteristics would coalesce around eight themes, the eight principles of the ALM. The ideas that came from the students fit nicely into our model.

Then we asked them, "What's missing? Is anything missing?" One of the students came to the front of the class and said what she thought our lists lacked: essentially, a sense of global vision. We're living in a world that's increasingly interconnected, she told the class, so it's important for us to broaden our perspective. When we're thinking about any of these principles and any of the ways we might act on them, we must consider the global implications.

In that moment, that young woman had crystallized two key tasks of the leader: to identify guiding principles, as we had done, but also to bring a vision that will animate those principles. That vision is the spark of ideas and beliefs, the sense of what is possible; it is a concept framed so persuasively that it pulls others along, seeing what the leader has seen.

Wherever that young Emirati woman is now, I'll bet she's providing leadership. I credit her with reminding all of us that in the twenty-first century as never before, our vision must encompass the world. As I reviewed and refined the ALM language for this book, especially the principle "foster collaboration," I thought of her. For the leaders of the future—leaders like that young woman—fostering collaboration most certainly will mean "valuing the gifts each individual brings, with a perspective that is global and a spirit that is inclusive."

WHEN CLEVELAND, OHIO, gave Rita Singh its ATHENA Award in 2004, she had a dream of sharing ATHENA with leaders, especially women, in her native India. Two years later, she was realizing her dream and for one glorious part of it, she took me along.

When Rita began thinking seriously of planting ATHENA in India, she first told her husband and business partner Nip, her grown daughters

Kavita and Anjulika, and her employees at the family business, S & A Consulting. "All my staff and my family were so supportive," Rita says. "My daughters said, 'Mom, you're going to be able to do this!'" She got much the same reaction when she approached ATHENA International's leadership and board with her idea. We were blown away by her energy and humbled by her devotion to bringing ATHENA to a new continent.

Rita was convinced that India needed ATHENA because "the economic and cultural situation is really a mix. There are women who are very powerful and successful and have everything they need, but also women in slums and sleeping in train stations, still struggling to meet even basic needs. Many of them need economic empowerment in education, skills development and eventually leadership skills. As we're becoming global in our thinking, products and services, the world begins to realize the enormous contributions of women in every sector. ATHENA connects every woman to the worldwide opportunities to learn from each others' experiences, knowledge and challenges and to give back to their communities."

On her own time and money, Rita began the kind of highly personal, labor-intensive process we used more than two decades earlier when we created the ATHENA Award program in Lansing. Ever the diligent researcher, Rita began identifying India's potential ATHENA leaders: "I started by conducting a countrywide search to see who were the top 200 women in the country who were making a difference in their cities."

She then chose the top ten leaders in that group and tried first to get them on board. She emailed them and sent them ATHENA literature. To reach people during India's daytime hours, she recalls, "I would be up all night on the phone convincing people that this is the right thing to do, no matter how many awards they currently have in their country. Under no circumstances was I going to take no for an answer . . . . I would say, 'Please take me seriously—I have something that will create a powerful connection'" between women in India and the rest of the world.

Rita Singh (left) with Bakul Rajni Patel, first recipient of the ATHENA Award in India, and Martha Mertz at the October 2006 award ceremony in Mumbai. Photo courtesy of ATHENA International.

Because leaders were busy and typically had not heard of ATHENA, "I had a very tough time convincing them" to get involved, she said. But ultimately, after investing countless hours of work and a significant amount of her own money, Rita had a core group of energetic leaders for an ATHENA program in Mumbai, and had signed a corporate sponsor, Infosys Technologies Limited, an IT firm in the forefront of employing and mentoring women. The crowning, inaugural event of this new program would be its first Award presentation. When Rita called to ask if I would accompany her to that ceremony in October of 2006, I jumped at the chance.

While my travel to Mumbai was twenty-seven tiring hours but relatively uneventful, Rita's was a trial by fire. She had planned to fly there with me but, thanks to an unseasonal Cleveland snow storm, ended up missing all her scheduled flights. She had to buy a new ticket, ran through the airport to avoid again missing her connection to Mumbai, and arrived there to find all her luggage had been lost, including the bag containing her speech notes and printed materials for the award program. The city that day was 110 degrees and stiflingly humid, but the event site Rita chose, the gorgeous Taj Mahal Palace and Tower, was a suitably grand and historic place to celebrate the dawn of new leadership. Clearing one last hurdle, Rita learned at the last minute that the scheduled master of ceremonies had not shown up for the award ceremony; with utter poise, and with me assisting, Rita ran everything on stage herself. "Nothing else mattered, except to do this with no signs of the stress, pain, or turmoil," she said later. "It came together and we had a beautiful evening with a hall full of people who acknowledged our efforts to bring this to India."

The first ATHENA Award recipient in India was Bakul Rajni Patel, an accomplished entrepreneur and executive who held top posts in financial, media and manufacturing companies before establishing her own consulting firm. Bakul not only pursued professional excellence herself but helped others achieve it. As chair of one of India's state financial corporations, she promoted programs that enable women to work home-based and to develop their own business and service organizations. Spending time with Bakul at the ATHENA Award event, I was struck by her elegance and depth.

During and since that inaugural event, India's ATHENA program has recognized other women who embody and promote the ATHENA principles. I've been fortunate enough to spend time with two of them, both standouts in the high-tech sector that holds so much promise for India in general and India's women especially. As an Infosys senior vice president, Priti Rao not only led her teams to unprecedented growth and worker satisfaction, she created an in-house volunteer organization through which employees can help underprivileged women and girls. Anupama Arya worked in Silicon Valley for a decade and launched a successful IT start-up there, but returned to India to be closer to family and now heads a thriving technology firm in the northern Indian city of Chandigarh. Priti is a quiet, deep and decisive person whose colleagues treat her with respect bordering on awe; she impressed me immediately with her commitment to helping women advance. Anupama is a bright, infectiously friendly young woman who epitomizes the ATHENA ideal of collaborating across cultures. Helping India's fledgling ATHENA program honor these women was in fact a great honor for me.

Rita's goal, ultimately, is to have "all of India know about ATHENA… Though the economic and cultural conditions have changed a lot since I lived there, women still are not where they should be. There are a lot of women who can do a lot of things but they don't get the opportunity because there's still this idea that the men are superior no matter what women bring to the table. So taking the concept we have for ATHENA, the concept of balanced leadership, really helps a lot of women who aspire to be leaders as well as those who already are leaders."

"As long as I'm alive and healthy, I want to continue to work with ATHENA—that's how I feel."

BIG SMILE, BIG LAUGH, BIG HUGS to greet everyone she knows. It quickly becomes clear that Janet Lister does almost everything in a big way, and that includes the ATHENA programs she helped introduce in the town of Rotherham, England.

In Rotherham, in England's South Yorkshire region near the city of Sheffield, "we really are in a man's world," says Janet. After more than twenty-five years as a professional midwife, Janet joined the engineering firm founded by her husband Andrew and "had a tough few years because there were no other women around," she says. So she founded an organization for local businesswomen and began scouting for opportunities to raise women leaders' profile. When a Rotherham official came back from a 2004 U.S. trip bearing literature about ATHENA, Janet was sold. "The thing about ATHENA is that it's not all about the individual who's doing great things. It's about creating friendships and picking up ideas and running with those ideas."

Janet jokes that she "took in washing" to get ATHENA started in her community; she also got backing from Rotherham's Metropolitan Borough Council (the equivalent of what in the United States would be the mayor and city council's office). In 2005 she spearheaded Rotherham's first ATHENA Award celebration. Two years later she was launching an

Janet Lister, who introduced the ATHENA Award in Rotherham, England, as well as an offshoot program for youth. Photo courtesy of Janet Lister.

offshoot called the Young ATHENIAN Awards, to honor youngsters who have excelled in some arena, supported their peers and given back to their communities.

For both the ATHENA and Young ATHENIAN awards, Janet says, organizers have made a point of choosing male as well as female recipients. "In Rotherham if you leave the guys out they'll come out fighting, so you've got to keep them sweet," she says with a wink. She's particularly proud of the Young ATHENIAN Award which in 2008, she says, "was a tearjerker. Of our fourteen nominees, four were living in children's homes" rather than with their families and nonetheless managed to achieve, thrive and give back. Janet beamed as she described honoring these youngsters at a grand ceremony and presenting awards including laptop computers.

In Janet's hands, the ATHENA principle of relationship-building has created a miniature international exchange program. She regularly "crosses the pond" to observe ATHENA efforts in various U.S. cities, bringing along Rotherham government officials to build their knowledge and support. And she loves to host U.S. and other international visitors at events in the United Kingdom. She chronicles all this connection-making in chatty, information-packed emails, her way of sweeping us all into her enthusiastic, ambitious plans.

I saved the email Janet sent in December 2007 after a particularly eclectic and high-energy event starring entertainer Dolly Parton. On an earlier U.S. trip, Rotherham officials had convinced Dolly to give their community the first United Kingdom franchise of Imagination Library, a literacy program Dolly founded to provide books to preschool children. When Dolly came to Rotherham for the kickoff, Janet took the occasion to tell Dolly—and all the media there to cover the star—about the ATHENA program as well.

"Just wanted you all to know about Dolly Parton's presence in Rotherham yesterday, for the launch of the Imagination Library," Janet wrote in her email. "Everyone had a fabulous time. Dolly was absolutely wonderful, she has a great sense of humour and was able to pronounce 'Rotherham' like a Yorkshire lass. There was media coverage from all over the world, including Australia. I was interviewed by BBC Radio 4 for a women's program, regarding ATHENA .... Later I was invited to join Dolly for a photo shoot, so I took the opportunity to say that all our friends in America were aware of her visit, I presented her with an ATHENA brooch and said that it was on behalf of all the ATHENA board. She said she would treasure it forever. There has been such great publicity in all the national papers."

The rest of Janet's email shared news about other work she was doing to spread ATHENA through the United Kingdom: a new program being planted in the Midlands region, a meeting to discuss possibilities in Birmingham. In any given year, she'll have a number of ATHENA World Cafés scheduled. And she brags like a proud parent about the UK's ATHENA Award recipients and PowerLink participants so far. One is a top manager for an international bank, and another runs a studio that brings affordable dance and theater arts to the children of unemployed workers.

The ATHENA work of Janet and her colleagues has changed the dynamics for women in their region. Women there have learned to trust each other, share their business concerns, celebrate their milestones; they have become a force to be reckoned with. Janet is the first from her country to serve on the board of ATHENA International, and her efforts have caught the attention of UK leaders as high up as the House of Lords. But through it all, Janet's leadership is not about what's in it for her. Perhaps that's why she is so effective.

THE LONGER I KNOW ROBIN KOTTKE, the more I appreciate how she and other young leaders like her are shaping the future of ATHENA.

We met in a classroom at Michigan State University. I had returned to academia seeking broader and deeper perspectives on the changing status of women that I had experienced in my own life. Robin was working on her undergraduate degree. She had long aspired to become a teacher and was a semester away from completing her education degree when she took a class in women's studies. It shifted her worldview; she wanted to learn more, and in summer 1999 headed to London for an intensive women's studies program. "Talk about hooked!" she says now. "I came home and announced to my parents that I was going to pursue women's studies." Her mother was excited, her dad wondered aloud how that major would get her a job, and the next semester, Robin and I wound up in a "Psychology of Women" class together, partnering on small group projects. It soon became clear she was as thoughtful as she was passionate, and committed to women's studies as a means to personal growth as well as a career path.

After she graduated in 2001, we'd get together occasionally for lunch or tea. I loved hearing her enthusiastic accounts of her work with women, at an organization that worked on sex education and reproductive rights issues. I had no idea whether Robin could envision herself working for ATHENA, but it was a notion I couldn't get out of my head. To thrive in the twenty-first century, ATHENA would need innovative, energetic advocates and Robin impressed me as just that. So one day I just sprang it on her, in a rather backwards way. "Robin, how do you feel about moving to Chicago?" I remember asking.

As Robin recalls it, "I really didn't know much about ATHENA so I started looking into it to get a better understanding. It was when I read the ATHENA Leadership Model that I knew I had to work for this organization. I remember sending an email to my family just before the interview in Chicago saying, 'I couldn't have articulated this before, but this model of leadership really speaks to me. This is exactly where I need to be.'" In April 2004, Robin and her new husband Steven uprooted themselves from their native Michigan and moved to Chicago, where Robin took on every management and administration duty that ATHENA gave her. Today she is the program director for ATHENA International and has been pivotal in the creation of the ATHENA Young Professional Award program that honors emerging women leaders ages twenty to forty. Due in large part to Robin's efforts, that "Baby ATHENA" program was embraced by a full quarter of ATHENA communities in just its first year of operation.

"I know every day how lucky I am, so early in my career, to be surrounded by these extraordinary women who've been held up by their communities as exemplary leaders," Robin told me when we spoke recently. "This may sound crazy, but one of the best lessons I've learned working closely with ATHENA women is this: They, too, are fallible and flawed." She laughed at herself in mock horror—"Did I just basically say all our leaders were flawed?"—and then explained. "That doesn't sound

Martha with Robin Kottke, director of ATHENA programs, at the 2007 ATHENA International conference award ceremony. Photo courtesy of ATHENA International.

like a compliment but it really is! As a perfectionist myself, I feel I've learned from all the leaders around me that you don't have to be perfect to be really, really effective. In fact, I feel that our flaws are a great opportunity to teach other people how to be and how not to be, and also how to be more forgiving of ourselves and others."

That kind of insight is what convinced me that although Robin is a young leader, she's a wise one. I was eager to hear her views on another question central to ATHENA's work. Over the life of the organization, from her generation to mine, how have the challenges and opportunities changed for women who would lead?

Robin identified two key shifts, both for the better. "I appreciate all the trailblazing that women of earlier generations did, often without benefit of formal mentors, and I see that as a huge difference, Martha, from your generation to mine. Women from the generation that founded ATHENA realize the importance of giving back, of helping other women along their respective leadership paths and lifting as they climb. So certainly the leaders of my generation have benefited from that mentoring in ways that were not possible for those who came before us.

"I would say, too, that one of the things we've learned from these mentors is that our unique ways—dare I say, our innate ways—of knowing and leading are really assets and not liabilities. I think so many women in generations before mine tried to take on those more traditional, 'male' leadership styles. But in my generation, I feel we've really been encouraged to cultivate our own unique leadership qualities."

Working at ATHENA's Chicago headquarters, Robin stays in close touch, literally, with the principles that drew her to the organization. "I have eight small frames lined up on my desk, each with one of the eight ALM principles, and whatever principle applies to what I'm focusing on at a given time, I pull that one to the forefront," she told me. "I love having them on my desk, like touchstones."

When she travels, Robin says, she hands out cards bearing the principles and finds they lose nothing in translation. "Wherever I've been in the world, I've seen this model embraced. It truly is global. In 2005, ATHENA Foundation became ATHENA International to better reflect our international mission and scope, and it's been such an exciting time to be involved. We're seeing this become the international program it is meant to be. It's really beginning to resonate worldwide, this idea that we need to create balance in leadership. But there's still a lot of work to be done."

FOR A SETTING in which to celebrate ATHENA leadership, it's hard to beat Nashville. To mark the city's centennial in 1897, Nashville built a full-scale replica of the Parthenon as it stood in ancient Greece, right down to its forty-two-foot-tall statue of the goddess Athena. The building now houses the city's art museum and hosts various events, including, every year, a gala for Nashville's ATHENA Award honorees.

In spring 2008 for its eighteenth annual ATHENA Award celebration, Nashville pulled out all the stops. At a reception before the Award presentation, a few hundred people mingled at the Athena statue's feet, nibbling hors d'oeuvres, networking, greeting old friends. Then came the ceremony, opened with a proud procession of the organizations sponsoring ATHENA Award nominees—twenty-nine in all! Brief videos on each nominee could only hint at the accomplishments of this talented group: educators and activists, lawmakers and communicators, CEOs and entrepreneurs. The 2008 recipient was Joyce Espy Searcy, president of a Nashville non-profit that provides job training, childcare and other support to women struggling to lift themselves out of poverty. Joyce shared the stage with other grateful honorees: two high school students, two college students, and two women entering higher education later in life, all going to school with a generous boost from ATHENA-sponsored scholarships.

The festivities also included out-of-town guests who represented, for

Above, the Athena statue in Nashville's Parthenon, from a past ATHENA Award program cover. Right, ATHENA International board members gathered in Nashville in 2008. Photos courtesy of ATHENA International.

me, a globe-spanning reunion. Janet Lister was there from the UK, and Priti Rao and Anupama Arya from India. ATHENA International board members came from all over the United States, and Robin Kottke and Dianne Dinkel (who later would assume the role of ATHENA International president) joined us from Chicago.

In the midst of the celebration, a sad but stirring episode demonstrated what is so precious about these ATHENA associates, not just their leadership but their humanity.

Everyone who knew Robin had been congratulating and hugging her. She was four months pregnant, expecting her first child! A gathering of ATHENA International board members took on the air of a baby shower, as maternal colleagues regaled Robin with funny and encouraging stories.

Back at the hotel after the Nashville gala, Robin felt unwell but tried to shrug it off. She said goodnight to Dianne Dinkel, her roommate for the trip, and went to bed. At two o'clock in the morning, Robin awoke feeling worse, and then woke again at four o'clock, vomiting and cramping as if with stomach flu. Dianne called Robin's doctor, who advised taking Robin to the hospital. As Dianne packed a bag, Robin continued to be sick, and then she felt a gush. Her water had broken; what she had mistaken for flu cramps were the pains of tragically premature labor.

Robin recalls the scene with almost unbearable clarity. "I said to Dianne, 'Call Janet' (the veteran midwife). Janet came immediately and knew right away what was happening. She told Dianne to call an ambulance. I was crying and having labor pains, huge waves. Janet had me sit on the edge of the bed, wrap my arms around her and just bury my head in her midsection. I was beside myself with the pain, and she was talking me through the breathing. The ambulance came and we went to the hospital, where they told me that I had miscarried.

"The baby was so far from viability that there was nothing anybody could do. Janet encouraged me to see the baby if I wanted to, and the nurses took me to him. Janet and Dianne stayed there with me and they cried with me. I will always remember them as sort of my guardian angels. I was with women who knew to honor me as a mother and who also advocated for me with the hospital, when I was too distraught to speak for myself. I consider it one of the great blessings of the whole experience that they were with me."

When Robin returned to the hotel after the miscarriage, she was surrounded by concerned ATHENA associates. Some knew her well; most knew only that one of us was in pain and needed support. As Robin marveled later, "There were so many women who came in just to be with me."

The morning after that loss, we learned of another. As Robin was heading to the hospital, Priti Rao's mother in India had passed away.

Priti confided this quietly, as if not to intrude on Robin's grief, but as soon as other ATHENA colleagues learned her sad news, they enfolded her, too, in their sympathy and concern.

We were back to the age-old circle, the place from which ATHENA leadership arises: the soul-deep sharing, the unity of spirit, together with or without words.

WORKING ON THIS BOOK through the thick of the 2008 United States presidential election race, I was bombarded by analyses and debates about leadership, including gender's role in it. Depending upon which pundit was speaking, we were told that Hillary Rodham Clinton's gender did matter to voters and that it didn't, that it should matter and that it shouldn't. For whatever combination of reasons, she failed, in her words, to "shatter that highest, hardest glass ceiling." Republicans, meanwhile, made party history by nominating their first female vice-presidential candidate. While exit polls showed Sarah Palin ultimately was judged on her perceived fitness (or lack thereof) for leadership, the campaign was full of irrelevant, sexism-laced digressions.

From early in the campaign, I scrutinized every would-be leader for signs of our ATHENA principles. The more I applied that ALM measure, the clearer it became that we've had it right all along. Leadership is not contingent on gender.

As the contests wound down, I was increasingly aware of two distinct leadership styles clearly on display for the world to compare and judge. One candidate exemplified the old style: command and control, hierarchical more than collegial, dividing more than uniting. That candidate was a man with much to recommend him, John McCain, a war veteran who had served his country well. But I looked in vain for the leadership traits I considered critical in these perilous times—authenticity, a commitment to collaboration, the ability to inspire.

Another candidate represented a very different approach. Expressive but not dogmatic about values and beliefs. Not all-knowing, but eager and quick to learn. Courageous and passionate in addressing issues others had long avoided. Drawing strength from conviction and consensus more than from military might. Pulling in populations that never felt included before, but that now saw the workings of the nation as their responsibility, too.

I saw so many ATHENA leadership traits in this candidate—in this man, Barack Obama. I am eager to see what he can accomplish as America's forty-fourth president, though not naïve enough to believe that either ATHENA's principles or his own will, by themselves, guarantee success. That said, I will always see the 2008 election as a watershed: a clear statement, in a precarious time, that a new and more balanced way of leading must replace an old and discredited one.

"OUR BEST LEADERS are like great gardeners. They cultivate and nourish a whole lot of new leaders to grow up around them." Back when Polly Bunting was using gardening metaphors, they were decidedly not the language men used in serious social analysis. But this comparison of leaders to gardeners was made in late 2008 by one of America's preeminent scholars on leadership, David Gergen. Adviser to several U.S. presidents, Gergen now directs the Center for Public Leadership at Harvard University. In recent years, Gergen has described a steady evolution toward what is, essentially, the ATHENA way of leading. Consider his point about collaboration in a 2007 essay on American leaders: "Who can forget the haunting picture of John F. Kennedy alone in the Oval Office during the Cuban missile crisis? But today's leader is usually the one sitting at a table with six others, sleeves rolled up, trying to solve a problem together."

When the fledgling ATHENA movement first embraced the quote

from Plato—"What is honored in a country will be cultivated there"—
we could only hope it would prove true. Today, we see clearly that it has.
The eight principles we claimed for ATHENA leaders are now embraced
at large, with different wordings and emphases but meanings essentially
the same. Our onetime "women's ways" have moved beyond gender to be
leadership precepts for all.

Pressing into the twenty-first century the promise is so great. My
generation of mothers, aunts and sisters have found our voices of leadership; we now recognize how effective our ways are, whether in the board
room, the back room or the living room. We have provided that model to
our children of both genders, raised them on it all their lives, and what
they've witnessed and absorbed they now expect and perpetuate. Our
voices are not just as audible as men's but, increasingly, as credible.

As women gain presence and prominence at all levels of leadership,
old pressures to "fit in" are falling away. If working in the ways we find
most comfortable, most effective and consistent with our values, causes
us to stand out—well, so be it.

For years I've contended that "When one of us succeeds, we all are
elevated." As I write this, many of us have succeeded and more are on the
way. As third, fourth, fifth waves of women leaders arrive, with waves of
children and protégés behind us, we're ushering in a new time.

The logical extension of this would be an ATHENA version of Mal-
colm Gladwell's "tipping point": so many of us promoting and aspiring
to these leadership ideals that their acceptance is assured. As a civilization, we'd turn to the strengths of relationships and collaboration to find
solutions for the worst of our problems. We'd replace the call to arms
with a call to hearts and minds, to reconciliation and commonweal. It is
a harder path. But the world may be able to walk it—away from destruction and toward fulfillment and greatness—if our daughters and sons
have learned to lead with principle.

Some months before this book was finished, I sent a few chapters to my three grown children, just to see what they would think. Michelle offered insightful feedback; Michael deepened the meaning of key passages. But what really connected ATHENA's past and future for me, in a deeply personal way, was the phone call I got from Chris.

My youngest child is a clinical neuropsychologist at a large medical facility in Minnesota. Every day Chris works with people who have central nervous system issues, psychological issues, or some tangle of the two that can leave them despairing. Chris jokes that he entered the field because it required the least number of math classes. But the truth is, he loves what he calls "making an impact in real time," sharing knowledge that can provide dramatic relief for patients. Chris is empathetic and creative, good-humored and naturally social; he is a devoted husband and a fantastic father to his son Calvin.

On this phone call as in many other conversations we've shared over the years, Chris had something important to offer. In so many words, he thanked me for pointing out that the ATHENA model of leadership is his as well as mine. He appreciated me underscoring how these principles belong to leaders of both genders. He even asked me to include a few more "not only to granddaughters but also to grandsons" references in describing how these teachings are handed from one generation to the next. The ATHENA leadership traits he has embraced, Chris says, are serving him well in life.

I take enormous hope from this. As much as we've tried, many women of my generation haven't fully shed that "less than" sense forced on us in the past. Sometimes it still gets to us. We're chafed or saddened by the injustice, the imbalance. But Chris, Michael, and Michelle aren't marked by that history. That's a legacy we did not pass on. Because we've worked so hard together for the last three decades, determined to change what didn't make sense to us, we are leaving our world with more balance than we found. Because we have taught these principles to our sons and our daughters, in the future they'll be able to exercise—and to teach to their children—enlightened, balanced leadership. ATHENA leadership, principled and true.

"It is the learners, not the learned, who shape the future." Dutch Landen left that wisdom with me. As I complete this book I revel in the prospect of all that's left to learn. I give thanks for wise and generous teachers, those whose stories fill this book and others I've yet to meet. I will find them, I am sure, on the road to our shared purpose: becoming ATHENA leaders who will transfigure the world.

Index